THE
GOSPEL
TIME
BOMB

THE GOSPEL TIME BOMB

Ultrafundamentalism and the Future of America

Lowell D. Streiker

Prometheus Books

700 East Amherst St.
Buffalo, New York 14215

Library of Congress Card Catalog No. 84-42793
ISBN: 0-87975-259-9

To my parents
Frederic and Alice Streiker

Contents

PART FOUR: DEFUSING THE GOSPEL TIME BOMB

Preface

In the affluent and sophisticated suburban communities of the San Francisco peninsula, the weather is pleasant the year round. The standard of living is extremely high (as is, alas, the cost of living). Cultural attractions abound. Natural and scenic beauty is everywhere. The northern California "mellow" lifestyle—with its constant creation of techniques for personal exploration, interpersonal experimentation, and social transformation—is legend. But behind the legend lurks a different reality for many people—a reality of disrupted families, dysfunctional lives, wasted careers, and desperate confusions.

Freedom Counseling Center, which deals with such problems, was founded in January 1979 as an outgrowth of my counseling of the survivors of the Jonestown massacre in Guyana. My intent was to operate a professional counseling agency that recognized the threats and dangers posed by fanatic groups, and yet which offered alternatives to the equally fanatic vigilantism of the deprogrammers. During the past five years, we have pursued our mission of reconciling families disturbed by the involvement of a member in a fanatic group, without resorting to force, violence, or other tactics of humiliation.[1]

Cults, sects, and mass therapies abound in California, as they do in every part of the United States. In the past five years, I have personally been involved with clients in San Mateo County from every geographic section, socioeconomic stratum, ethnic and age group. In addition, cases have taken me to twenty-five states, Canada, Japan, England, and South Africa. And families from every part of the globe have come to us seeking assistance.

A dramatic device for illustrating the problems found in this corner of the world is to invent a mythical "Holt family," and show the family members involved in all the strange cults we have encountered in actual cases with many San Mateo County families.

1

THE HOLT FAMILY

Howard Holt, age 63, is a banker in Palo Alto. His only direct experience with cults is with Moonie fundraisers, who have been blocking the entrance to the bank as they sell roses to passers-by. Among the depositors at his bank are a colony for the Children of God, which derives its income through "flirty fishing" (prostitution), and the Willows commune, which earns a million dollars a month through the operation of an allegedly fraudulent food-supplement sales-pyramid scheme.

Sally Holt, 61, has a dying mother, 89. Resisting her sense of hopelessness, Sally has been giving large sums of money to a local psychic with a reputation as a faith healer. Sally is thinking of giving the proceeds of a trust fund established by her late father to a spiritualist commune in Virginia, which communicates with the spirits of the departed. She and her husband have been arguing bitterly about her fascination with the occult. Her "gurus" have advised her to leave her husband.

The Holt's oldest son, Howard, Jr., age 35, is the founder of a successful computer-manufacturing firm. He is married and has two children, both in elementary school. He spends four nights a week and weekends teaching seminars in successful marriage and parenting for Creative Initiative, an ethical-ecological reformationist group. He intends to sell his business and devote his full time to the group.

Thomas Holt, 33, works as an engineer for Pacific Telephone. He is attending Wave of the Future seminars. As he gets more "in tune with his feelings," he has become increasingly accusatory and hostile toward his wife and children. Since he spends four evenings assisting at the seminars and the weekends attending advanced seminars, his family sees little of him. He speaks a language replete with touchy-feely cliches and pop-psychobabble. He is finding it difficult to communicate with his family, friends, and co-workers. He thinks he is in love with his workshop facilitator. He has become deeply estranged from his parents, upon whom he places the blame for an unhappy adulthood.

Mary Anne Holt Webster, 31, recently married a divorced dentist with two college-age children. Her eldest stepchild, Tony, 22, is a Hare Krishna. He lives at the Berkeley temple and sells forged oil paintings. Tony's sister, Amy, age 20, has been involved with the Way International for three years. She lives in a Way House in Washington, D.C., supports herself by working part-time as a maid at a Holiday

Inn and spends ten hours a day hanging out at doughnut shops and bowling alleys inviting high-school students to attend "Bible study classes" at the Way House. Last week she was sexually assaulted by her "Twig" (local group) leader. When she protested she was labeled a troublemaker and encouraged to leave. She is severely depressed.

Tamara Holt Andrews, age 29, has made a career of conversion. An artist, Tammy has abandoned her husband and eight-year-old son to join the Rajneesh commune in Oregon. Previously she had been part of the Tribal Thumb commune in Humboldt County and other radical groups. She participated in two armed bank robberies. Before that she lived with the Li family on Pacific Gas and Electric right-of-way land in Burlingame while waiting for a UFO from Venus. Earlier she had moved to Mi-wuk Village near Sonora to await the "great tribulation." She has also been reported to Child Protective Services for beating her child when she was a member of Faith Fellowship in San Jose. She spent $50,000 in eight months for auditing to become a "clear" in Scientology, and once nearly starved to death on a macrobiotic diet.

Turning from soap opera to reality, I note that during a recent year our real cases with Peninsula families have included the following:

• We located a missing college student, who left a "goodbye forever" letter at home. From phrases in the letter we traced him to the Hare Krishna temple in Berkeley. We persuaded him to leave the group.

• We helped a stepfather secure custody of an abandoned child, whose mother had gone to live with the Rajneesh commune in Oregon.

• We helped obtain a refund of four thousand dollars for a woman who had dropped out of Scientology and had difficulty getting her former associates to honor the "money-back" guarantee that had been made.

• We persuaded a college senior not to leave school. The leader of the seminar group which he had been attending had told him that a college degree was only proof of "conformity," and that the student could learn more in a weekend seminar than in ten years at a university.

• We talked to two recent converts to Way International Twigs (local groups). We persuaded one to leave the group and to return to college. The other case is still open.

• We have conducted reassurance counseling sessions with parents and grandparents whose loved ones are involved in fundamentalist Christian aberration groups (Faith Fellowship, Word of Life Fellowship, Children of God, the shepherding movement, and deliverance ministry groups).

During the same year, our activities in the remainder of the country included the following:

• Court appearance. Acting as an expert witness, we helped to smash a lawsuit brought by a cult group.

• Exit counseling. As the result of our efforts to mediate family differences, we challenged cult recruits to examine critically their commitments and the groups they had joined. During our discussions, more than twenty individuals decided to leave cult groups, including the Unification Church, the Hare Krishnas, Scientology, and deliverance/ shepherding groups.

• Ongoing counseling, locating missing persons, expert testimony, rehabilitation, and so forth have been pursued on behalf of individuals involved in Scientology, Rajneesh, Church Universal and Triumphant, Neuropsyches Institute, Children of God, Body of Christ, the Local Church, Free Communion Church, the Way International, East-West Center, Faith Fellowship, and several "no name" groups.

I cite these cases to give the reader a concrete feel for the ongoing work of Freedom Counseling Center. Since the beginning of 1979 we have assisted more than two thousand individuals and families whose lives have been disrupted by cults, sects, and other authoritarian movements. About midway through our five-year history, I noticed that there had been a definite shift in the composition of our caseload. During the Center's first three years, our client statistics were heavily weighted by persons associated with the Unification Church of Rev. Sun Myung Moon. Moonies accounted for more than half our cases. The Church of Scientology and the Way International combined constituted about one-fourth of our work. The remaining cases were distributed among nearly one hundred different groups including Eastern guru cults, Bible-based sects, Marxist communes, UFO followers, and so forth. By 1982 we were hearing less about the Moonies—fewer first time calls from anxious parents, fewer requests to reconcile families with Moonies—but more about fundamentalist sects. The figures, however, remained constant for the Church of Scientology, the Hare Krishnas, Way International, Divine Light Mission, Rajneesh, and Free Communion Church.

By 1983, I was so overwhelmed by the significant incidence of fundamentalist, charismatic, and deliverance sects in our caseload that I prepared a special memorandum, "The Gospel Time Bomb—The Threat of Ultrafundamentalism." Undoubtedly the most melodramatic document I have ever penned, it reflected a concern that had been gnawing away at me for months. The memo was sent to the anticult network (a coalition of small organizations that publicize the destructive aspects of cultism), cult-concerned professionals, and media acquaintances. This book is an outgrowth of the memorandum.

With the memo I enclosed a summary of ultrafundamentalist groups with which Freedom Counseling Center (FCC) has been directly involved and requested that the recipients forward any relevant data they had about similar groups in their respective areas. I stated that it was my intention to devote a considerable portion of my time to analyzing this information so that FCC may make recommendations for action by the churches, law-enforcement officials, mental-health authorities, and the media. This book is the result of that analysis. Finally, I advised the recipients of the memo—as I counsel the readers of this book—not to throw up their hands in despair. Although ultrafundamentalist groups are extremely frustrating and in many ways dangerous to deal with, it is not true that nothing can be done to prevent the deaths, beatings, serious illnesses, and other excesses caused by groups of this type.

Ultrafundamentalism is *not* an irresistible tide but a phenomenon that may be understood, addressed, and moderated by the application of appropriate measures. If nothing is done, however, we will soon discover that Jonestown was no fluke. More than fifty preventable deaths have occurred in one ultrafundamentalist sect. Fatal shootouts between police and religious extremists have not been uncommon in recent months. Strategic enclaves have been established by several sects. Two groups known to us have allegedly stockpiled enough assault weapons, ammunitions, and other military supplies to equip 45,000 troops. Training for guerrilla warfare is active and intense.

Those who have worked with me in the past four years know that I am prone to neither tirades nor jeremiads. I am writing this book out of an overwhelming sense that educators, clergy, mental-health professionals, public officials, and concerned laity must pool their talents, insights, and energies to deal with the threat posed by these groups. Unless effective countermeasures are taken, I fear ugly days ahead as ultrafundamentalist cults act out their apocalyptic fantasies.

What is ultrafundamentalism? I use the term to refer to a cluster of "Bible-based" sects that are grounded in the doctrines of American fundamentalism but which greatly exaggerate and elaborate upon these doctrines.

Although the theology of such groups may be described as "otherworldly," ultrafundamentalist sects differ from most Bible-based sects in that they are not passive with respect to the world in which they live. They are opposed to all agencies of human betterment—the government, the agencies of social welfare, and the mainline churches. They see the world as irremediably evil, tottering on the very edge of doom, and about to be destroyed by a wrathful God. Yet at the same time, the ultrafundamentalists are social activists, vigorously striving to impose their sense of order, justice, and morality upon mankind—saints and sinners alike. Since their vision is reactive and negative and their proposed approaches are repressive and violent, it is impossible for those who disagree with them not to respond.

Fundamentalism at worst annoys and frustrates those who do not share it. Ultrafundamentalism at its worst kills its adherents, their families, and its enemies. Its usual manifestations are a prescientific and antirational mythic world view, an obsessive dependence on ecstatic highs, the abdication of responsibility, the surrender to group control, and a childlike obedience to authority. The darkest side of ultrafundamentalism is a holy terrorism, which has its counterpart in the extremism of the Ayatollah Khomeini and the fanaticism of his suicide squads.

In the following pages, I shall explore the ultrafundamentalist phenomenon by presenting selected case histories derived from a quarter of a century of study of Bible-based sects, as well as from the case notes and research files of Freedom Counseling Center. Next I shall explain the history and significance of the central tendencies of ultrafundamentalism. Then I shall attempt to explain why such groups are flourishing at this particular time and in this particular society. Finally, I shall offer suggestions as to what can be done to defuse the destructive potential of the extremists, to moderate the fanaticism of these new sects, or, where amelioration is impossible, to respond humanely and effectively.

Even as I write, the gospel time bomb ticks away.

NOTE

1. The work of Freedom Counseling Center is chronicled briefly in my earlier book, *Cults: The Continuing Threat* (Nashville, Tenn.: Abingdon, 1983), and at length in *Mind-bending: Brainwashing, Cults, and Deprogramming in the 80s* (New York: Doubleday, 1984).

Part One

ULTRAFUNDAMENTALIST
GROUPS AND
THEIR BELIEFS

Introduction: Beliefs and Practices

It is difficult to summarize the beliefs and practices of the scores of groups with which I have dealt or of the thousands of ultrafundamentalist groups that resemble them. The account of Truth Station in Chapter One and the brief descriptions of a handful of other sects with which I have been involved may be more helpful than a precis. However, a few general statements about ultrafundamentalist groups may be made.

With few exceptions, the groups under discussion are *revivalistic* and *fundamentalistic*. They preach salvation by grace through faith and elicit an emotionally cathartic conversion experience. They espouse the doctrines of fundamentalist Protestantism, including the inerrancy of the Bible, the virgin birth of Jesus, substitutionary atonement, and the anticipation of a literal second coming of Jesus to earth. They require that their followers lead a "separated life," that is, one free of such "worldly" vices as smoking, drinking, extramarital sex, gambling, and so forth.

Most groups are *baptistic* and *charismatic*. They require adult-believer baptism by water upon profession of faith. They emphasize a "second blessing," the baptism of the Holy Spirit, which is characterized by such spiritual gifts as speaking in tongues, healing, deliverance, and prophetic utterance. Typically evil spirits are regarded as the cause of all negative human experiences such as sickness, anger, strife, crime, and war. Illness is cured by the laying on of hands and through the exorcism of evil spirits. Medical treatment is usually strongly opposed.

Ultrafundamentalist groups are *dispensationalist-premillennialist* in theology. They believe that the seven-year period of "tribulation" is about to begin or that it has already begun. The "rapture," the removal of true believers from the world either before or in the midst of the tribulation is expected. Many groups believe that only the members of their particular sect constitute the true church and that only they will

9

survive the tribulation. Other Christians are viewed as apostates and enemies of the gospel.

Most groups are *authoritarian,* believing that their leader or leaders are one of the following: (1) God's chosen apostle of the end-time; (2) God's major prophet of the last days; (3) one of the "two witnesses" mentioned in chapter 11 of the Book of Revelation. A few groups go further, regarding their founder as Jesus Christ returned.

The groups are *hierarchical* and *pyramidal,* demanding total submission to leadership. Members are often instructed to lie, steal, defraud, abandon marriages, change careers. Refusal to obey a leader's instructions is considered rebellion against God. Leaders are accorded special privileges and consider themselves above the laws of man and, occasionally, even above the teachings of the Bible. Their words and vision constitute a "third testament," which supersedes the Bible. Financial and sexual exploitation of members is common. Leaders often enjoy affluent lifestyles while the rank-and-file members subsist below the poverty line. Biblical justification for polygamy, incest, and prostitution is attempted in a few groups.

The *husband's authority* over his wife and the obligation of wives and children to be *submissive* are emphasized. Women and children are frequently beaten. Since medical attention is often discouraged or forbidden, many preventable deaths—particularly of mothers and infants in childbirth—occur. Failure to register marriages, births, and deaths with civil authorities is widespread.

Most groups are *communal,* maintaining only minimal contact with the outside world. Possessions, real estate, and financial resources are often "held in common," which in practice means that they are controlled by the group's leader. In several groups, marriages are arranged; children are viewed as property of the collective; and romantic love and parental concern for children are condemned as "idolatry."

In summation, ultrafundamentalists are, first and foremost, fundamentalists. The ultras accept the five "fundamentals" for which fundamentalism is named: (1) the virgin birth, (2) the substitutionary atonement wrought by the death of Jesus on the cross, (3) the resurrection of Jesus, (4) the bodily return of Jesus to earth, and (5) the absolute inerrancy of the Scriptures. In addition, there are five characteristics of ultrafundamentalists that set them apart from other fundamentalists. The "ultrafundamentals" are (1) communalism, (2) apocalypticism, (3) ecstasy, (4) authority, and (5) resistance to deprogramming. We shall explore the significance of all ten of these hallmarks throughout these pages.

Freedom Counseling Center has been directly involved with individuals and families whose lives have been disrupted by ultrafundamentalist groups in virtually every part of the United States. In addition, we have received telephone inquiries from concerned families and journalists regarding groups throughout the world. Some groups have between three and eight members; others have a few hundred; some have several thousand. The most typical group has about four hundred members. Some groups are only partially communal. A core membership lives together while persons peripherally involved maintain separate residences.

CHARACTERISTICS OF CONVERTS

The age of recruits to ultrafundamentalist groups varies from early teens to mid-seventies. In the last two years, the average convert reported to Freedom Counseling Center is about twenty-six to thirty-three years of age, married, the parent of one or two children, and college educated though usually not a graduate. Men and women are equally represented. Most were recreational drug users and sexual experimenters before encountering the group. Very few were political activists or student radicals during the 1960s. Religious backgrounds are diverse. Reform Jews, Roman Catholics, and evangelical Protestants are slightly overrepresented. Most members were converted to born-again Christianity within their particular ultrafundamentalist sect. A significant number are drifters who have belonged to more than one Christian commune. Many were divorcees at the time they became involved and met their current spouse within the group. Many separate from spouses as the result of religious disagreements arising from group involvement. When a married couple leaves a group together, the chances are ten to one that the marriage will fail—even if they were married prior to their participation in the group.

Typical recruits have a history of depression, low self-esteem, and unsatisfactory interpersonal relationships. Prior to their conversions, they were chronically anxious, starved for approval, other-directed, and eager to please. Their inability to set and attain goals is evidenced in frequent changes in career and educational directions. Their intelligence and mental stability is average. Single converts were usually recruited while vacationing or traveling in a strange locale. Lonely college students away from home are particularly susceptible, and many ultrafundamentalist groups actively recruit in college communities. Married couples were typically invited to a meeting by co-workers or friends.

Divorce figures prominently in the backgrounds of the recruits. More than half are the products of broken homes. More than half the converts have themselves been married previously or will be divorced within a few years of their conversion.

The turnover rate of recruits in ultrafundamentalist groups is high. Seven months is an average career. Half of all recruits have fallen by the wayside by the eighth month. Three-fourths leave within two years. However, about one convert in ten stays with a group for two years or more.

My encounters with a number of ultrafundamentalist groups are described in the following chapters.

1

The Truth About Truth Station

Diane is in her middle thirties, a bright, engaging person, eager to please, quick to smile, pleasant, generally open.[1] At one of our first counseling sessions she was self-conscious, very tense, and frightened. She was suffering tremendous ambivalence about seeing me, a fear that by talking to me in order to alleviate her own anxieties she was betraying the group she had left and, thus, was betraying God. (The first thing she did after we were introduced was to excuse herself, go to the women's room, and throw up.) She was afraid that God would punish her, that she would be killed for her failure to submit to His will.

At this point she had been a refugee from her group for two months, having run away in Las Cruces, New Mexico, where she had worked for room and board in a motel before finally making her way to El Paso, Texas, and flying to her brother's home in San Francisco. Her head was a hodgepodge of ideas about the need to be submissive, and in being submissive having to accept a life of humiliation. Her husband had long ceased treating her as his wife and as the mother of their four children. Because of her "willfulness" she had constantly been isolated from the group. She was placed in a kind of solitary confinement either in a tent removed from the tents of the group as it camped in the desert or in a special isolation cabin at the group's farm in Apple Valley, California. When Diane belonged to Truth Station, the group owned and operated a ranch and sent itinerant teams out to distribute books which had been written by the leadership of the group.

Diane was desperately trying to put her own life in order, to find a future, and at the same time to reestablish her fragmented family. Her three minor children remained with their father in the group. He was leading a literature team, which was hiding from the group's "persecutors," in the Arizona desert. In counseling Diane, who was a sincere born-again Christian concerned about finding the will of God, it was necessary to counteract the exaggerated biblicism of the group with a compassionate view of the Gospel. I put a great deal of emphasis upon forgiveness and attempted to counteract the group's strong emphasis on demonic possession, judgment, and condemnation, which were used as an excuse within the group for humiliating its members.

The major ritual of the group was ongoing "truth sessions" or exorcisms, often lasting twelve to sixteen hours. During these sessions, an individual member such as Diane would be violently upbraided by another member for some alleged sin, for example, willfulness. The criticized attitude would, in turn, be ascribed to diabolic influence, for example, possession by the "spirit of Jezebel." Screaming at the top of their lungs, the group would pray, speak in tongues, command the demons to depart, recite Bible passages, and exhort the demon-affected member to repent. The sinful member would often be beaten with a leather belt as further punishment in order to break a "haughty spirit." Subsequent shunning and isolation, during which the sinners were not allowed to bathe, change clothes, or groom themselves, were routine.

Diane had been repeatedly chastised for manifesting the "spirit of the Queen of Heaven." This spirit, the one most feared and hated by the leader, Ed Mitchell, is evident in a mother's love for her children and in a wife's love for her husband. Only God is to be loved in this manner. Crying infants, he teaches, are not to be attended to by their mothers. Their demands are evidence of their self-centered, rebellious, and sinful nature. If they persist in crying, they should be beaten until they learn to obey their parents so that in later life they will instantly respond to the divine will when they are spoken to by God's Holy Spirit. Diane believed that she was a God-rejected, unspiritual woman because she had been repeatedly targeted at the truth sessions. Her major sins were her persistence in attempting to care for her offspring and her feelings of rejection because her husband refused to sleep with her and instead spent his nights snuggled between two unmarried women so that they could protect him from the evil spirits that prowl the night. Diane's spirit had been crushed.

A turning point was a session in which I instructed Diane to tell me as loudly as she could, "in the eyes of God I am a person having worth, having value; I have been put down for too long and I am never again going to allow anyone to humiliate me." I would ask her repeatedly why she would never allow anyone to humiliate her again and she would, in a loud stage whisper which she assumed was a shout, tell me that she was a person of worth, and so forth. Finally, the message took hold.

As the counseling progressed, she became extremely concerned about the three young children she had left behind.

ENTER THE DEPROGRAMMER

At the very beginning of our counseling Diane's brother and sister-in-law reported to me that they had been contacted by Harley Davis, a self-styled deprogrammer. Despite my knowledge of the field of deprogramming and my acquaintance with several deprogrammers, I had never heard of Davis. Also, I thought it was strange that he was contacting the Wrights, attempting to solicit a deprogramming of some one who had voluntarily defected from the group. According to the Wrights, Davis had warned them that Diane would be subject to "post-hypnotic suggestions which had been implanted by the cult and that prearranged cues would send her into a trancelike state." In these states, she would be "dangerous to herself and others." Therefore, he recommended that he be retained for a fee of one thousand dollars and that he and an assistant should confine Diane and deprogram her as soon as possible. The Wrights and I were of one mind with respect to Harley's offer. We felt that we were dealing with an opportunist who could only harm her further.

I phoned Harley to find out what he was up to and because he had told the Wrights that he was working with defectors from Truth Station and with concerned relatives of current members of Truth Station. He told me that he had abducted and deprogrammed a member of the group a year before and that he planned to conduct further abductions and deprogrammings. His major interest in Diane stemmed from his belief that she (and she alone) knew the whereabouts of the group. For with the exception of two or three adults still in Apple Valley, approximately twenty members of the group had simply disappeared into the desert. Since my major goal was discovering the location of Diane's children so that I could help her remove them from the group, I decided to partially cooperate with Harley.

Financed by one of the parents of an adult member of Truth Station, Harley flew to San Francisco, where he met with Diane, the Wrights, and myself. We underwent an elaborate process of negotiation. I offered to assist the concerned parents so that they might discover the whereabouts of their children and grandchildren. I offered to provide them with information regarding my approach to problems similar to theirs. I refused to participate in any kidnapping or illegal or coercive activities they might undertake. Harley, in presenting himself to Diane and the Wrights, took a high-profile deprogrammer's line. He compared Truth Station with the Manson Family and warned that the total insensitivity of the group to human needs would lead them in the direction of murder and possible mass suicide. He described in graphic and horrible detail the murder of Sharon Tate and her unborn child in an attempt to persuade us of the seriousness of the matter. He would later make the same "gut-smut" presentation at a meeting of the concerned relatives in Thousand Oaks, California, in order to stampede them into action.

Harley's speeches about brainwashing and deprogramming were classic Ted Patrick, whose apprentice he had been for three years. Cults, he said, "are all the same." They are based on principles of "brainwashing, mind control and hypnosis" through which cult members become "slaves, mindless robots, and zombies." He stated that there were five thousand cults in the United States with millions of members, that he had been involved in seventy-five deprogrammings (or as he termed them "kidnappings" or "body snatches") without a single failure. At other times during the conversation he told me of cases assigned to him by Ted Patrick which had gone badly, at least two of which had led to his arrest.

In private conversations he told me of three years of his life from ages seventeen to twenty spent in a fundamentalist Christian "cult" in Tennessee, which lived communally and operated a restaurant. He was the first convert to the cult, having assumed a position of leadership second only to the group's founder; he told of having been responsible for the conversion of half the entire membership of the group, having married, having brought members of his own family into the group. He related depressed periods in which he no longer felt conviction or enthusiasm, of how he had fallen from grace in the eyes of the leadership, only later to have repented and been restored and, finally, because of the threat which his mood swings and volatile behavior presented, of having been expelled and told to turn himself over to law- enforcement authorities.

He narrated how he had left the group and had gone through a miasma of overindulgence, which led to the disruption of his marriage. He had been floundering and was headed for self-destruction when he stumbled upon Ted Patrick. He began assisting Patrick by making the arrangements for the snatches, and mimicking "Black Lightning's" rap and deprogramming style. For a few years, he found direction and purpose. However, he told me that in the end he realized that Patrick had ruined his life. Ted had exploited him, paid him miserably, and subjected him to such stress that he had become an alcoholic. He informed me that he had been Patrick's director of security, that he had done most of the work and assumed most of the risks, that Patrick grossly overbooked cases at ten thousand dollars a pop, leaving it to Davis and other assistants to improvise as best they could in impossible and dangerous situations while working for two hundred dollars a week—when there *was* work.

"Do you know how much Ted was making?" Davis asked. Without pausing for a response from me, he declared, "One year he declared $191,000 on his income tax. He lied. His take was more than twice that. Deprogramming is strictly a cash business."

Davis attempted to snare me in his own grandiose aspirations for fame and fortune. He was planning a "mass deprogramming which will make me and anyone who works with me world famous," he related. At the same time he expressed a deep desire for "a closer walk with God" and stated that through personal friends among the defectors from Truth Station he had "returned to the Lord." He confessed that in his earlier days with various big-time programmers he had gotten drunk, used drugs, and taken sexual advantage of at least one subject. In addition, he was attempting to promote his personal career as an actor, writer, and script consultant, having just completed work in a motion picture. I found him a not unattractive person, articulate, though with a limited stock of concepts. He was glib. Still he seemed to be genuinely questing and looking for a peer in his relationship with me.

Yet Davis and I were manipulating one another. I was attempting to negotiate through him with the concerned relatives for financial support for Diane's counseling so that I could afford to go into the field and help her find her children. He was attempting to find information about the group's whereabouts so that he could kidnap eight or more adult members of the group and a number of the children.

Finally, I went with my client to a planning meeting of the concerned relatives held in Thousand Oaks. The group was obviously floundering for lack of leadership. I audaciously offered myself to the group, explaining to them that I did not engage in coercive deprogrammings but that I could locate the group through legal and ethical means and attempt to extricate the minor children and as many of the adults as possible; that if it were necessary to conduct coercive deprogrammings I would not participate but would be available as a rehabilitation counselor to assist any defectors from the group of deprogrammees who required my services. I told them that I would only become involved in the project if I had total control. Harley supported my demand. A vote was taken, and with only one dissenting vote, I was asked to undertake the project.

Our discussion was interrupted by word that the location of the cult had been discovered near Blythe, California, in the Arizona desert.

With instructions from me to representatives of the concerned relatives, two volunteers were sent off to scout the terrain. I went to bed
that night believing that I would be assuming command of the operation—but one whose complexity and danger I was unaware of.

The next morning I was told the group had suffered "buyer's
remorse" overnight and that my services were no longer desired. It was
apparent that a particular pair of parents, the Longs, had assumed
control of the operation, that they deeply resented Diane and me for
having withheld information from them, and that they felt they could
manage the coordination of the operation quite well without me. I
remained at the Longs for the entire day, trying to lend what profes-
sionalism I could to an operation that was rapidly escalating toward a
mass foxhunt in the Arizona desert. Then I left and with Diane went
to Blythe, California, where I remained on the periphery of the operation, steadfastly refusing to participate in any plans for kidnappings,
but remaining where I could be part of the conversations and discover
what the group knew about the whereabouts of Diane's children.

Harley and I remained on good terms through the whole ordeal.
He repeatedly asked me to join the operation as a "deprogrammer,"
since if he were successful in taking eight or more adults he would be
hard-pressed to deconvert them without experienced help. I steadfastly
refused. He contracted with a large number of out-of-state deprogrammers to come to his aid as the need arose. And the group secured a
large commercial guest ranch in California as a location for the
planned mass deprogramming. Harley felt that he could win me over
by inviting me to participate in what he termed "the largest deprogramming in American history," one which would receive tremendous
positive coverage by the media, thereby insuring "fame and fortune for
anyone" who assisted him.

As the result of an aerial search from a rented airplane, the group's
encampment was discovered about an hour's drive from Blythe in
Blanton, Arizona, an extremely small desert town in a very sparsely
settled portion of southwest Arizona. It was Harley's belief that at this
campsite was the entire membership of the cult except for two or three
adult members who had remained behind at the Apple Valley ranch.
Harley kept me well informed of developments, probably because he
could not easily communicate with the collection of mothers, fathers,
brothers, sisters, aunts, uncles, and assorted "thugs." The word *thugs*
should be in quotation marks, for the group was rounded out with a
few born-again charismatic Christians (who went about praying aloud,
"Lord, deliver them into our hands"), housewives, one or two former
members of Truth Station, as well as construction workers and an

unemployed actor. Several of the participants had been promised a hundred dollars a day by Mr. Long.

From the beginning Harley was having great difficulty keeping this conglomerate army under control. When I arrived, someone had become drunk and unmanageable, and Harley almost had to resort to violence to keep him under control. It was also obvious that one or two of the group's "rednecks" had come armed and prepared for battle.

On Saturday morning I met Tony, a smiling, born-again Christian, equipped with a large study Bible crammed with all manner of letters, notes, and personal items. Tony would soon become an important part of the story. The appearance at Blanton of eight or more vehicles and numerous members of the hunting party had panicked Truth Station into making a hasty departure. The campers, with all but two adults and three children, had successfuly eluded the hunters and escaped into the darkness. The deprogramming party had rammed the vehicles of the fugitives in an attempt to force them off the road. A broken wheel on a trailer prevented the departure of the remaining Truth Station members.

The next morning I headed from Blythe to Blanton with Diane, whose children had disappeared from the campsite. We reconnoitered with Harley, the Longs, and others in Topaz, Arizona, which is little more than a gas station in the desert three and a half miles from the campsite where the cultists who did not escape—Hank Watkins, his wife Maria Watkins, two infants, and a nine-year-old boy—were surrounded by the hunting party.

I decided to assert myself and go into action. My decision was now supported by all bystanders including Harley and the Longs. Knowing of allegations of child abuse, which I had heard from defectors from the group (some of whom had left only days before the incidents herein related), I had originally planned to go to the Arizona child-protective services and ask for an investigation so that minor children could be placed in foster custody. After a number of phone calls I gained the ear of the county child-protective officer, who promised to send a sheriff's deputy to investigate.

I decided we should attempt to establish communication with Hank and Maria and/or the Keatons, the family with whom the Watkinses were staying. (The Keatons owned the property on which the Truth Station had been camping.) I instructed a very reluctant Diane that she, together with someone to be trained on the spot by myself, should attempt to enter the grounds. Since Hank appeared to be armed and threats of violence had been made during incursions by the deprogrammer and the families the previous day, this was a tense moment.

Guided by a sudden inspiration, I selected Tony and instructed him how to handle himself on the Keatons' grounds. I waited in Topaz for the arrival of the sheriff's deputy while Tony and Diane drove to Blanton. When the patrol car arrived, I explained to Deputy Sheriff Jeb Moore and his assistant the nature of my business in the area. Having spoken with the deprogrammer and some of the concerned relatives the previous night and during the day, Sheriff Moore was very suspicious. He drove off agreeing to meet me at the Keatons' later.

After an hour's wait my curiosity got the better of me and I had one of the relatives drive me to Blanton. As we approached I saw my car approaching at great speed from the opposite direction. Diane was at the wheel. Sitting next to her was a short, thin woman wearing an excessively large cross, who was waving her arms frantically as she spoke. I knew from previous descriptions that this was Tara Keaton, the wife of the rancher and miner, Tim Keaton. We met in the middle of the road and Diane quickly summarized her visit to the Keaton ranch. Much to her own surprise she had been able to stand her own ground against vicious insults from Hank and Maria, who had reviled her as a "demon-possessed Jezebel," an "unsubmitted woman," and a "traitor to the Gospel."

She and Tony had spoken to the Keatons and had explained our purpose for being at their ranch, and Tara had insisted on talking to me face to face. Tara Keaton seemed terrified. Gesturing wildly, she told me that her husband was "not quite mentally normal"; that he had been a self-appointed "preacher of great power," who had lost his leadership over a small group quite similar to Truth Station, probably as a result of an infatuation with a younger woman. Tara described this younger woman as a "witch." Her fear arose not only from the state of seige under which she and Tom and their ten-year-old daughter found themselves but because of the highly volatile and abusive nature of her husband. She welcomed my arrival and hoped that I could serve as a mediator and bring some peace to the situation.

The Keatons' "ranch" resembled a garbage heap of about two acres surrounded by a wire fence. The land was barren, except for a house trailer to which an extra room had been added. A number of dirt trails, suitable for off-the-road vehicles crisscrossed the land. Approximately a third of the way from the front gate to the house was a trailer and van belonging to Truth Station. Hank Watkins was busily engaged in attempting to repair the trailer, which had been severely damaged by Harley and his party. Adjacent to the Keaton property were an airstrip, a tiny bar, and several simple frame dwellings. Blanton appeared to be a town with a population of no more than forty.

Hank was in constant motion, either working on the trailer or running over to the bar or the home of the bar owner, in order to make telephone calls.

Tara, Tony, and I went directly to the Keaton home, where a lengthy conversation ensued. I introduced myself to Tom Keaton and explained that I was not a deprogrammer nor did I approve of the deprogrammer's techniques. He was very frightened and angry, having witnessed the previous night's attempt to run a camper off the road, with children and adults in it. As we talked we were surrounded and under observation by a number of people wandering around the periphery of the ranch, some of them spying on the house trailer with binoculars.

In a meandering dialogue Tom Keaton and I discussed the born-again experience, groups which attempt to proclaim the Gospel, and the difficulty of telling true groups from cults. I was finally able to gain the confidence of Tom Keaton, as well as Tara.

The Keatons had been given a book by one of the literature distribution teams from Truth Station, and they had sent them a letter requesting additional copies and offering hospitality. The group appeared in the area and conducted "praise and song" services, winning a number of friends among the Keatons' neighbors. The Keatons felt that something appeared quite abnormal about the family patterns within the group; there was a lack of concern on the part of individual parents for their own offspring and a general vagueness as to the whereabouts of some of the children. Also the relationship between Ed Mitchell, the group's leader or "apostle," and Jody Scharf, the group's "prophetess," was bothersome. Mrs. Keaton, who has a fear of strong-willed women, was turned off by Jody's bossiness. It was apparent to me that she saw in the relationship of Ed and Jody a replay of her husband's bewitchment by the "younger woman."

The general tenor of my discussion with Tom was as follows: "I am not a deprogrammer, I do not believe in using force to convert someone to my point of view or away from their own point of view. I believe that each individual must make his own decision before God." These remarks were also an education for Tony, who had been recruited by a friend to assist in the mass deprogramming. He had been led to understand that he was going to accompany people who would leave the group voluntarily. As it became apparent to him that he would be expected to take part in a vigilante hunt and attempt kidnapping, he became very uncomfortable. Hearing me express my non-coercive philosophy afforded him considerable relief.

After about an hour and a half with the Keatons, I felt that some attempt should be made to communicate with Hank and Maria, who were about a hundred yards away. I asked Tom Keaton to go and prepare the way for me and to explain who I was. Then I walked down to the area where the trailer and van were parked. Unfortunately, just prior to my arrival the sheriff's department had come to the scene in response to my child-abuse complaint and were in the process of examining the children with the Watkinses: Tommy Hendler, 9; Ruth Watkins, five months; and Benjamin Mosler, nine months.

I stuck my head into the police cruiser and asked if I could speak with the officers when they completed their investigation. They agreed. Upon seeing me, Hank had run off to the bar, leaving Maria and the three children. Maria appeared to be the very stereotype of a brainwashed cult member—rigid, spaced-out, and wide-eyed. She said to me: "My husband has told me not to talk to you. And I don't want to talk to you either."

I then returned to the Keatons' home, where we were joined by Deputy Sheriff Moore, a grizzled veteran, and his young assistant. At first the police officers were cold and distant, apparently feeling there was no basis for the child-abuse complaint. They had found no signs of fresh injuries to any of the children and, of course, were concerned about the activity of the would-be intruders.

I made an emotional appeal to the police officers, explaining that I had information from Diane and other defectors from the group indicating that the group was dangerous, abusive to an extreme, and that their activities toward the children could be considered life-endangering. Specifically I told them it was the practice of the group to isolate rebellious members in the wilderness for long periods of time and that beatings had become a staple of the Truth Station lifestyle. Tony told them an incident about a young diabetic adult who died.

Gradually the seriousness of the situation dawned on the officers and they agreed to reexamine the children, bringing Tommy into the house and allowing me to question him. A neighbor named Roberts, friendly to Hank and Maria, entered the room and was obviously spying on us. My conversation with Tommy was the turning point in the child-abuse investigation.

In a quiet, supportive, nonthreatening manner, I asked the boy about the group. He was surprisingly articulate and mature. He told of regular beatings and isolations. It was startling that Tommy related the beatings and isolations in a natural way, as though they occur every day in normal society. It was obvious that he was very frightened and had been warned by the group to mind what he said to outsiders. In our conversation he explained how he had often been isolated in the desert with a sleeping bag for three or four days at a time. "For what were you being punished?" I asked.

"For the sin of having a haughty spirit—for acting as if I were better than someone else," he replied.

According to a member who had been deprogrammed from the group a few days earlier, the truth of the matter is that the child had been isolated for three or four months at a time!

When I asked him who administered the beatings he replied, "God uses Hank"—at which point Hank entered the room.

He became very defensive and interjected, "Yes, of course we beat people or chastise people in the group. Why not? What's so wrong about that?"

Diane began screaming at Hank, telling him that what the group was doing was not right. I had to separate them. While I was trying to get Diane under control, I could scarcely control myself. I had become angered hearing of the abuses and was enraged by Hank, who was acting proud of himself. Hank then insisted that the questioning be ended and that Tommy leave the room. The sheriff's deputies nodded in assent and the boy walked to the trailer. The lawmen looked from face to face with incredulity in their eyes.

In these few moments they had become friends of Diane and mine and the group's enemies. They immediately undertook a house-to-house search of the small community in hope of finding other children. In addition to the three children with Hank and Maria, seven other minor children were still missing.

We did a thorough job of informing the local people of the true nature of Truth Station. Several adults told us of having spent considerable time "fellowshipping" with Ed Mitchell, the Watkinses, other adult members of the group, and about ten children who had been camping at the Keatons'. The locals stated that while the overall mood had been one of childlike frolic on the part of the adults and children alike, there was a disturbing undercurrent. For example, they had been told by Maria Watkins that she was prohibited from breastfeeding her daughter lest she become attached to the infant and hence not give her total love to God and her total submission to the will of God as revealed to Ed Mitchell. Instances were cited of negligent treatment of the baby by Maria.

The next morning Diane and I rushed to Blanton after a "come immediately" telephone call from Harley. The child-protection officer from Parker, Arizona, had arrived. She and the sheriff's officers moved in on Hank and Maria and took the three children into custody.

After I returned to San Francisco the next day, I learned through a phone conversation that it was the intention of the child-protective officer to ask the court to make the children wards of the state and to place them in a proper foster home. As it turned out, this hearing would be the only positive accomplishment of the elaborate and grotesquely expensive hunting expedition. At this point, Mr. Long was reporting out-of-pocket expenses of more than fourteen thousand dollars as well as other large bills.

Three days later I left for a case in Chicago, keeping in touch with the Arizona situation by telephone. Hank and Maria appeared the following day in Parker to be interviewed by the child-protection officer. After the hearing they were tailed by two grandmothers, little old ladies from Pasadena, in a yellow Cadillac. Subsequently Harley and Peter Finch, one of his stooges, took up the trail and apprehended Hank and Maria, forcing them to leave in one of the vehicles belonging to the hunting party and leaving other vehicles at the scene of the abduction. The kidnapping, witnessed by locals, was reported to the police, and Harley and Peter were arrested. During the snatch, there had been a struggle in the road. Peter got a firearm from the trunk of his car and subdued Hank, who was seen on his hands and knees in the middle of the road. Hank was tied and placed in the front seat of the car next to Harley, and Maria was in the back seat with Peter. They were speeding off through the desert at ninety miles an hour when Hank freed himself of his bonds, threw the ropes over Harley's neck, and began strangling him. Harley lost control of the vehicle, which careened off into the desert. Fortunately no one was injured. There was a hearing, but I believe that the kidnap victims failed to press charges or to testify.

After the initial kidnapping, there was a major falling out among the hunters. Harley was no longer speaking to the Longs, but he was retained by Walt Mosler, to continue on the trail of Mosler's son and grandchildren. One of his friends informed me that Harley was pressuring Mosler to support a television series based upon Harley's experiences as a deprogrammer.

Diane's reactions to the ordeal described were as follows: She went through an initial period of deep depression and despondency, during which she felt her inability to recover her children amounted to God's judgment upon her for having defected from the group. The more time that she spent with the hunters, the more she began to feel that it was the hunters who were insane and brainwashed. Further reflection upon the testimony that led to action by the child-protective services convinced her that the group really was evil and that she had done the right thing by leaving the group. When she arrived at this realization,

nightmares which had plagued her for three months suddenly disappeared.

Today she is fiesty, personable, and human. At times, she and I are
sorry we ever attempted to cooperate with the deprogrammer and the
concerned relatives. Had we pursued our original strategy, it is likely
that Diane's children would have been removed from the group by the
child-protective services. However, if we had not cooperated we would
never have known the location of the children and would have been
unable to have done anything. At least, we were able to rescue three
other abused children from a dangerous group. Alas, these children
were not my client's.

MORE TRUTH ABOUT TRUTH STATION

After the well-publicized kidnapping of a TV producer's son and
grandsons, Dennis Webster and his sons Todd, 9, and Benjamin, 9
months, and the arrest of a group of deprogrammers that included
Harley Davis,[2] Truth Station attempted an all-out media blitz to tell
its story, even though the membership had shrunk to only eleven
people. Press conferences were called, biblically documented statements
of beliefs made available, accounts of the kidnappings of sect members
distributed, and supporting statements by critics of deprogramming
disseminated. The parents and deprogrammers retaliated with their
version of the story, laden with charges of child abuse and brainwashing. Truth Station responded with doctrinnaire counterblasts. It
was a three-ring circus, shrewdly exploited by both sides. For example,
in a March 5, 1981, UPI article, Skip Webster, producer of *Fantasy
Island,* accused the sect members of being "robots" who "regularly beat
children and adults." He had learned from group defectors that his
"daughter-in-law and a 4-year-old girl have been beaten, that a 9-year-
old boy was left alone in an Arizona desert for a long period and that
his 15-year-old grandson had helped beat an older woman."[3]

On February 27, Webster's allegations sparked the removal by
sheriff's deputies, acting on behalf of child-protective services, of the
nine minor children from the group. Included were my client's three
daughters, ages nine, eleven, and thirteen. During subsequent hearings,
their father abandoned his rights, and custody devolved to the mother.
The thirteen-year-old's acting-out behavior was so vicious that the
mother later asked the authorities to return the child to the father. On
March 4, the sect issued more than seventy-six pages of statements and
press releases charging that they had been the victims of repeated

kidnappings, break-ins, and personal assaults. They maintained that their tormentors—not they—were the true criminals.

One of their statements said: "We believe that believers are to be baptized by immersion in water and baptized in the Holy Spirit which is a separate baptism." They reiterated their conviction that "these are the last days and that Jesus Christ is coming within this generation for His people." They declare themselves separate from all forms of "worldly religion" and denominations. The implication is that they alone are based upon the true doctrines of Jesus Christ as set forth in the Bible. It is their "rigid commitment" which has elicited "persecutions, false accusations, lies, rumors and evil plots. . . ."

The accounts by cult members Cynthia and Rod Crow and Julie and Peter Hughes of the February 21 kidnapping attempt are reminiscent of a terrorist attack. Cynthia recalls: "They grabbed me. Harley Davis put his hand over my mouth. The other two tried taping my hands behind my back as I was on my knees. My pajama top tore open. They proceeded to drag me out of the bathroom on my knees, grabbing my arms trying to tie my wrists. The tape kept breaking as I struggled to get free. They put tape around my head and mouth but I tore it off. They tore my top off and I was naked except for my underwear. I struggled and crawled to the foot of the bed." It took thirty minutes to subdue her. Her husband, Rod, was beaten into near unconsciousness and bound. Peter Hughes was repeatedly beaten and choked. Other members of the sect suffered similar fates. In sum, not a pretty picture.

Truth Station has dwindled to about eight members—four of the beseiged desert dwellers and four new recruits. They now live in Tucson, Arizona, where they support themselves and their ministry by buying and selling used tires. Ed and his wife Dorothy are divorced. The self-proclaimed apostle of the end-times has married Jody Scharf. The distribution of *The Truth* continues.

ONE FAMILY'S GRIEF

The family grief which a loved one's conversion to an ultrafundamentalist sect can elicit is well illustrated in the case of Ted Manners.[4] Ted has been involved with Ed Mitchell for three years. His father, Theodore Manners, Sr., is the president of a family-owned manufacturing business in Ohio. He is a calm, deliberate man, who handles enormous amounts of stress in his work and manages to keep his feelings to himself. But young Ted is the one subject on which his emotions cannot be concealed.

When I first met Ted, Sr., he began our conversation by taking out his wallet, removing two letters whose creases revealed that they had been scrutinized a thousand times, and reading them to me. The first letter, written by his then twenty-one-year-old son at the end of his junior year in college, closes as follows:

Thanks for your letter and the love that you have for me. I really love you, Dad. . . . Well, it's Wednesday night and there are six people in my room cranking out some music on the stereo. Yep, I'm having a lot of fun here at college. We're going to keep plugged in. I'll be seeing you when you get up here.

Much, much love from me to you.

Your son,
Teddy

As Ted, Sr., opened the second letter, he was doing his best to choke back tears. He read aloud from the second letter, which was written six months after the first. His son had written:

As I told you before, I refuse your love—because it does not come from a man submitted to God. And just as light has no fellowship with darkness, I have no fellowship with you.

I am not—neither do I want to be—Teddy Manners ever again. There is nothing in my former life that I want.

In the short time that I have been living for Jesus Christ, I have come from being a boy to being a man of God. This is the true state of my welfare in obedience to Christ.

Theodore Manners

It took Ted a moment to regain his composure. As he replaced the letters in his wallet, he chanced upon some photographs. "This is my family," he said. "We are a normal family," he continued. "This is my wife Luanne. And here's my older daughter, Beth. She's twenty-eight—an on-site construction coordinator for a large corporation—a graduate of Purdue University. She beat out three guys for the job." He handed me another photo.

"This is Lilith. She's twenty-five and is finishing her master's in zoology. She's on call with Marine World and Sea Land. She's one of the few experts on the parasites of whales. And she's a deep-sea diver."

He placed a final picture on the table between us. "This is Teddy," he explained. "This was taken just before he joined the cult. He was just a quarter of a semester away from graduation in business economics at the university. He was a top student, too. He'd come from a 2.0 average to a 3.0. He had laughed his way though high school—smoking dope with his friends. But he had become a born-again Christian. We thought it helped him a lot—it got him down to business. Suddenly he took on the reality of 'Hey, I've got to get an education.' I've never seen a guy working harder at school and for what he wanted."

The father went on: "Teddy was active at Calvary Chapel—it's what people call a 'charismatic church.' It's very good for kids—gets a lot of them off drugs. But it has its extremists. Teddy went there on Sundays and for Bible-study groups during the week. He had other interests—hockey and skiing. And he was a great communicator. Why he would warn other kids about the dangers of cults. He used to go around and speak about cults." Ted fumbled with a pack of cigarettes, lit one, took a puff and added: "He went to a meeting one night. And there was this older man there who jumped up and said, 'There is someone in this group who is not in step with the Lord.' He pointed at Teddy and yelled, 'And it's you!' That was the nudge. Here he was about to graduate and unsure of the future. So he looked up to this 'street Christian' he had met, preaching about being totally submitted to the will of God."

Ted and Luanne were away on a business trip at the time. A week passed after their return and there was no word from their son. Teddy had left for college two weeks earlier with his car and thirteen hundred dollars in cash for the rent of his off-campus apartment. Ted related, "So I called him and he announced, 'I have left college. I have gone with God.'" Ted demanded that his son come home immediately so that they could discuss the matter. Teddy arrived a few nights later and slept in his car rather than come into the house. (Neighbors who had spoken with Teddy conveyed this to his parents some time later.)

After Ted left for the plant, the young man knocked on the door. His mother found him distant and strange. She insisted that he see his father at the office. Ted, Sr., was also uncomfortable with his aloof, distant manner. A loud and heated argument ensued. Ted questioned his son about his new mission and his plans for the future. The young man leapt up, his arms crossed defiantly. "I stand on God," he would reiterate whenever challenged. He refused to answer any of his father's questions. As Ted, Sr., recalls: "I became upset—I struck him. And as I did I realized that I was swinging at a stranger." Teddy turned and left.

Ted has heard nothing from his son in three years—except for inquiries from attorneys who were seeking information about the young man's assets—the value of his stock in the company, his endowment, and the surrender value of his insurance policies. According to Ted, "the cult was trying to cash him out—trying to shake us down for anything they could get."

Ted remembers how he and Luanne reeled from the impact of what had happened. Half their time went into trying to understand the how and why of the experience. Through the impressions which Teddy's roommates and friends shared with them, they learned the identity of the group. Ted attended the press conferences called by the group as well as by its critics. He phoned former members, journalists, deprogrammers—anyone who could help him understand where his son was and what he was doing. He tried to arrange a "rescue attempt," getting together a number of Teddy's born-again college chums. He explains, "We thought that their love and mutual interests would pull Teddy out from under the influence of the group." But Teddy managed to hide from them.

From time to time, Teddy and his newfound "elder in the Lord," an erstwhile disciple of Ed Mitchell's, would surface on the streets at night, preaching their jeremiads against sin, the spirit of motherhood, the apostate churches, and lukewarm dedication to Jesus. They would invite others to join them in their mission, urging their hearers: "Repent before it's too late. For the Bible says that the world is coming to an end."

Their uncouth, hysterical, and hostile manner won little approval. But a few lost souls listened too long and were swept up—at least momentarily—by their fiery invectives. The two preachers would move in with them and share their food and resources, conducting frantic "truth sessions" and "deliverances," which disturbed the rest of neighbors and attracted the attention of the police.

I was able to locate them through a local contact. Luanne and Teddy's sisters attempted to talk to him. But he and his companion went berserk, shouting obscenities, scripture verses, preprogrammed rantings and ravings for nearly two hours. The police came to restore order. Seeing that she was getting nowhere, Luanne asked her son for the keys to the car that was registered in his father's name. He complied. She has not seen Teddy since.

"For a long time," Ted recalls, "my life was so obsessed with this problem I couldn't sleep or think about anything else. Luanne and I probably started drinking too much. I don't know how my business survived. I kept worrying about this kid—where he was and how he was." Ted spent quite a bit of time with the parents of other members of Truth Station. They advised him to have his son kidnapped and deprogrammed.

But even though he agrees with their assessment, that is, that his son has been brainwashed by the cult, that his mind has "snapped" as the result of the group's indoctrination—Ted rejects their counsel. When a friend asked him recently, "Does deprogramming work?" Ted answered: "Not as well as the deprogrammers would have you believe. Forcible deprogramming is questionable at best. There has to be an inner want by that child to come out. Even then there have been a lot of problems. Many hours of professional help are needed."

Like many parents whose child has become converted to a totalistic sect, Ted has become a student of religious cults. He gives talks to civic groups, distributes reading lists, and has tape-recorded an account of his experiences for other concerned parents. He maintains regular phone contacts with anyone who can provide him with information about his son's whereabouts and well-being. And he waits.

Fearing that his family's unwanted contact with him and his "elder" (who is about two years older than Teddy) was a prelude to kidnapping, Teddy and his companion made their way to the remnants of Truth Station at the height of hostile actions against the group. According to Ted, Sr., his son is now in a southwestern city, supporting himself and what is left of Truth Station by buying and selling used tires. About once a year, one of Teddy's sisters receives a curt note from the vagabond, telling her that he is still "walking in the will of God and growing in grace daily." In his letters, he scolds his parents and sisters for their lack of submission to God, and disappears once more into his mission to redeem souls—and tires—for the kingdom of God.

NOTES

1. All names have been changed except Ed Mitchell and Jody Scharf. "Diane" asked me to include her story.

2. "8 Arrested in Kidnapping Case," *Los Angeles Times,* Feb. 25, 1981, p. 24; *People,* April 1, 1981, pp. 51-52.

3. "Cult Accused of Creating Human Robots," *San Francisco Chronicle,* March 5, 1981, p. 6.

4. Names and places have been changed. I have my client's permission to tell this story.

2

Sally and the Shepherds

I have mentioned the flow from democratic to autocratic government in charismatic groups. The most developed, yet generally unknown, expression of pyramidal government is the fundamentalist/charismatic movement known as the "shepherding," "discipleship," or "submission" movement. There are several chains of shepherding groups as well as independent entities. Their upper-level leadership usually is drawn from the ranks of disaffected Assemblies of God clergy and newly charismatic Baptists. Many of my experiences have been with the Simpson-Mumford-New Wine chain, which has its world headquarters in Mobile, Alabama. This is an invisible denomination with tens of thousands of members throughout the United States and abroad.

The movement may be traced to six charismatic Bible expositors: Juan Luis Ortiz, Bob Mumford, Derek Prince, Charles Simpson, Don Basham, and Ern Baxter. Ortiz is an Argentinian, widely known for his writings and sermons on "discipleship." He does not seem to have any structural role in the shepherding movement. In about 1969, Mumford and the rest formed a group known as the Holy Spirit Teaching Mission, which in the early seventies became Christian Growth Ministries of Ft. Lauderdale, Florida. The group provided speakers for conferences, began to publish books and pamphlets, and founded the magazine, *New Wine*.

Mumford is a graduate of the Reformed Episcopal Seminary in Philadelphia, the school of a small evangelical denomination. Prince is the product of Eton College and Cambridge University. Basham has attended a seminary of the Christian Church. Simpson was a Baptist minister in Mobile, Alabama. Baxter was a pastor in Canada.

The shepherding movement, which in most respects is a cluster of conventional independent fundamentalist churches with dispensational and charismatic characteristics, emphasizes spiritual growth through discipleship, that is, through the submission of the individual Christian to a God-ordained elder. This elder, in turn, interprets the will of God for his flock. In the words of Derek Prince, "Whenever his (God's)

31

delegated authority touches our lives, he requires us to acknowledge and submit to it, just as we would to him in person."[1] The movement's teachings about discipleship are heavily influenced by Ortiz and the late Watchman Nee, whose followers have founded the equally controversial sect known as "the Local Church." By the mid-seventies the shepherding movement threatened to divide the charismatic movement from which it springs. In March 1976 leaders of the charismatic movement met in Oklahoma City in an attempt to resolve differences.

Mumford, Simpson, and the others are generally well regarded among evangelical Christians. *New Wine,* a well-edited, attractively illustrated, slick magazine, is published monthly by Integrity Communications, which is now located in Mobile. Simpson, Basham, Prince, Mumford, and Baxter are listed on the masthead as members of the board of directors. Mumford's "New Wine Tape of the Month," is listed as an associated ministry. Articles deal with salvation, the Christian life, gifts of the Spirit, parenting, and the Second Coming in a moderate and skillful manner. There is virtually nothing in these pages that would offend the most conservative evangelical. Now and then something slips in about the value of submitting oneself to the authority of one's elder. But such references are rare.

One occurred in the July/August 1975 issue in an "essay of the month," "The Birth of a Local Church," written by Michael Ford, who is identified as "an elder in the Body of Christ in Tuscaloosa, Alabama," who had just graduated from the University of Alabama Law School. Ford tells how a group of college students had bound themselves in a covenant to establish God's Kingdom in Tuscaloosa. He states: "Hot on the heels of covenant loyalty came submission." He explained that the group had learned that "people will quickly degenerate into either anarchy or spiritual democracy if they do not have submissive hearts and teachable spirits." He related the group's regular pattern of prayer and fasting, and their decision to merge with another similar group from another city. He mentioned in passing that each group was led by a "shepherd."

Reading between the lines it is easy to cut through Ford's pieties and infer that there has been struggle and strife for leadership, that the group has not been very successful in winning converts, and that their structure, which to quote Ford, "we could find no black-letter scripture to substantiate," was autocratic.[2]

In February 1984, *New Wine's* cover story, "Bob Mumford: Thirty Years of Ministry," dealt rather directly with the shepherding controversy without ever mentioning the word or fully explaining the concept. The article, in the form of an interview, contains the following exchange:

> NW (*New Wine*): We have often heard you mention the need for a nonreligious message. How do you see that taking shape among the people of God?
>
> BOB MUMFORD: We need to eliminate the feeling that my job, my home, and my family are different from my responsibility to God.
>
> The word *gospel* means "good news." When we say the "gospel of the kingdom of God," we need to understand that a *kingdom* is a form of government. We're really talking about the good news of God's government. It's a government that has dominion over *every area* of our lives. That's quite a contrast to an approach in which our spiritual activity is one small area that we dedicate to the Lord, leaving the other seven-eighths of our lives for us to run as we wish . . . there is a way of seeing the New Testament *governmentally*. It is seeing Christ as a king, seeing apostles, prophets, pastors, teachers, and elders in a governmental way.[3]

Mumford declares that it is his intention to place the teaching of God's government alongside the other fundamental truths of Christianity, in his words, the "truth about redemption, truth about healing, truth about prosperity, truth about the coming of the Lord."[4] He admits that the controversy about his teachings—particularly the accusations that he has been a divisive influence—have hurt him deeply. He also acknowledges that there have been extremists who have applied his teachings in a manner which has done much harm "to groups and individuals." For this, he states, "I am deeply sorry."[5] Yet, he admits no second thoughts on the matter and is, he says, content to leave it to God to cleanse his truth of imperfections. As a reader of *New Wine*, if I did not already know what I do about the shepherding controversy, I would not know what Mumford was talking about. I would simply interpret him to be referring to the government of God over the believer's life, which every Christian is expected to embrace on the basis of his own conscience.

I had never have heard of shepherding until the spring of 1981, when I received a phone call from a worried and frightened young woman in Nashville, Tennessee. The caller was Sally Watson, who was afraid that her two daughters were going to be illegally removed from her custody by an Atlanta shepherding group we shall call Bible Truth Fellowship.[6]

Sally, a slight, attractive woman, has undergone in less than thirty years experiences that would put a soap opera to shame. By age twenty-two, she had married her childhood sweetheart, seen him off to

Vietnam, been widowed, borne a posthumous child, remarried, and divorced her second husband, Bobbie Watson. After the birth of her second child, he had beaten her so severely that a hysterectomy had been required. A divorce was granted in 1972 on the grounds that Bobbie "has been guilty of cruel and inhuman treatment or conduct toward the plantiff and renders co-habitation unsafe and improper." Then he joined a shepherding group in Nashville.

Bobbie's efforts at reconciliation had been spurned by Sally. The Nashville group subsequently merged with a similar group in Atlanta, and Bobbie, together with the bulk of the Nashville membership, had relocated in Atlanta. They had been told that while the Nashville leader was visiting Alan Jenks in Atlanta, he had a vision of "a black cloud of sin," floating over Nashville and realized that "all good Christians should move to Atlanta." About fifty families left jobs, homes, schools, friends and relatives behind and moved to Georgia.

Sally was convinced that Bobbie had made at least two attempts to remove forcibly from Sally's custody both his own daughter, Kimberly (age 10), and his stepdaughter Mavis Watson (age 12). According to oral reports made to Sally by Mary Otman, Sally's now deceased, former mother-in-law, the leadership of the Bible Truth Fellowship had planned and attempted child snatching so that Kimberly and Mavis could: (1) be placed under the authority, discipline, and control of Bobbie; (2) be rescued from the "evil" influence of their "unsaved" and "worldly" mother; (3) be reared in accordance with the shepherd movement's concept of submission and obedience; (4) be hidden from Sally and the authorities within the international network of shepherding fellowships.

Sally believed that the group's motivation was financial. Her father is wealthy and the two girls will certainly be his beneficiaries. Also the support payments and medical-expense reimbursement made by Bobbie are costly to the group.

At the time Sally first contacted me, I had no acquaintance with the shepherding movement. For all I knew, Sally was an overprotective mother who wanted her ex-husband to disappear quietly from her life and was raising the "cult" threat as a smokescreen. The issue at hand was Bobbie's petition to liberalize his visitation rights so that his daughter could visit him at his home, place of work, and place of worship in Atlanta.

I started asking questions of my professional and anticult acquaintances, particularly of the staff of such evangelical organizations as the Christian Research Institute and Spiritual Counterfeits Project.[7] In short order, I was inundated with books, pamphlets, tapes, magazine articles, photocopies of letters from shepherding defectors, and the first-hand testimony of disgruntled former members. I had stumbled upon one of fundamentalism's classic internecine wars.

The editors of the *Christian Standard* identify Covenant Outreach Ministries as a California affiliate of Christian Growth Ministries. A minister of a California Christian Church warned in the journal that independent Christian churches are targets.

> The movement to which we are referring uses innocent and even Scriptural-sounding words like "shepherding," "discipling," "covering," and "covenanting" to describe its ministry . . . . Although it plays down affiliations that might label it as denominational or identify it as part of a larger organization, it is nonetheless highly structured and organized . . . . Five men form the upper echelon . . . . Under them are disciples who have been trained by them and who are "covered" by them (that is, each disciple is in submission to his designated covering). This "covering-submission" chain works its way down to the local congregation and eventually involves everyone within the church who is willing to submit to a covering.[8]

The California minister, Rev. Rick Hahn, described the movement as committed to charismatic gifts, extra-biblical authority (vision, dreams, and prophecies that supplement the Bible), overbearing shepherding programs, and exclusiveness. He finds them unsupportive of local church autonomy and disinterested in evangelism.[9]

The publication of this letter and another article evoked charges of defamation and a lawsuit for libel from the California group. In a letter to the managing editor of *Christian Standard,* Dennis T. Peacocke, chairman of the board of Covenant Outreach Ministries, lambasted the periodical for having ignored Matthew 18: 15-17, which admonishes Christians to settle their disputes among themselves and not in the secular law courts—a strange way of notifying the *Standard* that it is about to be sued.

In the September 14, 1980, issue of the same publication, a "clarification" appeared. The magazine retracted some of its statements but further indicated that its "opposition to the error of the Covenant/ Discipleship viewpoint is unchanged." The lawsuit was dropped.

In 1979, Christian Research Institute in Anaheim, California, a major evangelical, anticult organization, issued a brief pamphlet which includes the following warning:

> [We] do not believe the so-called "Shepherding movement," led by Bob Mumford, Derek Prince, Don Basham, Ern Baxter, John Poole, and

Charles Simpson, is working according to biblical principle. We believe that there are some clearly nonscriptural teachings involved, and that it is dangerous to the healthful growth and the spiritual maturity of the Christian. For this reason we oppose the movement.

The central teaching of the movement is the necessity of every Christian being submitted especially to a certain person, who plays the role of "shepherd." There is no scriptural support for this belief, while on the contrary the Scriptures say that all Christians should be submitted to each other. . . . The amount of control exercised by "some shepherds" is amazing, coming to the point of giving permission to marry, to have children, and to go to certain church fellowships. This is not scriptural.[10]

In 1976, the General Presbyteries of the Assemblies of God, the major charismatic and pentecostal denomination in America, adopted a highly critical report on the discipleship and submission movement.

My contacts within evangelical Christianity described the shepherding movement as authoritarian, inclined to utilize intense peer pressure, dangerously centralized, rigidly hierarchical, excessively controlling, and prone to bring lawsuits against their critics.

SHEPHERDING CRITIQUED

Evangelical Christian criticisms of shepherding have continued. Jerram Barrs attributes shepherding to the unfortunate tendency on the part of some evangelicals to "harbor suspicion of doctrine, suspicion of using one's mind to understand Scripture and suspicion of law or any human effort to obey the law of God."[11] The anti-intellectuality of this position is evidence in the reliance on intuition, "the hotline-to-heaven mentality."[12] Since there is always the possibility that one's direct revelations may in fact come from one's own wishes, the need develops for an authoritarian structure to confirm and regulate the flow of direct messages. Hence, Barrs observes, the greater the reliance on direct revelation, the more authoritarian the structure will be.

Barrs commends the stated motives of the shepherding movement: it has attempted to overcome oral permissiveness, strengthen marriage and the family, and encourage maturity through discipline. However, the claims of the leaders of given fellowships to total control over every aspect of the believer's life are unwarranted, unscriptural, and dangerous. Not only are there no checks and balances on the leaders within the community, but the act of questioning a leader's opinion is seen as rebellion against God punishable by excommunication. While a biblical argument can be raised that it is the responsibility of the elders of the local Christian church to discipline members for false doctrine or moral lapses, there is no scriptural authority for regulating the specifics of people's lives: "whom someone should marry, where people should live, what jobs they should hold, how much they should give to the church, whom they should go to for counsel."[13]

Barrs is especially critical of the tendency of the shepherds to control the lives of the sheep on the basis of the shepherds' use of the "gift of prophecy." According to the shepherding movement, this gift is required both to receive God's messages and to confirm them. In essence, this doctrine means that the leader has access to God in a way not available to the ordinary believer. Thus, Barrs contends, the whole intent of the "new covenant," which makes all Christians a "kingdom of priests," is annuled, and with it, the Protestant Reformation's central doctrine of the priesthood of all believers is discarded. The leader becomes a mediator between God and man. He not only speaks with the authority of God, but also claims that what he says is what God says. He does not merely advise or counsel the believer as a concerned brother, he tells the believer "Thus saith the Lord" when he instructs the believer whom to marry, where to live, and so forth.

Shepherding is one of the most serious challenges facing evangelical Christianity at this time in history. How can it deal with groups that are theologically orthodox but which operate like cults in their abuse of authority? Among evangelicals who are today wrestling with this issue, I would mention sociologist Ronald Enroth and college chaplain Harold L. Bussell.[14]

It is a simple matter for evangelicals to categorize as "cults" groups which deviate from the "fundamentals" or the Apostles Creed. Instructional materials are developed and missionary strategies employed to respond to non-Christian cults. But the evangelical response to so-called "Christian aberrant" groups is problematic at best. For the most part, evangelicals duck and take cover.

NOTES

1.Quoted by Ronald Enroth in "The Power Abusers," *Eternity*, Oct. 1979, p. 25.

2. Michael Ford, "The Birth of a Local Church," *New Wine*, July/Aug. 1975, pp. 18-19.

3. *New Wine*, Feb. 1984, p. 7.

4. Ibid., p. 8.

5. Ibid.

6. The names of Sally and Bobbie Watson, the Bible, Truth Fellowship, and its former members are all fictitious. Sally has asked me to include her story.

7. Several counselors of cult-distressed families informed me that shepherding cases outnumber all others. Agencies in New York and Pittsburgh told me that inquiries and complaints about shepherding groups constitute most of their current workload.

8. "Wolves in Wool Suits" (editorial), *Christian Standard,* June 1, 1980, p. 3.

9. "Christian Minister Issues Warning," op. cit., p. 5.

10. "The Shepherding Movement," a "fact sheet," prepared by Cal Beisner, Research Consultant, San Juan Capistrano, California, 1979.

11. Jerram Barrs, *Shepherd & Sheep: A Biblical View of Leading and Following* (Downers Grove, Ill.: Inter-Varsity Christian Fellowship, 1983), p. 28.

12. Ibid., p. 29.

13. Ibid., p. 70.

14. See Enroth, "The Power Abusers," *Eternity,* Oct. 1979, p. 22; and Bussell, *Unholy Devotion* (Grand Rapids, Mich., Zondervan, 1983).

3

Other Ultrafundamentalist Groups

During the past two years, a majority of our cases at Freedom Counseling Center have involved us with ultrafundamentalist sects—offshoots of older charismatic groups that practice speaking in tongues and "healing," and that believe in the imminent return of Jesus Christ. In several instances, extreme child abuse, wife beating, and avoidance of required medical treatment (such as innoculations, removal of operable tumors, setting of fractures, chemotherapy) have been reported to me by my clients. Other abuses are common. The following is a brief account of our dealings with these groups.

FAITH ASSEMBLY OR GLORY BARN

The saddest record of any of these groups is that of Faith Assembly or "Glory Barn," which has its headquarters in the Warsaw, Indiana, area. According to several newspaper accounts, at least fifty-two people—most of them infants and children—have died as a result of following the teachings of the group. Faith Assembly, which was founded ten years ago by the Rev. Hobart Freeman (and who is today its pastor), has about two thousand members. Members are discouraged from seeking medical attention on the grounds that only God can heal and that using medicine is evidence of lack of faith.

Reporters Jim Quinn and Bill Zlatos of the Ft. Wayne *News-Sentinel* disclosed the following:

> There have been twice as many medically unattended deaths as previously among those adhering to Freeman's teachings.
>   Only a small fraction of the 52 known victims were old enough to understand the teachings of Faith Assembly.
>   An even smaller fraction made their own decision to shun medical treatment.

One victim asked for a doctor a few hours before her death, but no doctor arrived because her husband and friends decided prayer was best for the woman. They prayed for her for hours after she had died.

Routine medical procedures could have prevented many of the deaths.

Faith Assembly deaths were found in Indiana, Illinois, Ohio, Kentucky, Michigan, and Missouri.

Seven families suffered more than one death. The(se) families accounted for 18 of the 52 deaths. Two of the families lost three members each.[1]

Other newspaper accounts report that a 20-week-old fetus was buried in a backyard in a shoebox; babies and their mothers were dying in childbirth while registered nurses looked on and did nothing; children have died of chicken-pox complications; one girl was denied treatment for a massive tumor which destroyed one eye and finally killed her; a 40-year-old diabetic stopped taking his insulin shots and died four days later. In November of 1982, Leah Dawn Mudd, 5, was removed from her home by court order so that doctors could remove a cancerous tumor as big as a basketball from her abdomen. Earlier the girl's 4-year-old sister had died of a tumor.[2] In July 1976, Alice Rogers, 23, a pregnant church member, bled to death after two days of labor. No doctor was called.

In the summer of 1981, I was contacted by a young man in the Midwest, who said that he wanted his wife "deprogrammed" from Faith Assembly. His wife had become involved in the group and was about to have her second child. He was upset because she insisted that he deliver the baby at home without medical assistance. Because of blood-type incompatibilities, there was a chance of complications. I explained to him that I am opposed to coercive deconversions and that I felt that any form of intervention would be inappropriate under the conditions he had described. Following the birth of their son in July (without complication), the husband lured his wife from the group "supposedly to talk." At a family-owned cabin, she was deprogrammed by a team of professionals. The couple has distributed an appeal letter describing their ordeal and seeking funds for a lawsuit. Their aims, they state, are to expose the group as "a destructive mind control cult"; to cripple the group financially; to educate the public; and to "serve as a deterrent to other cult leaders." Should they receive "a substantial settlement," they have offered to return all donated funds along "with 10% interest."

Meanwhile, Region V Resource Center on Children and Youth Services announced at its Milwaukee headquarters in May 1983 that it was willing to allocate up to $10,000 to stop the abuse and neglect of children in the Faith Assembly Church. According to Adrienne Heuser, director of Region V: "It's our position that more can be done for the children involved. If more people knew about the situation and how to deal with it, lives might be saved in the future."[3] The funds will be used for a public-education campaign intended to provide information to local prosecutors, public-health nurses, welfare-department officials, legislators, and members of the general public.[4] State officials have promised investigations of child abuse (since infants and children have accounted for twenty-eight of the fifty-two reported deaths) and in-quiries as to whether the "unlawful practice of medicine contributed to the deaths."[5] At least one legislator has indicated that he will introduce legislation designed to prevent the deaths of children whose parents belong to Faith Assembly.

I find it somewhat ironic that Hobart Freeman, the pastor of Faith Assembly, is a widely acclaimed preacher and writer in charismatic circles. His book, *Angels of Light,* is recommended by Father Dennis Bennett, the Episcopalian priest who is virtually the father of "charismatic renewal" in the United States, as a guidebook to the dangers of cults![6]

WORD OF LIFE FELLOWSHIP

Word of Life Fellowship was originally located in an ugly, utilitarian storefront in Redwood City, California, about twenty miles south of San Francisco. It is now located in Mi-wuk Village, in a remote and sparsely populated area. An independent charismatic church with over four hundred adult members, the group is headed by Jacqueline Thom-shaw, who is regarded by the group as a divinely inspired prophetess. Membership is diverse—former dopers, ex-convicts, aerospace en-gineers from nearby Silicon Valley, blue-collar workers, small-business owners. Former members who have turned to Freedom Counseling Center for assistance have reported that Thomshaw exercises control over every aspect of her flock's lives.[7]

According to my informants, peer pressure was intense; any evidence of independent thought was reported to Pastor Thomshaw. Sinners were publicly chastised and humiliated at worship services. God spoke through Thomshaw as to acceptable marriage partners, business ventures, and living arrangements. Dating behavior, social activities, and reading matter were scrutinized and regulated. One member returned from a prayer meeting to find his college textbooks, phonograph records, and photo albums reduced to a pile of ashes. The church couple with whom he roomed had feared the "satanic influence" of having these items in their home. They believed that having rock music, philosophy and psychology books, and novels in their home would corrupt their young children.

Medical attention was discouraged—some defectors say forbidden. Thomshaw's rationale was that if God wanted the believer to be healed, the believer would be healed through faith. Physicians were condemned as murderers. God, Thomshaw taught, is the only healer. Members were urged to receive healing by faith at the worship services. If an illness persisted, it was considered evidence of lack of faith or a divine punishment for sin (for example, criticizing Pastor Thomshaw).

When Thomshaw received a vision of the imminence of the Great Tribulation, she ordered her followers to relocate in Mi-wuk Village near Sonora. She also instructed them to stockpile food, arms, ammunition, and off-the-road vehicles. International Harvester Scouts were God's first choice, according to prophecies uttered by Thomshaw. The Word of Life parking area teemed with these four-wheel-drive vehicles.

The members pulled up stakes and moved en masse. Careers were abandoned; family ties sundered; homes hastily sold. Scarce funds were invested in freeze-dried survival rations. Further visions required members to take up new business ventures at their own expense. Most efforts were poorly suited to the local economy and failed. Some businesses were exploited by the church—material and manpower were diverted to complete the group's new sanctuary. Thomshaw's lieutenants interferred with business operations, ordering members (who retained full liability) into destructive courses of action. Evasion of state regulations was common. Required insurance was not purchased. Employees were not paid on time. Safety standards were lax.

When business concerns failed, the hapless and powerless owners were derided at church assemblies for sloth and lack of faith. In several cases, members lost everything they had amassed through a lifetime of effort. Bitterly disillusioned, they left the group or were expelled for their negative attitudes. Liabilities they had incurred in ill-advised business schemes were all they had to show for their years in Word of Life. Members of their immediate families who remained in the group were not allowed to visit them or speak to them on the phone.

Members were urged to invest in a real-estate development, to provide homes for Word of Life families. (When this book went to press, the project was under investigation by the California attorney general's office. Apparently scant attention was paid to statutes requiring the registration of securities.)

As a result of refusing medical attention, many members of the group have suffered needlessly and a few have died. A young mother "received a healing" for lung irritation. Her condition worsened and, several months later, she was admitted to a hospital. Her husband appeared and forcibly removed her, but a few days later, he abandoned her at her parents' home, where she died shortly thereafter of lung cancer. For several months, another member hobbled about on a broken and unset ankle.

The dreams of many faded. Defections and adverse publicity multiplied. Former members took their grievances to the media, law-enforcement authorities, and the courts. Other similar independent churches withdrew from fellowship with Word of Life and condemned Thomshaw's high-handed and dictatorial ways.[8]

The Rev. George E. Evans, pastor of another fundamentalist church, claims that he tried to discuss his concerns with Thomshaw, but that she refused to meet with him. He states that Word of Life has withdrawn from the collegial influence of other churches, ministers, and retreats, that no visiting ministers are invited, that discipline is "too severe" (particularly on the issue of relocation), that there is "too much separatism" and a lack of concern with the church's mission to the world. Finally, he accuses the group "of growing into a cult." He concludes: "We can no longer endorse WORD OF LIFE FELLOW-SHIP by our coming with your present program. May the Lord help you and your congregation to move on in His Will . . . not taking a road of isolation and defensive attitudes, but openness and unity to the whole family of God."[9]

Word of Life persists. New members have been recruited to replace the disaffected and excommunicated. Pastor Thomshaw recently returned from a leave of absence. The fellowship had granted her a one-year vacation because the "lies" and ingratitude of the former members had become more than their pastor could bear.

I have counseled more than twenty Word of Life defectors. The hatred and anger which they feel does not quickly subside. Three or four years after their departure, they remain obsessed with getting even with Thomshaw and her henchmen. Some, unfortunately, have sunk back into self-centered, indulgent ways, which they had spurned when they followed the guidance of Thomshaw. Very few former members have left the experience behind them and moved on to fulfilling and productive lives. Their spirits appear to have been broken by their years in Word of Life.

NORTHEAST KINGDOM CHURCH

Founded by Elbert Eugene Spriggs, "a Chattanooga carnival barker turned self-proclaimed Christian apostle,"[10] the group was previously known as the "the Yellow Deli" and was located in Tennessee. They once owned a number of small restaurant/coffee houses in the South, where they recruited new members for their Christian commune. Deprogrammers had accused them of brainwashing and had kidnapped a number of members. The fact that one of Ted Patrick's assistants was previously a key member of the group may account for their being singled out for special attention. Half of the deprogrammees have returned to the group and have remained among the faithful for years. During my visit to their new headquarters in Island Pond, Vermont, I met and spoke with several. On the other hand, at least three of those who have been deprogrammed are today full-time deprogrammers.

Media coverage of the deprogrammings was so adverse that the group decided to leave Tennessee. A member from Vermont offered them property he owned near the Canadian border. When I visited the group two years ago, there were more than two hundred adults and numerous children living in thirteen Victorian houses which the group had purchased and skillfully renovated. This strictly disciplined Jesus commune had taken over much of a small, depressed town. The local old-timers were generally hostile, and they opposed and harrassed the newcomers whenever possible. The locals have described Northeast Kingdom Church as "a Jonestown waiting to happen."

The business ventures of the group include a general store/delicatessen, a bakery, a gasoline station/garage, and a dulcimer-making cooperative. What I witnessed was that, for the most part, they were attempting to support themselves through arts and crafts activities. Most of their business dealings were among themselves. For example, one house would swap its services (for example, automobile repair) for firewood or groceries, provided by another house. The group lives at the poverty level. I was told by one of the "elders," a young man of about twenty-six, that food was ample in the summer but woefully sparse during the brutally cold winter months.

Since my visit, many allegations of child abuse have been made. Tales are being circulated by former members of the group of toddlers being spanked by the hour in the presence of all the residents of their particular house in order to teach them obedience. Juan Mattatall, who was reportedly excommunicated from the group, told me and the media that all the children receive "frequent and lengthy bare-bottom thrashings with wooden rods."[11] During my visit, I stayed in a house with four families and their children and found no evidence to support these claims, although one nine-month-old child appeared ill and underfed. His mother was feeding him nothing but breast milk in the belief that this would render the child resistant to allergies.

Local sources claim that the group's reliance on paramedics and a makeshift health facility have led to the deaths of three infants." [12] Vermont State Trooper Kathy Cunningham reports that one of the dead infants "weighed only 13 pounds at eight months but had never been brought to a hospital." [13] Also the group got itself into two child-custody suits, one involving Mattatall, who is the father of five children. Kingdom Church took it upon itself to hide children of members in violation of court orders. In two instances, minor children were removed from the country in order to conceal them from their custodial parents. A father in the group, convicted on felony charges for burying his deceased infant child in a handmade coffin on group property, justified his act as an expression of religious freedom because "God told him" what to do.

According to recent reports, the group is planning to relocate in Nova Scotia. Founder Spriggs and some members allegedly went to Portugal, seeking to establish a commune. [14] Northeast Kingdom Church maintains fellowship through correspondence and visitation with similar communes in other parts of the U.S. and abroad.

In theology and lifestyle Northeast Kingdom Church is unremarkable. They are communal fundamentalists with typical emphases: submission of believers to their "elders," male dominance and female submission in marriage, and strict discipline of children.

I visited the commune with a father from Texas, who is bitterly opposed to the involvement of his son, daughter-in-law, and infant grandson. The father, himself a fundamentalist, feels threatened by the communal lifestyle with its general poverty and by his son's lack of ambition. The son has been with them for eight years and is now an elder and a superviser in a group-owned business. His father wanted him to finish college and become a minister or a youth evangelist. And he expected his son to leave this "demonic and anti-American cult." The elder Texan could not stomach this "bunch of hippies rejecting the free-enterprise system which God has ordained." In the father's eyes, communalism is indistinguishable from communism. "My son is nearly thirty. He should own a home of his own. That's the American way," he insisted. In this divided family, the older fundamentalism with its uncompromising individualism and the new ultrafundamentalism with its pyramidal collectivism stand at loggerheads.

In June of 1984, Northeast Kingdom Church was raided by a

small army of state police and social workers. Apparently all of the Children (more than a hundred) and their parents were taken into custody so that the children could be examined for evidence of child abuse. This highly irregular and possibly illegal mass arrest was rescinded by a local court almost immediately.

DAYSPRING MISSION

Sheridan, Montana, is a small town in a sparsely populated area of the state. The local independent, fundamentalist Dayspring Mission has about sixty-five members. The minister, a self-educated and self-ordained zealot with a history of sexual escapades in earlier remote missions, had become obsessed with satanic and demonic forces. Several members of the congregation experienced severe paranoid reactions. They came to believe that evil spirits controlled their spouses, children, farm animals, and machinery. If a cow lowed in an unusual manner, it was considered a manifestation of an evil spirit, which would have to be cast out "in the name of Jesus." Exorcisms were also performed over a stalled tractor and a broken tricycle. The mission members accused their neighbors of witchcraft and black magic.

The pastor became increasingly authoritarian and self-justifying. Any criticism of his life and behavior was condemned from the pulpit as blasphemy against the Holy Spirit. Longtime members were publicly rebuked and humiliated. Several left the church. The minister abandoned his wife and family and disappeared with mission's choir director, an educated woman of means and a devoted mother, who left behind two children and all her material possessions. In the three years since their departure, not a trace of their whereabouts has surfaced.

A CHRISTIAN "HOUSE CHURCH"

This commune of twelve adults and their children was started in Columbus, Ohio, by a self-ordained college dropout. The group persuaded students from the local state university to leave school and give up everything "for the sake of the Gospel." The leader was taking sexual advantage of a twenty-year-old woman, claiming that their relationship was a biblically sanctioned, "spiritual marriage."

The young woman became pregnant. Her parents were desperate. They wanted their daughter out of the clutches of the "preacher" and would have killed to save her. They approached Freedom Counseling

Center for help. I was assisted in this case by Tony, my born-again friend from the Arizona episode. Our first task was to get the parents under control. Next, we met with the young woman and were able to appeal to her basic decency. She was suffering from an uneasy conscience and was also homesick. Finally, we met the preacher on his own turf. The Scriptures (as Tony and I presented them) were not too friendly to his way of life. We convinced him that his life was out of harmony with the Bible. Shortly thereafter the group repudiated his leadership and disbanded. He moved to the eastern United States and began a new "house church."

FAITH FELLOWSHIP

This two-hundred-member independent church meets in a public school in Milpitas, near San Jose, California. Faith Fellowship is a charismatic group whose "prophets" claim to receive direct revelations from God. The church has achieved a large measure of notoriety as the result of numerous instances of child abuse and wife beating, and their steadfast opposition to medicine. One member suffered a psychotic break, murdered her children and killed herself. Constant infighting has produced several schisms. The pastor has bragged that he beat his six-month-old son several hundred times to make the infant stop crying. His explanation: "Children must be taught obedience to their parents from birth so that they will obey God instantly when he speaks to them in later life."

While there has been no direct Freedom Counseling Center involvement with current members, we have counseled numerous ex members and parents of members. One of our clients sustained permanent hip injuries as the result of public beating with a wooden plank. This punishment was meted out of sins which she had confessed. The group teaches that it is better to be chastised for one's sins in this manner than "to fall into the hands of an angry God."

THE LORD'S BELOVED AND JESUS PEOPLE U.S.A.

My very first case involved a Jesus-movement commune in Little Rock, Arkansas. In early 1979, Everett Walkins, a member of a civic organization to which I belong, contacted me as the result of the concern he and his wife shared for their twenty-four-year-old son Dennis. Dennis and his wife, Sarah, were members of the three-hundred-member fundamentalist commune, Jesus People U.S.A., whose headquarters is located in Chicago. The commune is best known among evangelicals for its newspaper, *Cornerstone,* and for the tracts it publishes that deal with non-Christian groups.

Before Everett phoned me, I had been in correspondence with the group and was familiar with their literature, particularly their pamphlets on such "cults" as the Hare Krishnas, the Way International, and others. My impression of *Cornerstone* and the cult tracts was negative. The artwork and layout were crude, and the editorial content was poorly written, full of Jesus-freak cliches and bad grammar. No attempt was made to understand or explain the viewpoint of the alleged cultists. Convictions and lifestyles were reduced to pejorative stereotypes, and their adherents were threatened with eternal damnation—all with a flurry of biblical citations.

But it was not their evangelical theology that disturbed me (groups such as Inter-Varsity Christian Fellowship publish anticult materials which are attractive and professional); what bothered me was the hostile tone, the irrationality, and the sloppiness of their style. Their literature reeked with converted-hippie self-righteousness.

Dennis and Sarah turned up for an unexpected family visit, and I had the opportunity to spend an evening and an afternoon with them. Despite their self-consciousness, they were eager to communicate. As we spoke, the fourteen-month-old boy for whom they cared was never very far away. Their membership in Jesus People U.S.A. was not their first involvement with a Jesus commune. They had met in a similar "ministry" in Little Rock, which I shall call "The Lord's Beloved."

Dennis had been recruited by the group while a student at a small Christian college in the Ozarks. Although he considered himself a born-again Christian, his life was in bad shape. His marriage was not too stable; he was drinking and using drugs. An old friend of his was sent to the town near the campus to arrange for Bible-discussion groups and prayer meetings. He urged Dennis and the other students who attended the meetings to seek a closer walk with God by "giving up everything for Jesus." Dennis was invited to weekend assemblies held by the parent group in Little Rock. Soon he felt "called" to drop out of college and seek "God's will for his life" among the Lord's Beloved. He and his wife argued bitterly about his decision, and their marriage ended as the result of his new commitment.

Sarah had been reared in a Southern Baptist family in eastern Tennessee. In her mid-teens she had become "rebellious"—experimenting with drugs and living with a boyfriend for a time. Through the preaching of Brother Milt, the leader of the Lord's Beloved, she had been called "to dedicate her life to the Lord." In "full-time Christian service," her life found meaning and she felt forgiven for her youthful sins.

Dennis related, "The spiritual life was good when I came in." But in this new Eden there lurked a serpent. In order to support the hundreds of college students, ex-hippies, and homeless young people who were attracted to Brother Milt's mesage, it was necessary to find a regular source of income. Somehow they stumbled on the selling of imported paintings and pottery from Mexico. The evangelistic teams which fanned out to small college campuses were transformed into sales teams. Little by little, the focus of the group changed from prayer, Bible study, and Christian growth to commercial enterprise.

Outposts were created in several cities in Tennessee, Texas, and Florida. Most of the men in the group, single and married, were sent out for two weeks at a time, returning for a day's rest and spiritual rejuvenation every fourteenth day. Each member was given a dollar a day in walking-around money and was expected to provide his or her own clothing or other personal needs. If anything beyond the reach of their miserly allowances was required, the members had to make special requests of Brother Milt.

Dennis became the director of sales operations and Sarah was made the group's bookkeeper. In a good month, she reported, the group netted $40,000. Their gross sales were over a million dollars a year. As the cash flowed in, the married couples in the group drifted out. Soon word spread to the remaining members that Brother Milt was conducting premarital sex-counseling sessions with all the be-throthed young woman in his flock. And he was not confining his attentions to lectures; he was conducting demonstrations. As woman after woman complained to her prospective husband, the high spirits of the group diminished.

Brother Milt conducted regular "brothers only" meetings, at which he warned the men that women "have a nesting instinct and will say anything just to get you out of the ministry." Since Milt was twenty years older than anyone else in the group and had been "in the Lord" much longer than any of them, the members were inclined to accept his word for everything.

Shortly after Sarah and Dennis were engaged, Brother Milt at-tempt to "counsel" Sarah. When she reported the attempted seduction to Dennis, the sales chief was dumbfounded. He recalls: "I know that Sarah wouldn't lie. But I also remembered Milt's warnings about women. So I was paralyzed and just did nothing." As Dennis traveled from outpost to outpost, he heard new charges against Brother Milt.

Apparently Milt had confessed to similar sins in the past, long before Dennis and Sarah had joined the Lord's Beloved. Since Milt had "repented," his sins had been forgotten. But out in the hinterlands, Dennis met other couples who had departed because of Milt's unusual prenuptial counseling.

When Dennis confronted Milt, the leader gave Dennis the choice of forgetting the whole matter or leaving the group immediately. When Dennis opted to leave, Milt gave him an automobile, some cash, and "God's blessings." Although Dennis and Sarah headed north in search of a better opportunity for "full-time ministry," they maintained contact with friends in the Lord's Beloved for some time. There were fresh scandals, new repentences, and increased defections. Finally, Brother Milt was caught in the act by his own wife, who left him and the group. According to Dennis, membership in the group dwindled to ten.

Dennis' attitude toward his first communal involvement was summarized in his remarks: "Brother Milt is a man who made a mistake and kept making it. I make mistakes, too. Anyway, I think we should take the good points from the experience and forget the bad. I learned that a full-time ministry, a Christian community, is where the Lord is leading a lot of people. Without a Christian community, people fall into the temptation of getting caught up in spending money and having houses. A Christian community gives everyone the opportunity to maximize his own ability and to grow." Sarah added: "And there are definite advantages—sharing costs, buying food in bulk, making better use of everybody's talents."

The Walkinses were living in a seven-by-ten-foot room with their racially mixed "foster child," Ephraim. The infant's mother was a prostitute who found that caring for a child did not fit into her schedule—"at least for now." She had asked Jesus People U.S.A. to take care of the child, but she had refused to allow the Walkinses to adopt him. Sarah was filling orders for tracts in the group's publication division while Dennis put up dry wall as part of the commune's construction and carpentry business.

When I spoke with them, they had been in Chicago for two years and found the new group vastly superior to the Lord's Beloved. No one person "lorded it over" the rest. The development of stable family units was second only to devotion "to the Lord" in the commune's priorities. The group was perceived as a definite force for good in their neighborhood. "The presence of three hundred Jesus freaks," Dennis elaborated, "drove the gangs right out of the area. People feel safe for the first time in years."

When I asked the Walkinses if they could imagine what life would be like of they ever "felt led of the Lord" to live outside of the group, making their own plans and pursuing their own personal goals, they were discomfited. They stated: "We intend to stay with the group as long as they will have us because we have grown so much as individuals and as a family." And Dennis added, "Remember—I was a mess when I came here." I have heard nothing further from the Walkinses in the past five years, but their father keeps me informed. Nothing much has changed.

My born-again Christian acquaintances inform me that the group has its friends within the evangelical community, as well as critics who distrust the "extremism" of the group. I have found this same tension between those who extol the evangelistic success of Jesus-freak ministries and those who condemn such efforts as divisive, antichurch, and antisocial. The president of the local chapter of Citizens Freedom Foundation, the major anticult organization, publicly condemns the group as a "brainwashing cult," which regards the members children as belonging not to their parents but to the entire group. She also claims that the group encourages child abuse. Her son has been a member of Jesus People U.S.A. for some time.

GOD'S FAMILY

It was like a detective story on television. Eric had been missing for two years. One day his parents had received a letter that read: "You are no longer my mother and father. I am no longer your son Eric. My new name is Brother Caleb. Sister Faith is my new mother in God's Family." Eric's parents, Quaker schoolteachers from Delaware, became deeply concerned. When they tried to contact their twenty-three-year-old son, their letters to his apartment in Oakland, California, were returned marked "moved—address unknown." His phone had been disconnected, and none of his friends knew anything of his whereabouts.

They trusted him nonetheless. They believed that he would come to his senses and return to them. So they waited and wondered. Two years after receiving the letter, they drove to California and tried to pick up Eric's trail. A police officer referred them to me. They asked me to find Eric. They wanted to know if he was alive and in good health. They wanted to be sure that he was doing what he wanted to be doing. That was all.

In my files was a faded poster (taken from a lamp post in Berkeley)

with a photograph of a middle-aged woman wearing some sort of
nun's habit—a robe suggestive of the Hare Krishnas and a starched
collar with a scarflike head covering. Three-inch-high letters invited the
observer to "Hear Sister Faith, the Voice of God in the Last Days." A
Berkeley acquaintance told me that Sister Faith and her small following—fifteen or so—had lived in Sausalito two years ago.

Ross Vintner, a staff member at Freedom Counseling Center, took
a personal interest in the case. He began phoning small Jesus communes in various parts of northern California. He told whoever
answered the phone that he was an agent of a shipping company and
that he was trying to deliver a package insured for $20,000 to Sister
Faith. After a number of calls, he chanced upon someone in Ukiah
who remembered hearing that Sister Faith had relocated her group in
Hawaii. Ross reported the rumor to me.

A few days later, a friend, who is a family counselor, mentioned
that he was seeing a woman who had recently run away from a small
Jesus commune on the Kona coast of Hawaii. "Do they call themselves
'God's Family'?" I asked.

"Yes," he replied, and their leader is called————"

"Sister Faith," I interjected.

From his client, I learned that the group was living in a clearing in
a remote jungle area about forty minutes from the nearest city. She
was unable to tell me the exact location. But she did know that they
had a post-office box in town and that members of the group went
into town daily to work as domestics. I phoned Eric's parents with the
news. They asked me to go to Hawaii to find their son. Ross and I left
the next day.

On the plane we were studying our notes and examining the photo
of Sister Faith. I looked over my shoulder and, seven rows behind my
seat, spotted a familiar face framed in a starched collar and a scarf. I
looked at the weathered photo and back at the woman. By this time,
Ross had noticed her too. He was positive that it was Sister Faith.
Before we could exchange a word, he was on his way to her seat.

"Hi," he said. "My name is Ross and I'm deeply interested in
religion. And you look like some kind of nun."

She looked at him suspiciously and said, "No. I'm not a nun. My
name is Sister Faith and I am a prophetess."

Ross decided to level with her about Eric and our mission. It was a
mistake. She turned stone cold and stated: "Eric is dead to the old life.
Tell his parents that they are dead also as far as he is concerned. He
belongs to God and they are servants of the devil. Now get away from
me."

At Hilo, she was met by two women, two men, and a few children from the group. They wore cheap, white, pajamalike clothes. She must have told them about Ross and me. For when we took the shuttle van to the auto-rental agency, I noticed that we were being followed by a car full of white-clad men. They tracked us from the agency also. We lost them somewhere in Hilo.

The next day, we visited the police, the newspaper, and churches, trying to pin down their location. Now and then we waited in the post-office parking lot to see if anyone came for their mail. Several people had seen white-clad adults shopping at a health-food store. The owner told us that they had not been there in weeks. A church secretary had seen two who worked as maids in a neighborhood near the beach. Ross and I spent hours driving the poorly paved streets to no avail.

A local editor had interviewed their prophetess when they first arrived. She had told him that she was God's only true prophet of the end time, that the Great Tribulation was about to begin, that her followers were the remnant which would be faithful until the end. She declared that they had no interest in winning new converts or raising money on the Kona coast. She said that she expected persecution. For a while she had conducted Bible classes at a local auditorium. Then she and her followers disappeared.

A day later, I was visiting the staff of a large independent charismatic church. One of their members worked for a real-estate firm, which had leased some rough terrain to the "white sheets." A few phone calls and we knew the exact location. I returned to the Kona-coast police and asked that a police officer accompany us. A tall, husky desk sergeant, Helen Jenna, was assigned to the task. (She had not been in the field for years.) We explained that we wanted to see Eric and give him a letter which we carried from his parents. That was all we planned to do.

On our third trip around the area we found a narrow trail that led to a barricade of telephone poles. A single gap, barely wide enough for an automobile, was secured with chains. We continued on foot. Except for a worn footpath, there was no sign of life until we reached a clearing, where our way was blocked by a tall, muscular man, who held a snarling dog. Twenty yards beyond the man, scrawny, pasty-faced men and woman formed a line. A woman stepped forward and ordered us to leave immediately.

The police officer tried to intervene, explaining that "it would be a whole lot better for everyone if you just cooperated. Just let these men," she said, motioning to Ross and me, "see Eric so that they can tell his parents that everything is O.K." The spokeswoman grew angry and hysterical. She screamed at us: "You are trespassing and violating the law. If you don't leave immediately, we will call the police commissioner and Judge Hemsley and have you arrested."

While the debate continued between the officer and the spokeswoman, I stared at the empty faces of the group members. With the exception of the guard and the spokeswoman, they appeared gaunt, undernourished, and spaced out. Some of them held bamboo sticks that had been sharpened at one end into makeshift spears. The few dwellings consisted of wooden frames covered with vinyl tarpaulins. The arguing continued. This time Ross joined in, appealing to their "sense of decency."

A chill came over me. I was having a waking nightmare. Leo Ryan was my congressman and an acquaintance. The tales of concerned relatives of the Peoples Temple members at Jim Jones' jungle "utopia" had stirred my anxieties. I had offered to accompany Ryan's fact-finding mission to Guyana, but I had missed the plane. For a moment, I could not tell in which jungle encampment I was standing. The barking of the dog a few feet away brought me back to Hawaii.

A few days later, Eric's parents received a letter from their son. It was full of bitter invective and hatred. He accused them of hiring "bully boys to try to kidnap me." Months later, two members left. One of them was persuaded that her daughter would be better off with the group than with her "God-cursed, rebellious mother." The mother crept in one night and spirited her child away. Months passed and the group exhausted its financial resources. They returned to California and took up employment in a small farming town. They no longer live communally but they maintain daily contact with one another and their prophetess. Eric is with them. His parents have not heard from him since his angry letter.

SURVIVALIST GROUPS

God's Family (not the group's real name) is one example of ultra-fundamentalist survivalism. These types of groups are convinced that America is being taken over by the forces of communism and the Antichrist. Huddling together, they consider themselves the true saints of the approaching apocalypse. Groups range in size from a handful to hundreds. Some groups are heavily armed. They are practicing guerrilla maneuvers in the wilderness. They stockpile assault rifles, antitank weapons, and huge quantities of ammunition. They expect that they will be called on to defend their families and foodstocks from the hoardes of unbelievers and survivors of the impending outpourings of God's wrath.

Such survivalism is not restricted to ultrafundamentalists. Several large and well-financed cults do not expect mankind to make it into the twenty-first century. Followers of Bhagwan Sri Rajneesh abandoned California, predicting a thermonuclear holocaust in 1994, and have built a city on remote agricultural land in Oregon. The Hare Krishnas have well-organized and armed survival camps at three difference locations. The Brotherhood of the Sun, a group founded in Santa Barbara which fuses Christian and American Indian beliefs, has bought 740 square miles in Nevada, one of the largest ranches in the United States.

The Church Universal and Triumphant, headed by Elizabeth Clare Prophet ("Guru Ma"), who allegedly receives messages from ascended spiritual masters, has purchased a remote 12,000-acre ranch in Montana. Guru Ma terms the land an "inner retreat" for the survival of the human race. The Foundation for Human Understanding, which teaches a combination of self-hypnosis, Christianity, and yoga, offers survival training at its 378-acre ranch in Selma, Oregon. According to Russell Chandler of the *Los Angeles Times,* similar retreats are maintained by the 3HO Foundation (Espanola, New Mexico), the Fellowship of Friends (Yuba County, California), the Farm (Summertown, Tennessee), and the Ananda Cooperative Fellowship (Nevada City, California).[15]

Chandler also identifies several ultrafundamentalist groups as "religious organizations that own large rural retreats and either are self-sufficient communities or teach survival techniques based on the belief that civilization will soon collapse." He specifically mentions the following:

The Tony and Susan Alamo Foundation [Alma, Arkansas] . . . .

    Christian-Patriots Defense League—Headquartered on 55 rural acres outside of Louisville, Ill.—this militant nationwide network of defense and survival outposts offers franchised safe lodging at rural retreats to members—for a fee. Founder John R. Harrell, 59, and his allied Outposts of American and Conservative Churches of America have about 25,000 followers—Christian, patriotic and white.

    Zarapheth-Horeb—A six-year-old survivalist settlement of 100 people on the Arkansas-Missouri border awaiting the onset of the battle of Armageddon, the group has stockpiled arms, food and wilderness survival gear on a 220-acre retreat. Leader Jim Ellison, 41, runs the Endtime Overcomer Survival Training School attended by men wearing

Army-type fatigues and carrying rifles and Bibles.

The Way—This Christian sect, with an estimated 40,000 to 100,000 followers in 50 countries, sparked controversy when a directive to new students at its Emporia, Kans., college told them to bring, in addition to Bibles, "a rifle or shotgun (handgun also, if desired)." The Way . . . [has] a survival school in New Mexico.

The Walk—This organization . . . has about 100 small congregations worldwide . . . The hub of the organization is a 300-acre farm known as Shiloh in Washington, Iowa. . . . [They] also own a 1,100-acre farm known as Mt. Zion in Brazil . . .

Legion of Zion Army—Describing itself as a "Christian preparedness" organization centered in Auburn, in the Mother Lode country, this group proposes to . . . "outfit and train ourselves in a military fashion" against "rioting, looting, murder, robbers, general insurrection or foreign attack upon our soil."

Body of Christ— . . . it has an estimated 10,000 adherents who maintain two dozen "wildernes farms" dotted across Canada, the United States [including Alaska] and Latin America. Local groups are autonomous and the survivalist network is called End Times Ministry, the Movement and the Body.

Word of Life Fellowship—The small vacation town of Mi-wuk Village in the Mother Lode east of Sonora is jittery about this fundamentalist group of 300 led by Jacqueline Thomshaw, 63, who has encouraged followers to buy property in the area as a hedge against economic collapse and reportedly to buy guns and stockpile food. She denies weapons hoarding.[16].

Cult/ultrafundamentalist survivalism was a manifestation of the widespread spirit of gloom and doom which characterized many segments of society in the late seventies. An expression of a pervasive sense of dislocation and pessimism, it continues into the eighties. For the first time in our history, a majority of our citizens believe that things are getting worse, that their children will have harder lives than they do. As Chandler explains the trend: "A foreboding spirit broods over the survivalist band, stoked by economic doomsday prophets and purveyors of coming hard times. There is fear that the end of civilization is coming."[17] Every ultrafundamentalist tendency of which I write is fueled by that spirit of dread.

NOTES

1. Ft. Wayne, Ind. *News-Sentinel,* May 2, 1983; see also Associated Press,

May 3, 1983.

2. *Globe,* June 7, 1983, p. 7; Associated Press, Nov. 24, 1982.

3. American Family Foundation, *The Advisor* 5, no. 1 (Aug./Sept. 1983), p. 3.

4. Ibid.

5. Ibid.

6. Dennis and Rita Bennett, *The Holy Spirit and You* (Plainfield, N.J.: Logos International, 1971), pp. 51, 231.

7. Data on Word of Life Fellowship are based on my interviews with and counseling of about twenty former members of the group, a lengthy conversation with leaders of the group, media coverage in San Francisco, Palo Alto, Sacramento, and Modesto, Calif., as well as numerous conversations with concerned relatives of members.

8. Letter of George E. Evans, pastor, Bible Missionary Temple, San Diego, Calif., March 15, 1983.

9. Ibid.

10. Mark Starr with Marsha Zabarsky, "The Kingdom at Island Pond," *Newsweek,* Nov. 30, 1982, p. 6.

11. Ibid.

12. Ibid.

13. Ibid.

14. Ibid.

15. "'New Age' Religionists Head for the Hills," *Los Angeles Times,* Oct. 18, 1981.

16. Ibid.

17. Ibid.

4

The Children of God and the Anticult Cult

T he Children of God movement initiated by my father, David Berg, in 1968 has been known as Teens for Christ, the Revolution for Jesus, the Children of God, and now calls itself the Family of Love. In the media . . . it is now commonly referred to as "the sex cult of the 80s."

In the early days of its formation the Children of God to all outward appearance was a very strict, puritanical group of youth dedicated to preaching the gospel of salvation and condemnation of the morally corrupt American society and the established church system. We felt we were the radical avant-garde of the Jesus people . . . We had forsaken all to follow Jesus.

Today the Children of God's main practice of evangelism involves committing fornication and adultery to show the love of God . . . They call this doctrine "flirty fishing" . . . .[1]

This is part of a speech given at a conference of cults sponsored by a consortium of evangelical Christian groups in Santa Barbara, California, in November 1982. The obviously tense and emotionally over-wrought speaker was Deborah Davis, the daughter of David Berg, founder of the Children of God. The mother of nine, Deborah and her second husband, Bill Davis, had left the group in 1978. She was going public for the first time with revelations that she knew would humiliate her mother and embarrass her children. Several times as she read from her prepared remarks, she was forced to stop as she wept uncontrollably. She continued:

The Children of God movement now perpetrates all forms of adultery, fornication, deception, sodomy, homosexuality and lesbianism, child sex, adult-child sexual relations and teaches as doctrine incest. If I were able to make up a life story as wild and bizarre as this one, no one——
—(Her composure broke. For a minute, she was unable to continue. With coaching from a minister who had counseled her in the past several months, she went on.) No one would believe that it was true.

59

I sometimes find it hard to believe that it really happened to me. [She breaks down again. Pauses for a breath, and continues] Yet daily I am surrounded by the living scars and wounds to remind me that it's true.[2]

Again and again, she forces herself to "expose my father and myself," even though she knows that she is forcing herself to deal with dread- and pain-filled memories.

The turning point for Deborah was a traumatic experience in London in 1972. Although she had not left the movement at that time, it was the beginning of her departure. In a lavish ceremony, she had been crowned the "queen" of the Children of God by her father, who had himself adopted the regal name of "Moses David, God's endtime prophet and king." In the letters which the Children of God movement distributes, he signs himself "Mo." Shortly after Deborah's "coronation," the Royal Family, consisting of Berg's wife, children, and children-in-law, was convened for a special session on marriage. Berg declared:

The private family is the basis of the selfish capitalist private-enterprise system and all its selfish evils. The most successful communes either abolished all private relationships entirely and required celibacy or abandoned the private marriage unit for group marriage.[3]

Mo was determined to see to it that his children and disciples would be "successful for the Lord" and that not even marriage would stand in the way. He roared out:

God will have no other God before him—not even the sanctity-of-the-marriage God. If we broke up every so-called marriage in the revolution, and it did the work good, to make them put God first, it would be worth it. God is the greatest destroyer of homes and families of anybody. We are revolutionaries. We are not hesitating to break up marriages that do not put God first. Partiality toward your own husband or wife strikes against the unity and supremacy of God's family and its oneness and wholeness.

That night, Mo tried to seduce his daughter. She spurned his advances. Once again, a meeting of the Royal Family was called. This time he thundered:

The churches have gone astray in their puritanical interpretations of the Scriptures. God has been showing us the wonders and beauty of the freedom he has given us, and sex is one of God's greatest gifts to man.

And we are free under grace to enjoy the liberties of sexual freedom. "To the pure all things are pure."

But there are some here who have been resisting the Spirit of the Lord. And God won't have it.

He went on for hours as his family sat in stunned silence. He explained that in the Bible "God makes many exceptions to his own rules." Without incest there would be no human race. The sons of Adam married their own sisters. And Lot's daughters were another example. "If we take a closer look at Scripture, we find that in some special situations, God breaks his own rule."

His own wife was so ashamed that she could not look up as he ranted on. Because Deborah had refused his desire for an incestuous relationship, she was no longer fit to be queen. That honor passed to a younger daughter, Faithy, who had never rejected his demands. For, in reality, he insisted, Deborah had not spurned him as a man but as God's only end-time prophet. He elaborated: "The prophet did not act selfishly or for his personal desire or pleasure. He acts always under the direct inspiration of the Almighty. By turning against the counsel of the Lord, she had revealed that she was too rebellious and selfish to be queen any longer. You have lost your birthright and you will never have another chance."

She fled from her father's home to a cheap hotel room in London, where she thought of suicide. But then she remembered her children. Who would protect them from the monster her father had become? She knew that she could not run and she could not fight. In a few days, she returned. It took her six years to leave. In the meantime, her brother Paul (who was known as "Aaron" in the movement) was deeply troubled. He knew the Bible too well to accept his father's revolutionary teachings on sex and marriage. But he loved his father too much to reject him. After telling his mother of his doubts, he left Moses David's house. Four months later, his body was found at the base of a cliff near Geneva, Switzerland. Deborah is sure that he killed himself.

DEPROGRAMMING: ENTER TED PATRICK

I have followed the Children of God for years—since I first met them on the streets of Los Angeles in 1971. If it were not for this group and their extremism, there would quite conceivably be no such thing as deprogramming.

At a time when the covers of *Time* and *Newsweek* were plastered with pop-art renditions of *Jesus Christ Superstar* and the media were atwitter with "the Jesus revolution," Ted Patrick, a minor state official, and his family were enjoying a balmy day at the beach. His teenage son wandered off with a band of ultrafundamentalist proselytizers, and returned later in a dazed state. Patrick thought that his son had been drugged or hypnotized.

Spurred on by complaints against the group from other parents, Patrick decided to investigate. He allowed the Children of God group to pick him up and attempt to convert him. The endless exhortations and recitations of biblical quotations had the same effect on Patrick as he had noted upon his son. He became "mesmerized" and felt that he was losing his mind. As he tells the story, it was only by the most heroic effort that he was able to undo the spell and escape before becoming a "mindless robot."

Patrick developed a technique that combines intense questioning, insults, anxiety-induction, intimidation, and argumentation in order to produce a cathartic counterconversion. Patrick discovered that he could not get the attention of the young Jesus freaks unless he held them captive and gained total control over their environment. So Patrick began to kidnap converts and, with the help of the convert's relatives or paid helpers, he forced them to listen until the light dawned and they realized that they had been "brainwashed" by the "cult" and transformed into "mindless robots" and "zombies." One satisfied client, the father of a convert whom Patrick had persuaded to defect, said something to the effect of "I don't know what you've done. My son was certainly programmed before. But you have *deprogrammed* him." Hence, deprogramming, a controversial and extreme form of intervention, arose—in reaction to the equally controversial and extreme Children of God.

In response to the deprogramming–Children of God confrontation, an organization of concerned parents, FREECOG (Free our Sons and Daughters from the Children of God), developed to support Patrick's efforts. Soon new groups also called "cults" were added to the list of deprogramming targets: Moonies (followers of Rev. Sun Myung Moon's Unification Church), Hare Krishnas, followers of Guru Maharaj-ji's Divine Light Mission, members of the Church of Scientology and the Way International, and others. Groups of anticult parents popped up in more than fifty cities, finally forming a national coalition, Citizens Freedom Foundation. What had begun with Patrick's efforts to understand his son's bemusement is today the anticult network, a loose-knit confederation comprised of deprogrammers, parents of present and former cult members, former cult members, as well as cult-concerned professionals (lawyers, mental-health practitioners, sociologists, and physicians).

According to the anticult network, cult members are brainwashed. Their minds have "snapped." They have been enslaved by "technologies of mind control," which have induced trance states, produced "sudden personality changes," and robbed them of their freedom. And these helpless "victims" are doomed to remain the pawns of greedy, unprincipled cult leaders indefinitely—unless they are "rescued."

Ted Patrick is the product of the kind of frantic, catharsis-inducing revivalism that he opposes with his own brand of frantic, catharsis-inducing counterconversion. When he was a shy black child in the South, his mother dragged him to every manner of faith healer, tent evangelist, and deliverance fanatic she could find seeking a divine cure for the boy's speech impediment. Patrick grew up hating the frauds who gave his mother false hope and consumed the few dollars the poor woman had saved. He hates the Bible thumpers and yet he fears their power. He told me a few years ago that he believes "the Bible is the most dangerous book ever written." He said that it is almost "impossible to read it without being brainwashed," and that he advises his rescued cultists not to read it.

Although he has adopted the language of popular psychology and B-movies with his talk of the cults' mesmeric, ESP powers, which enable them to induce "on-the-spot hypnosis" that can turn anyone into a "mindless robot," there is a great deal of ultrafundamentalist rhetoric, style, and technique to his deprogrammings. Long before Patrick came to prominence, I encountered self-appointed deliverance evangelists who locked their demon-possessed subjects in closets, shouted Bible verses at them, prayed in tongues, and sometimes beat and starved the recalcitrant for days until the devils fled. Did the victims of these spiritual ministrations consent to such treatment? Not always. In many cases, the alleged demon-possession existed in the eye of the beholder—the exorcist—rather than the subject.

Patrick—consciously or not—uses the tools of revivalism against the revivalistic convert. Perhaps he is getting revenge for the bilking of his mother by the religious con men. Patrick undermines the subject's self-image, creates an unremitting stress-overload, and offers relief and release through confession and ecstatic reintegration into an earlier state of being—the subject's childhood (and childlike) dependence upon his or her parents.

Once "saved" through Patrick's techniques or those of the dozens of deprogrammers who have followed in his wake, the apostate is received into a glad and joyous new family consisting of deprogram-mers, other deprogrammees, and the anticult network. He is given permission to enjoy the pleasures which the cult had denied him—recreational sex, alcohol, cigarettes, junk food, entertainment, sports, and leisure. And he is enlisted into a new and parentally acceptable holy crusade—deprogramming—a crusade with its own scriptures, sa-cred duties, saints, and devils.

Deprogrammees are loaded down with Robert J. Lifton's *Thought Reform and the Psychology of Totalism: A Study of Brainwashing in China* and *Snapping: America's Epidemic of Sudden Personality Change* by Flo Conway and Jim Siegelman. They are encouraged to give their testimonies at anticult meetings, church services, on radio and television, and before high-school assemblies. They are enlisted as low-paid aides by deprogrammers in attempts to deconvert other members of their former groups. Some are asked to write accounts of their experiences by book publishers. Others appear as cultists, as deprogrammers, or as themselves in motion pictures. Those who con-vert to socially acceptable forms of evangelical religion become youth-affairs experts and banquet-circuit stars. Their stories of forsaking the false gods for the true gospel are incredibly popular. At least one self-professed "ex-cultist" completely counterfeited a past in a satanic cult so that he could win an audience in the world of born-agains.

Above all, the former cultist is warned by the deprogrammers that the group will stop at nothing to win him back or keep him from exposing the mind-bending, money-gathering apparatus of the cult. The deprogrammee fears that there is a cultist behind ever tree, ready to remesmerize and capture him for the cult or to kill him so that he cannot tell what he knows. The message to the ex-cultist is: Trust no one but the anticult circle; cults and their fellow travelers are every-where, waiting to destroy the unwary; sometimes they even infiltrate deprogramming operations and parents groups. Soon deprogrammees associate only with other deprogrammees, work only with deprogram-mees, date and marry only deprogrammees. Their language is replete with deprogramming cliches. Their way is often lonely, narrow, and paranoid. They have joined the anticult cult.

NOTES

1. Speech by Deborah Davis during a panel, "Coming out of Cults" at a Conference on Cults, Santa Barbara, Calif., Nov. 1 and 2, 1982. Tape re-cordings were provided by Joseph Hopkins and Ron Enroth.

2. Ibid.

3. This and the following quotations from David Berg (Moses David) are as cited by Deborah Davis in her 1982 speech. I wonder if she remembered her father's teachings about marriage or if she, at least partially, reconstructed them from the "Mo letters." Much of what Deborah says that Mo taught at the Royal Family meeting appears verbatim in "One Wife," published in Oct. 1972. See Moses David, *The Basic Mo Letters* (Geneva, Switzerland: The Children of God, 1976), pp. 1366-74.

Part Two

RELIGION
AND REVIVALISM

Introduction: The Conversion Experience

Most forms of intervention undertaken by families on behalf of a loved one in a religious sect or cult treat their problem as if the following were true: (1) only the *subject* is in trouble—he has become dysfunctional, irrational, harmful to himself; (2) his religious conversion is a psychological aberration; and (3) his conversion and subsequent experiences are not authentically the subject's but represent a state into which the subject has been manipulated by powerful agents of mind control.

The only trouble with this analysis is that it is false. When a family is distressed by an individual member's conversion, we are encountering a family dysfunction, often a manifestation of long-time disturbances. If the family of a cult member realizes this and approaches the estranged member on the basis of the admission, *"We* have a problem," satisfactory results can be assured 90 percent of the time.

Further, conversion in itself is not aberrational. It is commonplace and an essential element in the religious lives of millions of Americans. The intensity of the experience may throw the individual off balance for awhile and the individual may incorporate into his interpretation of his experience elements derived from his group which may prove within a few days or months to be unacceptable to the individual, but the conversion itself is the subject's and remains the subject's, no matter what the group or its critics may claim. A religious conversion is no more a mental disorder than is falling in love or feeling impelled to volunteer to work in a political campaign or having a sudden urge to paint a picture. It is what the individual does as the result of the experience that counts.

Group persuasion is powerful. Individuals in religious groups may surrender to the group an enormous amount of decision making and reality defining. But groups are not as perfect in their manipulation nor are individuals as capable of handing over control of themselves as they believe or as the critic outside the group believes. There is an automaticity to human consciousness which absorbs, compares, judges, and discriminates even when we consciously order it not to. How else are we to account for the 75 to 95 percent turnover rate of recruits in even the most sophisticated and manipulative sects and cults? If we are to develop a clearer conception of the conversion process and the limits of group control, we must have a precise understanding of the nature of religious experience.

5

The Nature of Religion

The dictionary definitions of religion emphasize the familiar elements: belief in a supernatural being, attendant rites and rituals, appropriate patterns of behavior, personal values and attitudes, as well as the institutionalized forms in which beliefs and practices find expression. According to the *Merriam-Webster New Collegiate Dictionary,* religion is "(1) The service and worship of God or the supernatural; commitment or devotion to religious faith and observance . . . (2) A personal set or institutionalized system of religious attitudes, beliefs, and practices . . . (3) A cause, principle, or system of beliefs held to with ardor and faith." *Webster's New World Dictionary* defines religion as "(1) Belief in a divine or superhuman power or powers to be obeyed and worshipped as the creator(s) and the ruler(s) of the universe. (2) Expression of this belief in conduct and ritual."

The Comprehensive Dictionary of Psychological and Psychoanalytical Terms defines religion as "a system of attitudes, practices, rites, ceremonies, and beliefs by means of which individuals or community put themselves in relation to God or a supernatural world and often to each other, and from which the religious person derives a set of values by which to judge events in the natural world." *The Columbia Encyclopedia* notes that "when a man becomes conscious of a power above and beyond the human, and recognizes a dependence of himself upon that power, religion has become a factor in his being."

As a counselor and scholar who attempts to understand what religion is, how it works, what it does, I find it necessary to place myself within cultural and social circumstances other than my own, to feel empathetically what it is like to exist within the skin of another person. It is not enough merely to study how others conceive of the divine, the accomplishments of their founders and leaders, the contents of their confessions and scriptures, the nature of their ceremonies, their understanding of the "good life," and their anticipations regarding human destiny. For religion is much more than the data that fill such categories. Religion is a complete restructuring of all elements of a per-

71

son's experience. An individual's religion is his relationship with that which he regards as central to the nature of things, that which, despite all efforts, he can neither doubt nor elude. And this relationship shapes his thoughts, his feelings, his actions, and the society in which he lives.

Religion cannot be reduced to concepts or abstractions, for it does not exist in concepts or abstractions but only *in, through,* and often *despite* specific living human beings. Religion is an individual's response to that which he experiences as ultimate, as most valuable, as dearest to that person, as most real and intense. Religion is a person's relation to ultimate reality in his specific socioeconomic-historical context. Sometimes an individual's religion is derived from and underwritten by that context. I have met my share of religious types who uncritically worship the status quo: Americanism, with its accompanying tenets, the work ethic, and the inferiority of other nations and non-middle-class lifestyles, and so forth. Sometimes a person's religion operates at variance with the values of the age and society in which the individual lives. I have encountered alienated individuals in virtually every religious group I have studied who are in a permanent state of war against everyone and everything—in the name of God, of course.

Much of the time there are subtle tensions between the individual's religion and the society in which he lives, just as there are constant stresses and strains between religious and social institutions. Religion is a dynamic living with the gap between the way things ought to be and the way they are. Religion is the impossible dream, the very quest for which gives meaning and dignity to a person's life—even though it can never be attained.

Every religion consists of the manifestation of ideals as well as the betrayal of ideals. Since such ideals are impossible by definition, their realization may never be more than approximated. A person's religion is based on the awareness of a gap between *is* and *ought to be*. Moreover, it is the gradual, progressive, and asymptotic restructuring of life to bridge that gap. I have borrowed the word *asymptotic* from mathematics, for the goals of religion are approached gradually and progressively throughout an individual's life, but they are never reached. Therefore, to attempt to understand religion, it is necessary to study a person's conspicuous successes, failures, and evasions of his ultimate goals. As one human activity among others, religion evidences the ambiguities from which all human pursuits suffer. There are tensions and problems which have never been resolved by human beings. Why should we expect religion—either the individual's or the group's—to be all bliss and perfection? The actual religions of actual persons, like the times in which we live, are determined by struggle, progress, betrayal, and renewed struggle.

Religious experience is the awareness of something ultimate in power and meaning, of something holy or divine upon which all beings depend, of an extraordinary other which transcends, judges, and yet sustains the everyday world. Religious experience is the encounter with this mysterious but ineludible something; it forms the basis of all religious activity—even though such activity is conditioned by the circumstances of the individual's existence.

An individual's religion is his experience of, response and commitment to Ultimate Reality in his specific socioeconomic-historical situation.[1] Now, let's unravel this thought a bit. Religious experience is the individual's relationship to whatever he regards as having ultimate importance for himself and as being permanent and central to the nature of things.[2]

In our society we are used to speaking of an individual's religion as the worship of God. If we understand by *worship* the granting of value or worth to something and if we expand the term *God* to mean not only whatever concept we may have learned in Sunday School or in our homes as children and, further, realize that an individual's "God" is whatever that person places at the center of his life, then we are well on the way to understanding what religion is.

Each person must answer for himself: What do I most value? What is vital? What really counts? What is worth doing, worth having, worth being, worth living for? Or to approach the same issue from a slightly different perspective, ask the following: When I am my authentic self, I live as if certain things were true—about myself, about the world in which I live. What are these things? The answer to these questions is never a set of formulas, a neatly stated creed. For religion is a lifestyle based upon that something which is of ultimate importance.

The religion of an individual is what psychologists term a "master sentiment"—that is, an organized motive or disposition developed through experience to respond favorably and habitually to those conceptual objects and principles which are of greatest importance to the individual and which he considers ultimate, unconditional, and absolute in the greater scheme of things.[3]

There is another important consideration in defining religion. The expression *religious experience* may refer to one of two contexts. Religious experience is any state of consciousness in which one becomes aware of and responds to that which is ultimate, permanent, and central to the nature of things. Religious experience is also the progressive structuring of all experiences in response to this awareness. Thus crisis conversion (being "born again" or "saved") is a religious experience in the sense that in a moment of personal intensity the individual finds himself directly confronted by a reality which the subject may or may not have previously conceptualized as being central to the nature of things. As powerful as this experience may be, if it does not become the basis of a new lifestyle, it is only of momentary significance. Most intense experiences simply evaporate in the light of the next day's sun. Unless a given religious experience becomes the basis of new feelings, attitudes, and behavior, it too will melt away. Most recruits walk away from the Moonies, ultrafundamentalist sects, the Krishnas, guru groups, mass therapies, and so forth after a few days. If such groups had the irresistible "technologies of mind control" with which deprogrammers and the anticult network credit them, there would scarcely be a soul not in a cult today.

Religious experience is also the whole life of the religiously motivated individual. When the sect or cult member who lives in a community of like-minded and like-converted brothers and sisters, whose entire life is an attempt to recapture the ecstasy of the original religious experience in every experience of every kind, then the total life of such a person and such a community is a constant religious experience.

To summarize, the religious life ("religious experience" in the broadest sense) is grounded in special moments of awareness or intense aliveness ("religious experience" in the narrowest sense). To express this in a somewhat awkward manner, it is necessary to distinguish between *experiencing the religious,* that is, those rare and intense moments in which one finds himself in relationship to religious objects, powers, and the like; and *the religionizing of experience,* the progressive transformation of all of a person's experiences under the impact of his encounter with the objects of religious experience.

REALIZATION

Religious experience, in the broadest sense of the term, refers to the progressive religionizing of all the experiences of an individual. As such it may be divided into three categories—*realization, articulation,* and *routinization.*

Realization refers to the relation of the individual and apprehended reality—the powerful sense of the presence of a holy God, who judges us as sinners yet calls us to fellowship; a sense of profound oneness with reality; an encounter with a charismatic individual felt to be an instrument of God.

ARTICULATION

Articulation is the process of expressing, explaining, and justifying all that has happened to an individual during his moments of religious realization. After all, if an experience is not articulated, it cannot be communicated. Articulation takes such forms as doctrine, dogma, symbol, mythology, even dance, liturgy, and sacrifice. Although it is directed by the one who has had a religious experience to other individuals in an attempt to express the experience, it is ultimately self-concerned. The individual must say something about the mysteries of religious realization not only to his fellows in order to justify his social nature, but to himself as well. Intensity without interpretation evaporates.

The articulation of a religious experience begins with "symbol-pictures," images of the world as meaningfully related to the individual. All religious rites, myths, statements, beliefs, and theologies arise from "symbol-pictures." The subject's sense of new relatedness to the ultimate or of restored relationship to the divine, notes Peter Munz, is so "opaque, so tenuous, vague and fluid that we should not be aware" of it at all "except for this symbolic expression."[4] The symbol-picture is prior to all religious thought. Munz asserts:

> The common view is that both ritual and myth are men's response to religious beliefs. We think of religious duties as flowing from the dogmatic truths we accept. We think that the primary datum is the belief in a religious theory, and that all religious behavior, all rituals and all myth, are derived from belief. We think that myths are illustrations of beliefs and that rites are actions which we expect, on the assumption that the belief is true, to yield certain results.
> I propose to argue the reverse. . . . .[5]

Consider the statement, "God is a loving heavenly father." The individual who utters it has had certain feeling-states which were extremely vague, tenuous, and fluid. But because he lives in a given religio-social context, namely the Christian Church, he interprets these momentary states as "the love of God for me." Now if it were not for the concept, "the love of God for me," the experience would never be tied down and would disappear. Experiences evaporate all the time. Intense sensations drift away. We forget that we felt anything. But because of this image of the world as meaningfully related to ourselves, or to put it the opposite way, of ourselves as meaningfully related to the world, these feeling-states, which we would not be aware of except for their symbolic expresssion, are now securely anchored in our consciousness.

Symbol-pictures are "food for thought, not substitutes for thought," as Robert Lawson Slater has observed.[6] A sect or group can subject us to stress and offer us commitment, but it cannot tailor-make our response. It can offer symbol-pictures, doctrines, and ethical maxims, but it cannot control the outcome. Predisposition, personal idiosyncracy, and individual expectations are more powerful in the fashioning of the individual's religious articulation than all the tools of group manipulation.

Slater comments that symbol-pictures are "so pregnant that they allow for and even encourage variety of interpretation."[7] Just as some-one in a different religious tradition might interpret the same feeling-state though a different image of the world as meaningfully related to him, so also members of even the most authoritarian and dogmatic sect entertain a remarkable and bewildering profusion of personal in-terpretations. Symbols are not arbitrary. They are not consciously chosen. Rather, they emerge from and reflect an immediate awareness of the real. The convert's symbol-pictures become translated into asser-tions, which then are subjected to logical and historical criticism. Or they are translated into moral maxims, which may turn out to be rele-vant or irrelevant to the convert's ongoing life.

ROUTINIZATION

Routinization is the process through which special isolated experiences become the basis for what a person does in all aspects of his life. First, there is the religious experience, in the narrow sense of the term, producing a sense of hallowedness, that is, an emotional tone, a sense of harmony with that which is encountered in the religious experience. Next, various symbol-pictures rise in the consciousness, images which depict the relationship between the experiencing subject and the object of religious experience. Such feeling-states suggest statements, the con-tent for which is drawn from the individual's life and general expe-rience.

For example, the individual feels comforted and accepted, and associates such feelings with the maternal love he received in childhood. He is actually associating the divine with a loving mother, and, if his culture has concrete images of a divine female principle, he adopts these images and the language in which they are expressed. The wor-shiper has come to conceptualize that which is hallowed. Finally, he addresses himself to a pattern of behavior, a program of activities, in which a sense of harmony is to be progressively or asymptotically achieved, together with ideological references to the object of his devotion.

Though reasons are given for characterizing particular acts or programs as "right" or "wrong," it is the sense of harmony that determines the evaluation. In practice, it is impossible to separate one's realization and articulation in any strict fashion. The individual responds to the reality which he experiences and selects some "key" term for his articulation according to the specific circumstances in which he first or habitually experiences the religious reality.

Starting with the "key" experience, the convert frames all other experiences by reference to it. The key may be derived from the circumstance of the individual's conversion. The convert may be forever dependent upon the group-induced crisis and the doctrines espoused during his moment of catharsis. His articulation and routinization may always preserve elements of the original moment of surrender. Or the key may be some image or picture which the individual brings with him from the distant unconscious past, a symbol which perseveres in his religious development whether or not it is underscored by the ideology of the group. Having been overwhelmed by the central element, it is then the vocation of the religious individual to "compose" in his actual existence—intellectually, emotionally, sexually, aesthetically, economically, politically—a world view which, on the one hand, satisfies his rationality by its inclusion of all experience, consistency, and simplicity and which, on the other hand, is intensely satisfying.

Ultrafundamentalism is a systemized form of religious experience based on revivalism, a distinctively American form of religion. Since ultrafundamentalism cannot be understood apart from revivalism, a phenomenological account of this central form of religious experience follows.

NOTES

1. Joachim Wach, *The Comparative Study of Religions* (New York: Columbia University Press, 1958), pp. 30-31; Joseph M. Kitagawa, "The History of Religions in America," *The History of Religions, Essays in Methodology*, ed. Mircea Eliade and Joseph M. Kitagawa (Chicago): University of Chicago Press, 1959), pp. 28-29.

2. Gordon W. Allport, *The Individual and His Religion* (New York: Macmillan, 1960), p. 56.

3. Ibid.

4. Peter Munz, *Problems of Religious Knowledge* (London: SCM Press, 1959), p. 65.

5. Ibid.

6. Robert Lawson Slater, *World Religions and World Community* (New York: Columbia University Press, 1963), p. 196.

7. Ibid.

6

Revivalism:
A Phenomenological Account

Revivalism is, first and foremost, a religion of personal transformation. It is the conversion *experience* that is essential, not doctrine or morality—although this is not to say that doctrine and morality are absent from the experience. They are present in the context of the experience—preaching, testimonies, and hymns of the evangelistic rally or the revival or the tent meeting.

The implicit ideology of the powerful emotional conversion state includes: (1) acceptance of Jesus Christ as personal Savior and Lord; (2) acceptance of the authority of the Bible as the word of God; (3) acceptance of the authority of the preacher, church, evangelist, evangelistic organization, gospel-tract publisher, youth leader, sect or cult as the mediator of the presence of God and the authoritarian interpeter of the Bible; (4) a pessimistic view of one's own nature and of human nature in general; (5) renunciation of control over one's life and the acceptance of divine control as mediated by intense feelings, the Bible, the church or sect, religious leaders, and so forth; and (6) the repudiation of vices—for example, smoking, drinking, gambling, promiscuity, and various other "worldly" deeds and thoughts which are condemned by the evangelist, church, or sect. All of these elements and more are implicit in the conversion experience itself and are usually proclaimed immediately prior to conversion. After conversion has occurred they begin flowering like so many previously planted seeds. The elements are worth considering one by one.

JESUS CHRIST AS PERSONAL SAVIOR AND LORD

Just prior to and during the conversion experience, acceptance of Christ means only the recognition of one's own dilemma as described by the revivalist and a personal resolve to accept the offered conversion experience as a means to resolve this dilemma. Often the conversion experience is accompanied by the recitation of a prayer of contrition. The moment of conversion is typically characterized by a profound sense of relief or release, and a sense of inner warmth and security, interpreted by the revivalist as a signal of the indwelling presence of the Holy Spirit or of the divine Christ.

Under the guidance of the revivalist, the convert learns that acceptance of the conversion experience is equivalent to acceptance of Jesus Christ as Lord, which further implies the willingness of the convert to live in accordance with the will of Christ as revealed in the Scriptures and through an inner sense of assurance that accompanies certain acts, thoughts, plans for the future, but which is absent from others. What the convert is being told is that he should think, act, and feel in such a manner that he preserves the powerful and distinctive affective tone by which he has been overcome during the conversion experience, so that he can attain this same inner state in all subsequent experiences.

As a general rule, I have discovered that unless the conversion experience is routinized, it will fade within days. For at its outset, conversion is almost totally self-centered. Masters and Houston have observed in their studies of drug-induced religious experience:

> However awe-inspiring the strictly religious elements of the transforming experience, the subject's most immediate interest is almost always in himself and the way he feels when he has been changed. Later, when some of his euphoria has passed, he returns to a more sober consideration of those moments . . . that were truly profound and climactic. For the present, however, the subject is intensely happy, even blissful as he continues to discover and itemize the various signs by which he knows he has been transformed.[1]

Has the subject really been transformed? We have only his subjective certainty to vouch for it that it occurred at the time of conversion. With the passage of time we will be able to see whether or not behavioral changes occur which support the certainty of transformation. The observer may find these changes positive or negative in accordance with his own personal values. But such changes *are* evidence that a transformation has taken place.

However, if the conversion experience is made the basis of a daily routine for at least three weeks, it becomes firmly anchored in the life of the individual. Given twenty-one days of wholehearted dedication to a new style of life, to the maintenance of religious activities such as prayer, Bible reading, regular attendance at religious services, the new world view takes hold and begins to transform all of the individual's experiences. The total transformation of experience, influencing all values, attitudes, and motivations, is a much more gradual process taking several years—if not a lifetime.

The revivalistic conversion experience marks the initiation of the convert into a fundamentalist sect. The individual undergoes a deliberately induced catharsis. The evangelistic rally atmosphere is recreated in miniature with its exhortations, Bible quotations, personal testimonies, and pressure to conform to the will of the group. And the smaller the setting, the more personal and intimate the experience becomes. The prospect is directly confronted with his sins. His physical and psychic space are invaded by these self-confident strangers. He is discomforted and thrown off balance. He becomes anxious. The group tells him that his feelings are caused by his sinfulness. He is overcome with guilt and sadness. He realizes that his life is not working. Eagerly he confesses his shortcomings—sexual lapses, lies, petty thievery, drug abuse, and so forth. Guided by the group, he prays that God will forgive him and receive him as His child. He is urged, "Ask Jesus to come into your heart." He does, and the inner turmoil subsides. The recruit senses an inner release and relief. The hugs and congratulations of the group tell him that he belongs, that he has identity, that he is accepted. Many ecstatic converts report, "It was as though a great weight had been lifted from my shoulders."

I wonder what this stage-managed catharsis has to do with genuine spiritual experience. The possibility remains that most conversion experiences that follow this model are not so much personally integrative transformations as artificial crises resulting from the deliberate arousal of anxiety in the subject, followed by permitting him to enjoy the relief that comes when the stress-inducers are removed. Crisis conversion of this type distorts human nature, appealing only to the emotions, exploiting vulnerabilities, and demanding instant conformity. As we shall see, it has a great deal of similarity to the induction of catharsis in nonreligious areas of life. When Jesus told Nicodemus of the need to "be born again" he did not badger his hearer until he underwent a group-coerced, programmed, stereotyped purgation.

THE BIBLE AS THE WORD OF GOD

Since the proclamation of biblical text was the source of the conversion experience and since the revivalist based his claims to authority not upon his ability to arouse emotions but upon the authority of the

Bible, it is natural for the convert to regard this book as unique and authoritative. For the logic of conversion is simple: either the book and the convert's experience are valid or both are false. The intensity of the convert's personal transformation will allow no other possibility. Guided by revivalistic teachers and preachers, the convert begins to read the Bible regularly, both in privacy and under their tutelage. He is told that the Bible is a divinely inspired, error-free, comprehensive, and unambiguous message from God to man.

Although there are many theories of inspiration, the very essence of revivalism is the claim that the original documents of the Scriptures were inerrantly dictated by God to the prophets and apostles and that everything contained in them is infallible. In extreme form, this means that the Bible is the final, if not the only, authority in all matters— history, geography, chronology, biology, zoology, geology, physics, as well as matters of faith and morals. It is not unusual to encounter fundamentalists who believe that the only education men need is biblical education and, preferably, biblical education in accordance with a given sectarian interpretation (for example, dispensationalism) and that modern colleges and universities are "satanic" entrapments that destroy the faith of Christian young people with the "lies" of modern science.

The convert is told that it is his duty to read the Bible regularly, and to seek therein guidance for his life. "God will speak to you through the Scriptures," the revivalist tells the convert, "revealing His will for your life by granting you a sense of assurance and comfort or by striking you with feelings of conviction and discomfort as you read His Holy Word." The convert is urged to read the Bible "devotionally," that is for his personal comfort and guidance.

Little importance is attached to studying the Bible as a historical document. The Scriptures are not to be *understood* through historico-grammatical exegesis. They are to be *obeyed* as God's message to the individual reader. At times, this technique degenerates into a divine lottery, in which the Bible is regarded as a source of magic answers. Instead of carefully considering the possible alternatives available to him in a given situation, the convert merely throws open his Bible and immediately finds "God's will" in the first verse that strikes his eye.

The ultrafundamentalist not only accepts the authority of the Bible, he worships it. He is so filled with awe and devotion that he scarcely reads the printed words at all. He collects and memorizes passages out of context, stringing them together to form intellectually unassailable systems of infallible teachings. Whether he realizes it or not, he accepts on faith what his leaders tell him. And since scattered verses from the Bible can be assembled in support of anything, the canny manipulator

is at a distinct advantage in arranging the Scriptures to suit his pro-
clivities.

Many fundamentalists are safeguarded by the checks and balances
provided by pastors, seminar professors, and dedicated laity who have
studied the Bible for decades. There is for them a moderating body of
believers. The ultrafundamentalist is the lone wolf of biblical interpreters, accountable to no one but himself. His private interpretations
are like the secret ingredients in commercial products that make them
new and improved even though they are indistinguishable from the old
and inferior versions. By adding a remarkable discovery (for example,
that Jesus was crucified on Wednesday not Friday) or a novel interpretation (some are called to be apostles, and these modern apostles
have as much authority as the bishops of the various churches claimed
in the second century), the ultrafundamentalist offers a new, improved
gospel for those bored by the previous versions of the product.

THE LEGITIMACY OF "RELIGIOUS AUTHORITIES"

In seeking a local church with which to affiliate, the convert may be
directly advised by "counselors" at the evangelistic meeting or he may
drift from group to group until he finds a local congregation which
supports and encourages his new world view. Converts tend to associate themselves with the group headed by the revivalist through whom
they were converted. This provides the convert with the greatest sense
of continuity.

But what of the converts of itinerant tent evangelists or such not-
able nondenominational crusaders as Billy Graham or the television
evangelists ranging from Graham to Oral Roberts, Jerry Falwell, Rex
Humbard, and the rest? Obviously the traveling evangelist's organization or the electronic revivalist's headquarters cannot look after its
converts. Nor can the evangelistic organization recommend churches
to its converts if it is to maintain the impartiality it owes to the many
different churches that sponsor its mass meetings. (Billy Graham's evangelistic rallies, for example, are sponsored by local churches representing every ray of the spectrum of organized religion from Unitarian
to Roman Catholic.) It is the convictions implicit in the conversion
experience and the recommendations of chance acquaintances that
guide the convert to a local congregation supportive of his experience.
Conversely, the convert will not stay long in a congregation which
provides an adverse setting for the preservation of his newly found
inner state.

Just as the focus of the crisis convert is on his own experience, so also his understanding of the church is equally egocentric. The church is seen as a local assemblage of persons who validate his experience both by their testimonies of equivalent catharses and by their efforts to win others. A basic weakness has always afflicted the revivalistic notion of the church. Since it is easier to recognize and condemn the errors of established churches than to establish positive alternatives, the revivalist has found it simpler to attack his enemies—real or imagined—than to deal creatively with society and its problems. Likewise, the convert finds it easy to attack the religion of his past or youth as nothing more than "churchianity and not truly Christianity." Rapidly recruited converts, whose religious knowledge is limited to a few intense hours of experience, are loath to settle down in established congregations. They distrust traditional creeds, formalized worship, theological discussion, or anything which might distract Christians from their major responsibility—the conversion of sinners. For only if the conversion experience is the remedy to every person's problem can the convert really believe that it is the solution to his.

The church which most appeals to revivalistic converts is one characterized by three essential elements: excitement, contrast identity, and lack of ambiguity. The recruit feels most at home where the emotional excitement of group activities mirrors the programmed enthusiasm of the evangelistic meeting. As we have stated above, revivalism is first and foremost a religion of experience. Of course, this reliance leads in many cases, to a virtual addiction to ever-increasing doses of emotional arousal. Hence, the Christian life is regarded as a state of recurrent (if not constant) spiritual hyperactivity. Such addiction leads inevitably to the experiential excesses of ultrafundamentalism.

In revivalistic churches, the contrast between one's former "sinful" life and one's new identity is constantly reinforced. In every way possible the old—life, past values, associates, beliefs, and attitudes—is derided and devalued. At the same time, conformity to the beliefs, attitudes, and patterns of behavior of the group is fostered. The convert's guilt over his past life is intensified under the tutelage of the group to include all aspects of the everyday, secular world with its accompanying attitudes, patterns of behavior, and sources of information. Everything and by extension, everyone outside the circle of faith becomes associated with the pain, sorrow, and uncertainty of the convert's former life. With the new group helping him to reconstruct his memory of the past, the convert is unaware that much of the unhappiness and confusion concerning his past life is a back-formation.

What is happening to the convert is that he is moving from a momentary experience of ecstasy to the attempt to routinize his life with this ecstasy at the core. The real leap of faith is not from spiritual indifference to faith in God as much as it is from lack of uncertainty to dependence on the beliefs, attitudes, and patterns of behavior encouraged by the revivalist.

The preacher, who previously elicited an affective state which the preacher interpreted as the presence of God, now offers his idiosyncratic interpretations of the good life as though they alone mediate the continuing divine-human bond. In the eyes of the naive convert, the conversion-inducing revivalist is prophet, priest, example, sage, mentor, and seer. There are few human relationships with such power. The abject openness of the convert to the revivalist and the shameless manipulation of that openness by the self-confident conversion-inducer constitute an awesome potential for good and evil.

PESSIMISTIC VIEW OF HUMAN NATURE

Not only does the preacher proclaim that man is by nature a rebel against the will of God, but also that the depravity of the individual dooms to futility all human undertakings aimed at the betterment of man's state. Social work, psychiatry, politics, mass movements, and, in extreme cases, medicine cannot improve the human condition or alleviate mankind's suffering. For the "real problem" is sin. Human nature is perverse and irremediable. The world is destined to become worse and worse until the second coming of Christ. According to one revivalist: "When the Lord returns, there will be no racial strife, there will be no poverty or hunger, there will be no air pollution. Jesus is really gonna get it together." The impending doom of the world is seen as an occasion for rejoicing: "Maranatha! The Lord is coming!" The church, according to revivalism, is not an agency for the amelioration of human misery but an ark through which a select number of righteous souls can be saved from the impending cataclysm. The world is lost; prepare to leave.

But not only does the convert come to view the world as doomed, he sees his own essential selfhood as perverse and beyond remedy by human action. Unable to trust his own reason, affections, and will, he must completely yield control of himself to the dictates of an external force deemed to be the voice of God.

All too often, creativity ceases with conversion. Once they are born again, poets lose their rhymes, singers their voices, actors their craft, dancers their dance. Talent is "worldly" except when it is restricted to

the creatively sterile forms used in evangelism. Fundamentalism in
America remains largely devoid of culture. Almost without exception,
it builds no cathedrals, commissions no great works of art, tells its
story in no worthy theatrical vehicles or artistically valued motion
pictures. It is known for its evangelists and not its theologians or
philosophers. For the use of one's ability is denigrated as pride and
arrogance.

The human mind is condemned as the one place where Satan can
control us. The revivalist counsels the convert to abandon deliberation
and to float on successive waves of strong feelings, which the revivalist
interprets as the "leading of the Lord." In ultrafundamentalist groups,
divine guidance is sensed by the entire group or, in the case of larger
groups, by the group's elders or prophets. Soon every decision—what
to eat and to wear, whom to marry, whether or not have children,
where to live and work, what to read and think—is being determined
by those with direct lines to Heaven.

This tendency to abdicate responsibility by relying on fleeting emotional states ("I feel led of the Lord to say . . .," "God put it in my
heart to do . . .") is bad enough in fundamentalism. In ultrafundamentalism, human beings scarcely exist at all. They are blank screens upon
which the feelings, words, thoughts, and deeds of spiritual entities are
projected. God and Satan are the only realities, both proximately and
ultimately. Thinking is spiritually dangerous. The free play of the imag-
ination must be drowned out by the repetition of Bible verses, religious
cliches ("Praise the Lord," "Thanks be to God," "Jesus, Jesus, Jesus")
or nonsense syllables (speaking in tongues).

RENUNCIATION OF CONTROL OVER ONE'S LIFE

The notions of the depravity of mankind and the ultimate futility of all
human efforts hardly elicit self-confidence or self-assertion in the young
convert. After all, where has autonomy gotten the convert in the past?
If his freedom has not brought him an intense sense of failure and
self-dissatisfaction, conversion would never have occurred in the first
place. Therefore, the convert places his life in the hands of a higher
authority. In psychological terms, this means that ego-control is surrendered to the demands of the superego. For the convert had been
carrying with him for years a sense of dread and discomfort. This sense
is derived from the habitual violation of values he had unconsciously
regarded as sacred for years. Finally dread becomes intolerable, demanding a resolution. The solution is the conversion experience and

the commitment on the part of the individual to obey the internal injunctions that were previously spurned and violated. Thus brought into consciousness and enhanced, these prohibitions become more vivid than ever.

REPUDIATION OF VICES

The convert adopts a way of life structured according to specific do's and don'ts determined by two sources: (1) the mores which he had previously violated and in consequence of which he had felt enormous guilt and dread (one convert may be aware of the need to overcome lust; while another may focus his repentence upon previous acts of greed or dishonesty); and (2) the rules and regulations of the religious group which he has joined (one group will condemn social dancing and rock music while the next group may approve those but condemn mixed swimming at beaches and swimming pools). The convert's new group requires such practices as regular Bible reading and prayer, attendance at church services, participation in the sacraments or ordinances of the sect, and financial contributions, as well as the avoidance of "worldliness." Prohibited by most groups as "worldly" are gambling, the use of profanity, the use of tobacco and alcoholic beverages, attendance at movies, sex outside of marriage, and so forth. The specifics differ from group to group.

"BRINGING IN THE SHEAVES"

Above all, the convert is required to evangelize others. Some converts engage in such soft-sell forms of "soul-winning" as merely allowing their acquaintances and relatives to see the transformation of the converts' lives. After all, the rose does not conduct an advertising campaign for its perfume. Others will use every method, fair or foul, to reproduce their experience in the lives of others. In the words of one Jesus-movement leader: "So we sow the seed by any means—by force, by compulsion, by fad. It doesn't make any difference—just so the seed is sown."

A college professor in California wrote to me: "I just dismissed from my home two teenagers who gained entrance on the pretense of taking a religious-affiliation survey—only to end up trying to 'sell' me on the 'four laws' of God's wonderful plan for my life. They admitted they had entered my home on false pretenses but rationalized that in most cases they would have been turned away if they told the truth to begin with about their real objective when they introduced themselves."

In some suburbs of Philadelphia, which are heavily populated by Roman Catholics and Jews, a consortium of evangelical churches rented motion-picture theaters, advertised a G-rated "motorcycle" action picture. No mention was made of the fact that the film was evangelistic in content nor that theater doors would be locked after the film so that evangelists and counselors would attempt to get the audience, composed mostly of unaccompanied young children, to "come forward and make a decision for Christ." When I criticized this covert evangelism as unethical, I was accused in the media by the film's sponsors of being mentally unbalanced, soft on communism, a drug pusher, and a fan of pornography and free love. I received more than a hundred letters, reminding me that Jesus taught: "Suffer little children to come unto me and forbid them not."

It is with their "bring in the converts at all costs" mentality that revivalism and ultrafundamentalism begin their slide into the "ends justify the means" moral abyss. The rationale is simple: We are offering the cure to the world's ills. Satan has darkened men's minds so that they do not recognize their own need. The argument runs: If a Christian saw his neighbor's two-year-old son playing in the road with a truck bearing down on the child, would he need his neighbor's permission to rescue the toddler? So if he sees his neighbor's ten-year-old son in danger of spiritual death, of spending an eternity in the fires of hell, is it not his duty to save that child—whether his neighbor approves or not?

The revivalistic Christian never accepts the possibility that he can be wrong when he undertakes to do unto others for their own good whether they want to be done onto or not. He reasons that his chosen course of action is more than justified; it is mandatory. He believes that the Bible is infallible and that his understanding of the Bible is equally inerrant. The revivalistic Christian simply cannot realize that manipulating others for their own good is intrusive upon and destructive to the freedom and responsibility of the other person. Once deceit, unfair advantage, and undue influence are justified, it is a short step to the totalism, totalitarianism, and elitism of the ultrafundamentalist sects.

THE SIMPLE FORMULA

The revivalistic convert lives by a simple formula: submission to total demands equals total fulfillment. Like all intense experiences, crisis conversion must be routinized if it is to be of any permanent significance in the life of the individual. Unless new states of affective tone and heightened awareness find ritualized patterns of expression, they will fade away within days. On the other hand, if they are channelled according to forms of articulation and action approved by the community or faith, they may become the basis for a total transformation of the individual's personality and way of life.

In general, there is a ratio between the demands which the community makes upon the individual and the degree of personal transformation which is possible. In other words, the more total and involving the commitment of the individual, the greater will be the personal satisfactions which he finds. Moderates in all spheres are at an extreme disadvantage. Their constituency has neither the zeal nor the intensity of the extremists. Liberalism, humanism, middle-of-the-road Protestantism, Reform Judaism, and Vatican II Catholicism are constantly outflanked by high-demands groups. Moderates often fail to appreciate the appeal of fanaticism, and they offer few emotionally fulfilling alternatives.

But there is another side to the "high demands bring personal satisfaction" coin. For as the degree of commitment and personal satisfaction increases, so does the possibility of delusion and self-destruction. Ultrafundamentalist sects are the most common, rapidly growing, and intense of today's high-demands groups. When it comes to vitality, power, and pervasiveness, they are where the action is in North American religion. They are particularly fascinating to the uninvolved observer, uniquely significant to the experiencing subject, and overwhelmingly exasperating to the bewildered family and friends of the convert. And they are potentially hazardous to the mental, physical, and spiritual well-being of all who are attracted to them.

What need do these groups serve? The need for constant reinforcements of one's level of certainty, passion, and unambiguity. How do they satisfy this need? Usually by the creation of a controlled and controlling environment. For in such an atmosphere the features most cherished by the revivalistic convert—authority, approval, community, identity, and ecstasy—may be structured, routinized, and protected.

THE UNCONDITIONALITY OF RELIGIOUS COMMITMENT

Revivalistic commitments are "all or nothing." The revivalist evokes a picture of hopelessness without the Gospel and a future bright with hope for those who accept this "once in a lifetime offer." How well I remember the evangelist's arguing with the unspoken hesitancy of the unredeemed as the congregation sang endless choruses of "Just As I Am" and "Almost Persuaded." The evangelist would intone: "You say to yourself, 'Not now. I'm young and want to have a good time. There will be plenty of time to become a Christian when I am older.' But who can say that you will not be killed in an automobile accident on your way home or die in a month of a fatal disease?"

The revivalist evokes a tension in the listener which demands resolution—now. For the elicited pain mirrors the potential convert's own accumulated grief, guilt, alienation, loneliness, boredom, and unrest. The commitment which the evangelist demands and the dedication with which the convert wholeheartedly responds is "once and for all." It is an act of faith. The revivalist has offered the convert an interpretative framework which, it is promised, will make sense of all his experiences. The convert grabs hold of that interpretation with all his might. He unconditionally and irrevocably commits himself to this interpretation as a frame of reference that gives meaning to all of his existence.

But have I not just described a fanaticism that can never be broached by reason or circumstance? Not at all. Because for the convert's experience to have meaning, it must be personalized—just as an off-the-rack garment must be individually tailored. The convert's commitment, whether he realizes it or not, is constantly restructured in accordance with the individual's basic motivational principles and values. Conversion only appears to be an instantaneous process. It is the conscious expression of many years of inner struggle and turmoil. Likewise an unconditional commitment is unconditional only in the sense that it is not based upon the consideration of probabilities. It is an act that ends deliberation and despair. But faith does not end with the suspension of critical examination and surrender of oneself to the revivalist's way of life. Conversion is not a product. It is a process. With the act of commitment, it has only just begun.

NOTE

1. R. E. L. Masters and Jean Houston, *The Varieties of Psychedelic Experience* (New York: Delta, 1966), p. 296.

7

Fundamentalism

During the twentieth century, revivalistic religious experience has been promulgated by a vast movement known variously as fundamentalism, born-again Christianity, evangelicalism, and conservative Protestantism. Revivalism has branched off into several experientially based tendencies (for example, pentecostalism, charismatic renewal, and deliverance) and has produced a movement of social and political reactionism known as the Moral Majority. An understanding of these revivalistic offspring is the sine qua non for the interpretation of ultrafundamentalism as well as for a proper perception of the religious shape of the 1980s.

In the words of America's best-known revivalist:

The world longs for authority, finality, and conclusiveness. It is weary of theological floundering and uncertainty. Belief exhilarates the human spirit; doubt depresses. . . . [1]

Just before the first tent meetings in Los Angeles I became absolutely convinced that the Bible was the Word of God. Today my convictions concerning the Bible are much stronger. I have seen the Word of God penetrate the hearts of people and transform and change them. I know that this Book was inspired by the Holy Spirit. It is a supernatural book. This is a Living Word.

The events we see happening in our world today are the fulfillment of prophecies made centuries ago by the prophets of Israel, by Jesus Christ Himself, and the apostles. Everything is falling into position with almost frightening precision. Prophecy is being fulfilled to the letter. . . .

We do not know the hour that our Lord is to return, but we are told to watch the signs. They are pointing in one direction, the soon coming of the Lord Jesus Christ. . . . If ever there was an hour when you needed to repent and believe and make sure of your personal relationship with God, it is now.[2]

Repentence and conversion, a personal relationship with God, the final authority of the divinely inspired Word of God, the imminence of the Second Coming of Christ, belief which exhilarates the human spirit—for more than thirty years this had been the message of Billy Graham, preacher to millions, counselor to presidents, and the chaplain of middle America. But as modern as his methods have been, as distinctive as is the personality of the preacher, there is nothing new or startling in Graham's message. For America has heard this evangelist in every generation since the mid-eighteenth century. In the twentieth century, we have grown accustomed to calling this gospel by a name born of religious controversy: *fundamentalism.*

What is fundamentalism? A movement? A creed? A mentality? A way of life? Clearly, it is all of these.

Fundamentalism arose in the late nineteenth- and early twentieth-century as a movement of reaction to the introduction of the theory of evolution, the "social gospel," and the application of historical and literary scholarship to the Bible. Darwinism cast doubt upon the creation accounts of the Book of Genesis. The social-gospel movement supported the progressive reform of government, business, and other institutions as the means of establishing God's kingdom on earth. By abandoning faith in the imminence of the Second Coming and by encouraging human effort toward the amelioration of human predicaments, the social gospelers undercut the necessity of personal salvation.

Fundamentalism is a combination of revivalism and reaction. It emphasizes man's sinfulness, his need for redemption through repentence and faith. Faith is both a heartfelt catharsis, a sense of being accepted by God and filled with his presence, and an objective content which is believed. The experiential elements have been central to American Protestantism since before the American Revolution. The objective elements or cardinal doctrines, the "fundamentals" of the faith were drawn up in 1895 at a conference held at Niagara Falls. They were: (1) absolute belief in the Virgin Birth; (2) literal payment for man's sins by Christ substituting in death on the cross; (3) the physical resurrection of Jesus; (4) the visible, bodily return of Jesus on the earth; and (5) the absolute inerrancy of the Scriptures.

The doctrinal foundations of the antimodernist forces were elaborated in twelve volumes of pamphlets, *The Fundamentals,* the publication and distribution of which were underwritten by two wealthy Californians, Lyman and Milton Stewart. Their purpose was to defend the five "fundamentals" of the Niagara Falls statement and to attack biblical criticism, evolutionism, and social democratic ideals. The term, *fundamentalists,* refers to the defenders of these fundamentals. The years of the fundamentalist-modernist struggle were 1918 to 1931. The issue best known to the public at large was evolution.

The most illustrious fundamentalist of these years was William Jennngs Bryan, the thrice-defeated presidential candidate, who aided in the prosecution of John Thomas Scopes, the young teacher accused of violating the Tennessee Anti-Evolution Act of 1925. But the bitterest strife occurred as the orthodox within major Protestant denominations, such as the Presbyterian Church, U.S.A., attempted to impose their doctrinal standards on clergy, seminaries, and mission boards. Their initial victories were soon reversed as the tide turned against them. By the mid-thirties, those who remained within the denominations were largely without influence and many had departed to preserve their purity within newly established church bodies (for example, the General Association of Regular Baptist Churches, the Bible Presbyterian Church Association, the Reformed Presbyterian Church, the Independent Fundamentalist Churches of America).

After 1931, fundamentalism survived largely as an attitude of vigorous reaction and protest. *Fundamentalism,* a term by which the orthodox had proudly identified themselves, became a term of opprobrium—even among conservative Christians. By the mid-fifties, the term *neo-evangelical,* or simply *evangelical,* was preferred by those who maintained the orthodox theology of the fundamentals but rejected the raucous cacaphony of the self-righteous separatists. A more moderate, socially concerned, and relevant stance was being sought. Much of the change was attitudinal rather than substantial—an alteration in style as much as content. The Gospel as the answer to the problems of the postwar era was being presented by Billy Graham and such parachurch agencies as Youth for Christ, Inter-Varsity Christian Fellowship, Campus Crusade, and Young Life. The emphasis was upon overcoming anxiety by attaining "peace with God" (the title of a Graham bestseller in the mid-fifties) and participating in the church of one's choice, community and business affairs, and the political arena as a spirit-led child of God.

The old revivalistic individualism—that is, God will solve our problems for us if we will repent of our sins and turn to him—had returned. By setting themselves above and apart from the ecclesiastically divisive and socially irrelevant struggles of the fundamentalists, Graham and the new evangelicals won themselves an audience which has remained intact for a quarter of a century.

By the late 1970s, one-fifth of all adult Americans, thirty million individuals, would identify themselves as evangelical Christians. One-quarter of our population, nearly forty million men and women, would claim to have undergone a conversion experience that included asking

Christ to be their personal savior. Sixty-five million adults would declare that they believed the Bible to be inerrant. *Christianity Today* commissioned the Gallup Poll, which gathered these surprising data, and solemnly exclaimed:

> . . . the *conservative* churches . . . are growing fastest, while the liberalizing denominations are moribund. . . . most evangelical and Pentecostal groups are growing. . . . evangelicals must make their influence felt in society at large now, or lose an opportunity that might not come for another hundred years, if ever.[3]

While evangelicalism was winning the multitudes, the older fundamentalism degenerated into little more than a reactive mentality. For it was not the fundamentalist's faith that set him apart from other Christians so much as his attitude. His life consisted largely of maintaining "status by negation." The good life became the separated life—separated from the world and its vices. The good man was one who *avoided* tobacco, alcohol, gambling, dancing, and sex outside of marriage.

The fundamentalist became much more concerned about the way in which he was perceived by other fundamentalists than in his impact upon the society in which he lived. He shunned movie attendance, for movies were considered the devil's instrument to tempt us with the "lust of the eyes," but watching a movie on television in the privacy of one's living room did not harm the viewer's "testimony" and was allowed. The Christian life was seen by the fundamentalist not as partnership with God in the ongoing redemption of society but as avoidance of prevailing social mores. Neo-evangelical theologian Edward John Carnell observed twenty-five years ago:

> Whereas Christ was virtuous because he loved God with his heart and his neighbor as himself, the fundamentalist is virtuous because he does not smoke, dance, or play cards. By raising a scrupulous demur over social mores, the fundamentalist can divert attention from grosser sins— anger, jealousy, hatred, gossip, lust, idleness, malice, backbiting, schism, guile, injustice, and every shade of illicit pride. . . .
>
> Fundamentalists defend the gospel, to be sure, but they sometimes act as if the gospel read, "Believe on the Lord Jesus Christ, don't smoke, don't go to the movies, and above all don't use the Revised Standard Version (the "modernists'" translation of the Bible)—and you will be saved."[4]

With the inevitable decline of liberal theology in the face of the stubborn realities of human perversity (continuing warfare, nuclear threat), fundamentalism no longer had an enemy with which it could contrast itself. It developed no world view of its own, contributed nothing positive to society, cut itself off from science and learning, spurned the arts and philosophy, and became distrustful of other fundamentalists, who were seen as "worldly" or "compromisers." Fundamentalism, noted Carnell, became a "lonely position." He explained:

> And when there are no modernists from which to withdraw, fundamentalists compensate by withdrawing from one another. They dispute whether the rapture takes place before or after the tribulation. Status by negation must be maintained or the *raison d'etre* of fundamentalism is lost.[5]

But fundamentalism never turns completely inward. The negativity of its mentality eagerly awaits social issues as well as theological concerns. The fundamentalist not only achieves status by negation with respect to other fundamentalists; he also offers his leadership in reactive campaigns to the broader populace. The champions of sawdust-trail revivalism readily espouse the antivice positions of others who do not necessarily share their theology. In the 1920s, Billy Sunday, the leading evangelist of the day, was a major force in the Prohibitionist crusade. In the 1950s, many fundamentalists embraced anticommunism. In the 1970s, the preservers of the values and mores of former times when youth, women, and minorities knew their place found a voice and a leader in Jerry Falwell. And there arose the Moral Majority, an essentially negative, repressive reaction to ethical humanism, sexual permissiveness, liberalized abortion policy, and open homosexuality.

Ultrafundamentalism is last-ditch fundamentalism. What is distinctive about the ultrafundamentalists is that which they add to the five fundamentals both ideologically and attitudinally—in a word, their extremism. They set themselves apart from other evangelicals by their unwillingness to compromise about theology, politics, or style, and by their excessive vituperative hostility toward any who fail to meet their standards of faith, conduct, or social philosophy.

An evangelical mass evangelist such as Billy Graham will cooperate with Christians from a vast variety of ecclesiastical and theological camps in order to obtain the widest possible audience for his message. Jerry Falwell's Moral Majority is led by doctrinnaire evangelicals but it welcomes the participation of men and women of similar concerns from every segment of the population—Protestant, Catholic, Jew, or unaffiliated. To the ultrafundamentalist, such cooperative effort smacks of heresy, hypocrisy, compromise, and outright spiritual perversion. Ultrafundamentalists inveigh against Billy Graham's "fellowshipping with unbelievers" and his unwillingness to follow the separatists' example and counsel ("Come out from among them, and be ye separate" [2 Cor. 6:17]) and treat Graham with the hostility usually reserved for the National Council of Churches and the Vatican. Indeed, some ultrafundamentalists go so far as to condemn Graham, the National Association of Evangelicals, *Christianity Today,* and most fundamentalist churches as allies and agents of Satan in their expectations of the emergence of the Antichrist and the Great Whore of Babylon (Rev. 17).

Ultrafundamentalism sprang into being with the "Christian anticommunism" of the fifties. Fundamentalist opposition to labor unions, the social-welfare programs of the New Deal, racial integration, and any other form of collective action to improve the human condition has been vehement throughout the twentieth century. Equally abhorrent has been the ecumenical movement for the reunification of Christendom, as well as the increasing dialogue between the Vatican and other Christians.

It was fairly easy for Bible-belt evangelists to regard the "godless Marxists" as pawns of Satan, and to picture "God-fearing, Christian America" as the chosen instrument of God's purpose. The myth of America as a Christian nation, God's new Israel, is deeply entrenched in the American psyche. The American Revolution was seen as our exodus from old lands, old institutions, and old identities. The Declaration of Independence and the Constitution were lauded as our sacred scriptures and Washington as the divinely appointed Moses who led his people out of tyrannic bondage.

The Abolitionists saw the Civil War as "the glory of the coming of the Lord." President McKinley decided not to liberate the Philippines, inadvertently won as a prize in our war with Spain, partially out of concern for the spiritually benighted Filipinos to whom missionaries of the Gospel (and of American imperialism) could be sent. In 1917, the churches all but enlisted soldiers as they urged the nation to do its "Christian duty," to take up arms against despotism, and to "make the world safe for democracy."

Throughout our history, we have tended to see complex issues in overly simplified, black and white dualities. We are the "good guys"; those who oppose us are "baddies"—whether they are Tories or Mexicans or Indians or Spaniards or Germans or Japanese or Vietcong. Our cause is just. God is on our side. And when our blood is hot, any of our citizens who advise us to cool our ardor and seek moderate solutions are regarded as dupes and agents of the bad guys. At our best, we are guardians of personal liberty, freedom of choice, and fair play. At our worst, we are atavistic crusaders who will countenance any evil means in order to preserve our way of life and to impose our values upon other cultures.

Often we have failed to see that our means were inconsistent with the values which we were attempting to preserve. A case in point is the manner in which most of us reacted to McCarthyism. Many Americans endorsed, supported, cowered before, hid from, or remained silent in the face of the anticommunist witch hunt. And when this disgraceful period in our history was over, when McCarthy was finally discredited and disowned by his colleagues and the media, did his version of the just war against the enemies of our way of life fade with him? Of course not. Our anxieties and inadequacies require scapegoats to explain and justify them. If life is less than utopian, someone must be to blame. And the history of America in the twentieth century proves that there is no scare like the red scare. When the left and center escaped from McCarthy, the "Christian right" pressed him to their bosom, combining his opportunistic paranoia with their own biblicistic apocalypticism.

As Erling Jorstad documents in his book, *The Politics of Doomsday: Fundamentalists of the Far Right,* the theological foundations of the Christian right rest on three notions: the verbal inspiration and inerrancy of the Bible, separatism, and premillennial apocalypticism.[6] Although these doctrines are derived from fundamentalism, they are interpreted in such a radical manner that they set the Christian right apart from the vast majority of American evangelicals. The mainstream born-again Christian regards the Bible as the inspired Word of God, the final source of truth, and the guidebook to human existence. Most evangelicals believe that God spoke through the prophets and apostles in a way which preserved the personality, idiosyncracies, and general world views of His chosen instruments. They realize that essential doctrines are clear and that the remainder is subject to interpretation. Hence, most evangelicals shun strict creedalism, the insistence that any one system of propositions can adequately decipher all the mysteries of God's revelation and command unquestioning assent of the faithful.

As the observer moves from the majority toward the right, he encounters the dispensationalists, whose system is more complete and airtight. Within the Bible-institute movement and such dispensationalist institutions as Wheaton College and Dallas Theological Seminary, disagreement about biblical interpretation is taken with greater seriousness. Belief in the essentials, the fundamentals, is paramount, to be sure. But exposition of the details (for example, how and in what manner the Bible is inspired; whether Christ will return before, during, or after the "great tribulation"; whether the Lord's Supper may be offered to any believer or only to those known by the elders to be of upright character) is scarcely unimportant. Bullingerites, or ultradispensationalists, who believe that the only portions of the Scriptures operative today are the prison epistles of the Apostle Paul, have little to do with dispensationalists, who insist that "all scripture is inspired of God and is profitable . . ." (1 Tim. 3:16).

The ultrafundamentalist views the Bible as though it were a letter dictated by God, each sentence of which is a separate proposition or truth, the sum of which can be arranged by the interpreter in a system of truth which is just as infallible, inerrant, and authoritative as the Author's. The essential teaching of fundamentalism is the claim that the original documents of the Bible were dictated by God to His spokesmen and that everything contained in them is infallible. The innovation added by the ultrafundamentalists is the notion that *their interpretation* of the Bible is equally infallible and, hence, cannot be debated or questioned. The ultrafundamentalist preacher thus becomes as authoritative as God.

The arrogance of this position inevitably leads to schism, abuse of authority, and sociopolitical reaction. Clustering around the personality and teachings of charismatic interpreters of the fundamentalist heritage, ultrafundamentalist churches see themselves as keepers and preservers of the Gospel in the midst of an apostate and hostile world. To question the expositors of the Bible is tantamount to rebellion against God. To deviate from the community's understanding of the separated life is to court excommunication and being delivered "onto Satan for the destruction of the flesh" (1 Cor. 5:5).

Leaders escape such drastic condemnations through an ingenious cop-out: God forgave his prophets and apostles their human failings. David remained "a man after God's own heart" even though he was an adulterer and murderer; Peter denied Christ three times and yet remained the "rock" upon which the church was built; many of the patriarchs were God's chosen instruments despite their treachery, duplicity, and sexual sins. If a leader "repents," he or she is to be instantly forgiven. No punitive action is to be permitted or criticism voiced, for "Thou shalt not touch the Lord's anointed."

Rank and file who cannot submit are ostracized or leave of their own volition when they can no longer tolerate the abuse of persons and property that inevitably crops up in groups with inadequate checks and balances. The defectors' tales combine with outsiders suspicion of the ultrafundamentalist group to produce hostility toward the group. The group welcomes such reaction as evidence of its own theological and moral superiority. "So persecuted ye the prophets who were before us." It is the lot of every true Christian to suffer persecution. The group more sharply defines the line that separates it from the dominant culture, other fundamentalist churches, and former members. Social contacts shrink. Children are removed from the "permissive and morally corrupt" public schools so that they may receive a "Bible-based" education. Politicians are supported only if they oppose the group's enemies or espouse its reactionary fear of those who attempt to change the world for the better by any means other than calling for repentance in the face of the impending end of the world.

Now and then issues emerge to which the ultrafundamentalist can address himself. For example, he can oppose the sale of *Playboy* or *Penthouse* at local stores, rail against movie houses that feature X-rated movies, or agitate against fluoridation as a harbinger of socialized medicine. He can campaign for the rare political candidate who shares his theology. Otherwise, ultrafundamentalism retreats from politics, public concerns, and the culture almost entirely.

The confusion of the inerrant book—itself a troublesome notion with which we shall deal elsewhere in these pages—with an inerrant interpreter is nowhere more obvious than in the apocalypticism of ultrafundamentalism. All fundamentalists expect and await the Second Advent. This belief is shared by (1) conservative denominations ranging from the Southern Baptist Convention to the various Dutch Reformed groups to the Plymouth Brethren; (2) evangelical wings of "middle-of-the-road" denominations such as the Presbyterians, the Methodists, and the Lutherans; (3) thousands of independent Bible churches; (4) pentecostalism in its organized and disorganized forms; and (5) even by such heretical "cults" as Jehovah's Witnesses and the Worldwide Church of God.

Once again, the ultrafundamentalist position is more extreme than their competitors. Fundamentalists passively await the end of the present evil world system. The ultrafundamentalists actively encourage it—some by provoking the forces of law and order into killing their members; others by insisting that Christian America use its thermonuclear power to destroy its godless enemies; others by plotting to enlarge present conflicts in the Mideast into global war; still others by pulling their members out of mainstream society and moving them to heavily armed and well-supplied "end time" enclaves.

The ultrafundamentalists of the fifties and sixties spent their energies and substance in a propaganda battle against apostasy and collectivism. Their dispensational apocalypticism convinced them that American society would be taken over by Satan's agents (modernists, liberals, ecumenists, integrationists, the United Nations, and other elements of "Communist conspiracy"). Yet in the attempt to restore America to its "Christian foundations" (which the ultrafundamentalist defines as republican government, laissez-faire capitalism, and thermonuclear militarism) they fought on against the war on poverty, Medicare, the lifting of restrictions on immigration, urban renewal, the liberal Supreme Court, the desegregation of the public schools, academic freedom, rock and roll music, the fluoridation of water, the income tax, as well as "giveaways, federal subsidies, welfare, deficit finance, consensus, bureaucracy, red tape, new taxes, unlimited credit, installment buying, and pay-as-you-go tax collections."[7] Their theology requires that they must lose these battles. Things must get worse and worse. The Bible, as they interpret it, says that the forces of the Antichrist (collectivism, the welfare state, communism, ecumenism and so forth) will triumph. Then God will intervene by ending human history and establishing his reign.

When the sociopolitical balance listed to the left as it did during the Roosevelt, Truman, Kennedy, and Johnson administrations, there was a small but supportive audience that revered the Christian right whether they agreed with its theological presuppositions or not, because it was practically the only organized form of response to frightening changes in the society. With the backlash of the sixties, the Nixon victories, and finally, the Reagan landslide, the entire society seemed to tilt toward the preservation of older certainties and the rejection of the Great Society. The Christian right found itself outflanked. A president of the United States unself-consciously mouthed platitudes about the historic importance of the Scriptures. He declared 1983 "the year of the Bible" and explained escalating warfare in the Near East as the fulfillment of biblical prophecy. It would be hard for the Christian right to condemn this president.

Many of the targets of the ultrafundamentalists' bitterest rhetoric seemed to lose their vigor with age. The National Council of Churches, most established denominations, the Roman Catholic Church, the supporters of the United Nations all seemed in decline. The left was withering. The coalition of Democratic social activists, big-city machines, labor unions, and Southern conservatives no longer ruled Congress. Many of the gains made by blacks, women, the poor, ecologists, and the other activists of the sixties seemed to slip through their fingers. But if the society appeared tilted to the right, much of the past half century's reforms and social innovations appeared firmly entrenched. There appeared no momentum propelling us in the direction for which the Christian right had so long agitated. Prayer was still banned from the schools. Communism remained unchecked in Cuba and Indochina. Busing to achieve racial balance continued. Homosexuals did not return to the closet. The nation appeared confused and divided.

By 1980 the left and the center were virtually leaderless. A new evangelical leader concerned more with the slipping away of moral values than the advance of collectivism emerged and with him the so-called Moral Majority. It is so much easier to recognize and respond to sexual laxity, liberalized abortion, and homosexuality than it is to spot collectivistic inroads. There are millions more in this country who want a channel to protest sexually explicit material on television than the presence of the United Nations in New York.

But as one group of ultrafundamentalists faded into ever greater obscurity, a newer and more dangerous movement was coming into being. It began with the Jesus movement of the late sixties and early seventies. They were young. They were zealous. They looked like hippies. They had "turned on" to Jesus. They were as fanatic for the Gospel as many of their peers had been for drugs and sex.

While conducting reserarch for my book, *The Jesus Trip: Advent of the Jesus Freaks,* I interviewed hundreds of Jesus people and their leaders. Their style and argot was counterculture but their message was fundamentalist to the core. Every one of the five fundamentals was essential to their lives. Their message was simple: Accept Jesus Christ as your personal savior, read the Bible, pray, tell others about Jesus, give up drugs, avoid sex outside of marriage, and mellow out.

When it came to the fundamentals of the faith, the Jesus people were theologically orthodox. But they differed in one important respect from conservative Protestant denominations and sects. The Jesus freaks were willing to abandon the sins of their former lives, but not their youth-culture lifestyle—hence the hippie appearance which many conservative Christians found reprehensible.

At first glance, they seemed to be converted junkies, bikers, bank bombers, and radicals. Their standard costume included long hair, beads, ponchos, overalls, workshirts, fatigues, and sandals. For many Jesus freaks this was more disguise than personal statement. The majority of them were recruited from cozy, middle-class, suburban evangelical churches. They were initiated into the youth culture by the very movement which rejected that culture. By adopting the antiestablishment uniform of the sixties, the Jesus movement made itself relevant to street people, drug-culture burnouts, and other social refugees. But the cost of this relevance was alienation from mainstream evangelicals, who were threatened by the style.

Also the Jesus people took their premillennialism much more seriously than other evangelicals. I heard Hal Lindsey tell an audience of Jesus people at the Jesus Christ Light and Power House located on the UCLA campus: "When the Lord returns, there will be no racial strife, there will be no poverty or hunger, there will be no air pollution. Jesus is really gonna get it together." The Jesus movement had a superb rationalization for ignoring the duties of Christian citizenship in a perplexing age. Leave it to Jesus. He is coming—soon.

Their focus was not only apocalyptic, it was sensate. Becoming a Christian meant getting "stoned on Jesus," "grooving on God," attaining "a permanent high." Pentecostalism was rampant among the Jesus freaks. Getting high once and then studying the Bible and doctrine was not enough for most of them. They needed renewed hits. The baptism of the spirit, speaking in tongues, healing, prophetic utterance, and deliverance soon followed. Pentecostalism was a mixed blessing to the Jesus movement. The leaders who received the most attention from the mass media were fundamentalist revival preachers in the Billy Graham tradition. They ignored so-called manifestations of the spirit or they actively opposed them.

The evangelists tended toward a "once-saved-always-saved" doctrine. The pentecostals often taught that the Christian can lose his salvation by his postconversion sins. The alienation of the Jesus freaks from their families and mainstream society, as well as their marginal employability, soon led to communalism. Once again, the form was countercultural but the distinctive content was fundamentalist and pentecostal. Instead of joining local churches as earlier converts to revivalism had done, the Jesus freak often migrated toward "Christian houses" and "Christian communities." As the leaders of the movement moved farther apart on theological issues, many became self-proclaimed "apostles," while others were simply regarded as father figures by the tribal bands that clustered around them.

Outcasts, derelicts, and drifters, who found a sense of identity and belonging in the born-again communes, were dependent upon their new brothers and sisters in every respect. Their resources were scant. They needed housing, food, and medical care. Time hung heavy on their hands. The leaders of the groups were much more than evangelists; theoretically they became loving and demanding parents, who supported the recruits physically and spiritually as the converts cleaned up their act. The converts' newly found self-respect and impulse control was a gift of God which they had received through his earthly representatives. High demands were imposed on the convert by the groups and their charismatic leaders.

An economic base had to be established. Some Christian houses were supported by donations from wealthy evangelicals, others by contributions from conservative churches. Some communes turned into cottage industries—poster publishing, music recording, health-food restaurants, and so forth. Larger groups sent members out to sell literature, imported pottery, and other goods. Some groups tried farming or providing stoop laborers for farmers.

Doctrinal distinctions that set groups apart from one another were accentuated. The Christian World Liberation Front of Berkeley fractured over Jack Sparks' claims of apostolic authority. Sparks and his followers founded the Evangelicals Orthodox Church. According to Sparks and the EOC, the true Christian subscribed not only to the Bible but to the ancient creeds of Christendom. Youth evangelist David Berg promoted himself to Moses David, God's end-time prophet. His group, the Children of God, accepted Berg's "Mo Letters" as superior to the revelation found in the Bible. Victor Paul Wierwille of the Way International emphasized Bible study and speaking in tongues but denied the Trinity and other orthodox doctrines.

At the height of the Jesus-freak fervor, Tony and Susan Alamo's Christian Foundation, then based in Saugus, California, "rescued" dopers and drifters from the streets of Los Angeles. Susan proclaimed not a God of love but a God who hates sin. Several hundred recruits were put to work in Alamo-owned enterprises. When Susan died of cancer, a twenty-four-hour-a-day chain of praying followers was activated to insure her resurrection. For two years they maintained their vigil before her embalmed remains in the living room of the Alamo's home in Fort Smith, Arkansas. Meanwhile, Tony barnstormed northern cities, seeking unwed mothers who would give their infants to the Christian Foundation. Frustrated in his efforts to continue the movement without Susan, Tony and his inner circle reportedly have fled to France.

The past ten years have produced hundreds of groups based not only on the five fundamentals but on what may be termed the four "ultrafundamentals": *communalism, apocalypticism, ecstasy,* and *authority.* And a word has achieved new prominence to describe this plethora of authoritarian, totalistic, totalitarian, paranoid Bible sects. The word is *cult.* Before the emergence of these sects, the most common use of the term *cult* was by evangelical Christians to refer to groups whose theology was considered heretical. For example, courses on Christian apologetics (the defense of the faith) at Bible institutes dealt with such "non-Christian cults" as Jehovah's Witnesses, Christian Science, and the Mormons. In the evangelical catalog of spiritual counterfeits, a "religion" was a cult if it denied the Trinity, the divinity of Jesus, the virgin birth, human depravity, the substitutionary atonement, salvation through faith, the necessity of personal conversion, and so forth.

As various factions of the Jesus movement became institutionalized as disparate sects, a movement of reaction developed. It began with the clearly extremist Children of God. Ted Patrick began forcible kidnappings and deconversions of COG members. Since COG was feared and hated by other Jesus-movement groups for their confrontive conversion tactics and the hostility they evidenced toward other Christians, the Jesus people cared little. Patrick justified his "deprogramming" tactics" as necessitated by the "brainwashing" or "hypnosis" techniques allegedly employed by COG to destroy their recruits' freedom of will and to turn them into "mindless robots and zombies." He contended that his remorseless cross-examination of his subjects, his threats and bullying, his deprecation of cult leaders and doctrine, and his castigation of the converts forced them to "think for themselves" and reject the cult's "mind control."

In support of Patrick, the anticult network arose. The network is a loosely knit coalition of deprogrammers, parents' groups, former sect members who had been successfully deconverted, information and referral sources, and concerned mental-health professionals. Within a decade Patrick had kidnapped nearly three thousand adult converts from hundreds of different groups. His tactics were imitated, refined, and applied by scores of new deprogrammers—many of them Patrick proteges or Patrick deprogrammees.

Soon the application of the term *cult* spread to any "heavy" involvement with a nontraditional or traditional religious group, mass therapy, political cell, commune, meditation society, sexual preferences, or romantic relationship undertaken by a young adult *contrary to the wishes of that individual's parents.* If the subject's behavior could in any way be described as evidence of a sudden personality change and that change could be attributed to the agency of a movement, an ideology, a practice, or a person, the subject was deemed "brainwashed." Once the subject had been so branded, a coercive deprogramming could be arranged for a fee averaging more than ten thousand dollars.

Since the subject's parents were said to be acting to prevent a greater harm (continuing brainwashing which, according to the expert testimony of anticult experts, could lead to insanity or suicide) from befalling their child (usually a young adult of about twenty-three), police and courts were loathe to interfere. In those rare instances in which arrests occurred, parents and deprogrammers were usually acquitted on the basis of the doctrine of justification: At the time of the kidnapping, the parents believed that their actions constituted the lesser of two evils. The deprogrammer was merely their agent in attempting to rescue the subject from what was perceived as greater harm. It is not my purpose to deal with the deprogramming controversy in these pages. I have done so at length in three earlier works.[8] My point is that defense against deprogramming has become as essential to ultrafundamentalist groups as the fundamentals that have been set forth. *Resisting programming* has become the fifth "ultrafundamental."

Blood of the martyrs is the seed of any church. Persecution is the sine qua non of ultrafundamentalist sects. If there were no opposition, they would create it. But they do not have to at this time in history. That's what deprogramming does. To the ultrafundamentalist, the deprogrammer is Satan incarnate, the lion waiting to devour the unwary. Resisting this demon is a test of character. Ten of thousands of converts to ultrafundamentalist sects have been snatched. Probably half have returned to their respective sects, where they are treated as heroes and examples. The convert's new-found brothers and sisters warn him to trust no one. Satan and his agents are subtle. The recruit hears repeatedly of what has befallen others who trusted their parents or friends.

The recruit lives constantly with the fear of being kidnapped for his or her faith, having been told that he could be imprisoned for months, drugged, tortured, deprived of food and sleep, beaten, reviled, shamed, stripped naked, sexually abused, threatened with death, and tempted to sin. For just as deprogrammers concoct tales about each sect that embody every negative experience ever reported, so the sect leaders combine every repulsive detail of every shameful tactic ever employed by any deprogrammer. Unfortunately such warnings are not totally unfounded.

NOTES

1. Billy Graham, "Biblical Authority in Evangelism," *Christianity Today* (Oct. 15, 1956), reprinted in Frank E. Gaebelein, ed., *A Christianity Today Reader* (New York: Meredith Press, 1967), p. 21.

2. Graham, *20 Years Under God: A Pictorial Review of the Billy Graham Ministries,* ed. George M. Wilson (Minneapolis: World Wide Publications, 1970), pp. 152-53.

3. "We Poll the Pollster," *Christianity Today* (Dec. 21, 1979), p. 10.

4. Edward John Carnell, *The Case for Orthodox Theology* (Philadelphia: Westminster Press, 1959), pp. 120-21.

5. Carnell, "Fundamentalism," in *A Handbook of Theology* (New York: Meridian Books, 1958), p. 143.

6. Erling Jorstad, *The Politics of Doomsday: Fundamentalists of the Far Right* (Nashville: Abingdon Press, 1970).

7. Ibid., p. 149.

8. For a complete discussion of the deprogramming controversy, see *Mind-bending: Brainwashing, Cults, and Deprogramming in the 80s* (New York: Doubleday, 1984). My position is also delineated in *The Cults Are Coming!* (Nashville, Tenn.: Abingdon, 1978) and *Cults: The Continuing Threat* (Nashville: Abingdon, 1983).

8

Dispensationalism, Pentecostalism, and Deliverance

Most fundamentalists are followers of the "dispensational premillennialism," a theology introduced by two nineteenth-century British religious dissidents, John Nelson Darby and William Kelly, leaders of the Plymouth Brethren. This theology maintains that the church will be removed from the face of the earth and that the Jews will resume their role as God's chosen nation before the establishment of the kingdom of God.

Needless to say, premillennialists despair of mankind's ability to resolve personal, community, national, or international problems. They believe that the end of the world as we know it and the violent destruction of the social order are imminent. They interpret obscure passages in the Old Testament Book of Daniel and in the New Testament Revelation of St. John as predicitons of the "end time," which is presumably being fulfilled even as I write these words. Jesus is coming—soon—within the next few years. As a matter of fact, dispensationalists have believed this for a century and a half!

Premillennialism was well-suited to the period of eschatological expectation in the mid-nineteenth century that produced the Millerites, Seventh-Day Adventists, Mormons, and Jehovah's Witnesses. These groups share many dispensationalist notions—as do such present-day cults as the Worldwide Church of God, headed by Herbert W. Armstrong, the Children of God, and even the Unification Church.

Dispensationalism resurrects itself as though newly discovered whenever renewed societal stress (depression, recession, threat of war) elicits the belief that things are getting worse and will probably stay that way. Virtually ignored today by Protestant theologians in Europe, dispensationalism was popularized in this country by the Scofield Reference Bible, a study edition of the King James Version of the scriptures; it is printed in such a manner that the dispensational commentaries are virtually indistinguishable from the actual biblical text.

Dispensationalism is also the dominant theology of the Bible-institute movement, which includes, for example, Moody Bible Institute, Biola College (Bible Institute of Los Angeles), Philadelphia College of the Bible, Wheaton College, Dallas Theological Seminary, and several similar institutions. Numerous biblical sects, fundamentalist associations of churches, and missionary organizations espouse dispensationalism as do such prominent evangelical writers as Hal Lindsey, author of *The Late Great Planet Earth*.

Dispensationalism is based on the notion that the history of mankind as recorded in the Bible has been divided into seven distinct periods, during each of which God deals with the human race on the basis of one specific principle or means of "dispensing" grace. Although there is disagreement among the dispensationalists as to the number and characteristics of these periods, they usually agree with respect to the last three: the dispensations of Law, Grace, and the Kingdom. According to this viewpoint, Jesus offered the kingdom of God to the Jews, who were then under the dispensation of Law, a covenant that required ritual sacrifice for the expiation of sin. It was God's plan that the Jews would accept Jesus as their messiah and king and that through them He would rule the nations of the world in peace, harmony, and justice. However, the Jews upset the divine plan by rejecting Jesus' offer. Although the final purpose of God is a restored Jewish theocracy, He has been forced to institute the Christian church as a "temporary" measure. The hands of the prophetic clock are stopped "until the times of the Gentiles be fulfilled."

At some date in the near future, Jesus shall return secretly and "rapture" the church, that is, remove it from the world. The Jews will then be converted, and be subject to the "great tribulation," a seven-year period of persecution at the hands of the forces of the Antichrist. But Jesus will again return to establish his kingdom—a thousand-year reign with its center in the renewed nation of Israel, whose capital is Jerusalem. The dispensationalist has a high regard for the Jew, since he will play an important role in restoring the kingdom of God. Like the traditional Christian Jew-baiter, the dispensationalist regards the Diaspora and Holocaust as divine punishments for the rejection of Jesus. However, the dispensationalist believes that the sufferings of the Jewish people were imposed by Satan rather than God.

The Jews, the dispensationalist asserts, remain the chosen people of God. Most traditional Christian theologians *regard the church* as the new or spiritual Israel, and believe that God has no further purpose for the Jewish people unless they convert to Christianity on a one-by-one basis. The modern return of Jews to Israel is taken by dispensationalists to mark the beginning of the fulfillment of God's plan to restore his ancient people to their land and their special place of service and witness. Dispensationalists are strong supporters of the state of Israel, often espousing an uncritical pro-Israeli and anti-Arab viewpoint. Rumors abound of a fundamentalist-sponsored conspiracy to seize the Temple Mount area in the Old City quarter of Jerusalem, where the Dome of the Rock Mosque of Omar stands (the third holiest site in Islam), so that Solomon's Temple may be reconstructed in order to hasten the Second Coming. There is a fear in some quarters that dispensationalist meddling with Near Eastern politics will trigger international conflict. To some dispensationalists, that is the point.

The dispensationalist notions that mankind is growing ever more sinful, that history is a one-way street leading to disaster, and that there are conspiracies of powerful political, industrial, and religious leaders led by the forces of evil, which shall soon rule or destroy mankind, readily combine with American populist concepts of unseen powers that manipulate the economy, control public opinion, and undermine traditional values.

The late Gordon Kahl, leader of Posse Comitatas, a right-wing organization whose cells honeycomb the agricultural heartland of America, combined dispensationalist, anti-Communist, antigovernment, anti-Semitic, and anti-Black ideologies. (After being involved in a shootout with U.S. marshalls in South Dakota, during which two marshalls were killed, Kahl and a county sheriff were killed in a subsequent episode in Arkansas.)

Each successive dispensationalist leader conveniently forgets to tell his followers that his basic scheme is a variant of the Plymouth Brethren/Bible-institute theology. Hence, converts to the ever-growing number of dispensationalist sects are convinced that their leader is the first to "rightly divide the word of truth," and the only one to realize that "Jesus is coming—soon." Dispensationalism is easily franchised. The self-appointed leader reads the notes in the Scofield Reference Bible, or takes a Scofield Correspondence Course offered by Moody Bible Institute, buys a dispensational chart at a Christian bookstore, simply picks up the lingo from a "Bible expositor" at a "prophecy conference," listens to a radio preacher, or reads *The Late Great Planet Earth*. Minimal exposure to this rather simple interpretive scheme is all the training required to start one's own dispensational sect.

The strength of dispensationalism as a scheme of biblical interpretation is in its attempt to account for the discontinuities in the Bible. It obviously begins with the conception of an older and a new convenant

or contract between God and man, which is explicit in the teachings of
Jesus and the apostles, but then undertakes to expand the notion.
However, much of the Bible remains outside airtight compartments.
Where does one place the books of Job, Esther, Proverbs, or Ecclesi-
astes? Also it is a strange system that places the teachings of the
apostles above the words of Jesus as reported in the four Gospels.
According to the dispensationalist, the Sermon on the Mount, the
parables, and the other messages of Jesus clearly pertain, not to the
church, but to the Jews as citizens of the kingdom that Jesus offered
them, which they rejected, and which God will reinstitute in the last
days.

The dispensationalist notion of the rejected kingdom would seem
to indicate that God never intended for his Son to die, that the gospel
of salvation by grace through faith, the giving of the Holy Spirit, and
the life of the church were all compromises or improvisations on the
part of God. Dispensationalism is a shallow theory of religious evolution or progressive revelation. It admits that the Bible is a record of
God's progressive self-disclosure but does not seriously wrestle with the
significance of this admission.

Perhaps the rules of the divine-human encounter change, not
because God arbitrarily changes the nature of the game but because
different human beings living in different epochs have disparate under-
standings of the world in which they find themselves. Dispensationalists
would never acknowledge it, but their system opens the way for viewing
the Bible not as a seamless garment of inerrant propositions but as (1)
a collection of narratives, poetry, writings, letters, liturgical instructions, and apocalyptic warnings which reflect the idiosyncracies as well
as the insights of their respective writers and (2) an attempt on the part
of two ancient religious communities (the Hebrews and the early Christians) to codify and preserve their heritage.

The dispensationalists are right in one respect: everything in the
Bible is *for us* but it is not necessarily *to us*. The problem is that their
system does not provide a sufficient basis for discerning the difference.
Further, dispensationalism's overly simplified scheme of the rapture,
the tribulation, the millenium, and so forth, is arbitrary and capricious.
It is not—nor has it ever been—the only way of systematizing the
prophetic passages in the Old and New Testaments. Even among
evangelicals it is a minority position—one that can be regarded with
interest but scarcely the key which opens the last recesses of the mystery
of God's plan for the ages.

The dispensationalist overemphasis on the timetable of the "end
time" produces an eschatologically based irresponsibility that destroys

careers, family ties, and friendships. Several of my clients have spouses or children who have fled to some enclave with like-minded prophecy students to await the Second Coming. The abandonment of all human duties—business obligations, the rearing of one's children, the needs of elderly parents, the commitment to one's husband or wife—are justified by the group-held assurance that Jesus is returning in a few weeks.

Hundreds of small groups and dozens of major sects watch and wait, confident that there is no future for the human race. They refuse to allow their potential as individuals or the needs of their loved ones to distract them as they read their Bibles, pray, evoke hysteria in one another, search the daily newspapers for some fresh confirmation (an earthquake or a war), listen to the recorded messages of their respective seers, and permit life to run through their fingers like sand through an hourglass. "What are your plans? What will you be doing this fall?" I asked a young Jesus freak whom I met in Los Angeles in 1971.

"What do you mean?" he replied, "Like getting a job or going to college? Hey, man, what's wrong with you. Don't you know the Lord is coming?" By now he is in his early thirties. I wonder if he is still living with his parents and waiting.

I suppose I could praise the dispensationalists for having refused to spiritualize and ignore the apocalyptic element in the New Testament, as most other Christians have done. Jesus and the early church lived with the expectancy that the Kingdom of God was at hand, and this conviction is the sine qua non for interpreting much of the New Testament. However, most Bible scholars would contend that their expectations were disappointed and that the church had to face the alternative of either reinterpreting its initial millenialism or going out of business. The Book of Acts represents one solution: the Holy Spirit is depicted as the invisible Jesus, carrying on the work of the ascended Christ by empowering the apostles as missionaries and wonder-workers. The confusion between the concept that Jesus would return during the lifetime of his first generation of followers and the realization that the church is the leaven which throughout coming ages must leaven the loaf of human history was never satisfactorily resolved within the apostolic church. As the early church developed its manifold traditions, denominations, sects, and so forth, the eschatological urgency faded, the Jesus of the Gospels became the mystical Christ, the inaccessible king, or the humane moralist of liberalism. Only in some sects, the cults, and dispensationalism was his millenarian message taken seriously—though often with less than salutary effects.

To a counselor of families distressed by fanatic groups, dispensational apocalypticism is much more than a question of how to interpret passages from the Books of Daniel and Revelation. Apocalypticism is a way of experiencing life with accompanying attitudes and patterns of behavior. It is a not unexpected outgrowth of the current "evangelical upsurge." For whenever there is an outpouring of revivalistic piety, we find that millennarian excesses are not far behind. Today—as in the past—American revivalistic preaching is creating a climate of enthusiasm from which cults, sects, and utopian communities are emerging. Moreover, the elements of the apocalyptic mood are pervasive: religious excitement, social disconnectedness, uncertainty, distrust of established authority, and pessimism.

As exasperating as it is to deal with the personal, interpersonal, and social disruptions occasioned by the messengers of dispensational gloom and doom, it should be borne in mind that most apocalyptic groups are short-lived. They are soon consumed by their own essential negativity and failure of their prophecies, and they fade into oblivion, while the world and its evils stubbornly persist. Since the dispensationalists have been wrong in their predictions of the end of the world for more than a century, it may be predicted they will be wrong again in our day, and will probably be wrong yet again a hundred years hence when their scheme of biblical interpretation is "discovered" anew.

PENTECOSTALISM

The most significant twentieth-century contribution to American religious experience has been pentecostalism, an ecstatic, experience-based form of spirituality characterized by speaking in tongues, spiritual healing, the casting out of evil spirits, and special revelations. There are today more than 150 different pentecostal bodies in the United States with a combined membership of about two and a half million. Almost all pentecostals are fundamentalists (and revivalists)—although very few fundamentalists (approximately one in fifteen) are pentecostals. In addition to the many pentecostal denominations and sects, there are numerous independent pentecostals in storefront missions, communes, and sects, as well as thousands of neopentecostals in major Protestant denominations and within the Roman Catholic Church. (Neopentecostals are members of mainline churches who preach "charismatic renewal" and gifts of the spirit, usually in less frenzied and antisocial ways than the sectarian charismatics. They are not necessarily fundamentalists.)

What is pentecostalism? Like revivalism, pentecostalism is first and foremost a religion of profound, shattering, and heartfelt experience. Experience is primary; theology secondary; ethics tertiary; and relevance to the everyday world of little consequence. Pentecostalism is revivalism with a secret new ingredient—*the baptism of the spirit.* This second blessing or renewed conversion experience bestows upon the believer various gifts of the spirit.

For all practical purposes, the principle gift and sole criterion of whether or not the individual has received the spirit is "speaking in tongues." According to charismatic evangelist Kenneth Hagin's reading of the Bible, tongues are important for ten reasons including the following: (1) Speaking in tongues is evidence that the believer is filled with the Holy Spirit. (2) Tongues are spiritually edifying. (3) Tongues remind us of the spirit's indwelling presence. (4) Speaking in tongues keeps selfishness out of our prayers by making it impossible for us to pray and think at the same time. (5) Praying in tongues strengthens our faith. (6) Speaking in tongues can be used to fog our minds so that we can keep from being disturbed by church services, our jobs, or risque jokes at the barbershop. (7) Praying in tongues enables us to have telepathic knowledge of distant events and to affect their outcome.[1]

Dennis and Rita Bennett emphasize that the gift of tongues is (1) a sign of God's presence to unbelievers, a powerful means of calling their attention to Him; and (2) a means of edifying the church.[2] Robert Brandt stresses that God's control of our tongues, our most difficult member to control, is evidence that the Holy Spirit controls our entire being.[3]

From my point of view—and I have attended many pentecostal services, prayed with friends who "have tongues," and researched the phenomenon for many years—speaking in tongues is a form of incoherent babbling, induced by stress; it is regressive in nature (and, hence, suggestive of baby talk) and an imitation of the rhythm and intonation of speech without an authentic spoken language's syntax, vocabulary, grammar, or semantic structure. It is often intense, exciting, moving, but it is disorienting; certainly it is involuntary and spontaneous. Although it usually takes place in a communal setting reinforced by the frenzy of hand clapping, shouting, arm waving, hymn singing, preaching, testifying, and miracle working, it is also common where two or three people are gathered for prayer, and it is not exceptional during private acts of devotion.

The worshiper believes that he is being possessed by the spirit, that he is being filled and energized by God, that God is speaking through him for the edification of the faithful. The messages vouchsafed to the congregation by these means are customarily translated into the language of mortals by a second ecstatic believer, one who is said to have the gift of interpretation.

Like all ecstatic experience, speaking in tongues affords the subject the opportunity to get out of himself, to escape momentarily the tensions and contradictions of his everyday existence. Appealing primarily to the estranged and lonely, the experience grants the subject instant status among the faithful, bestows a sense of self-esteem upon the worshiper as an instrument of the divine power, and channels suppressed emotions, ranging from terrifying anxiety to profound joy.

The experiencing subject believes for the most part that he or she is speaking an intelligible language. Reports have been rampant for nearly eighty years of individuals speaking foreign languages they had never learned, including such archaic tongues as Coptic Egyptian, classical Greek, and ancient Syriac. Such stories are nonsense—supported by not a scintilla of evidence. Pentecostal utterances have been repeatedly studied by linguists throughout the world. So far, it is the universal opinion of scholars of the structure of language, as well as experts in foreign languages, that the ecstatic utterances of the pentecostals bear little resemblance to language, apart from the fact that both ordinary language and the so-called spiritual tongues are vocalized. Further, it has often been observed that the same message in tongues may be translated into several different messages by different interpreters.

At the last pentecostal service I attended, an independent group in Santa Barbara, California, I estimated that the spiritual message took one minute to recite but that the interpretation, delivered at the same rate of speed, took three to four times as long. Further, as is usually the case, the message was a rather trite recitation of biblical simplisms. It was scarcely the stuff of a special revelation.

But we must not lose sight of the fact that it is the *context* and the *consequences* rather than the *content* which is important to the pentecostal. His experience unites him with other ecstatic believers, it admits him to the realm of miracles (a kind of mythic universe in which the ordinary laws of nature and society are suspended), and it initiates him into a wisdom that ordinary consciousness cannot attain. The mythic universe is animistic, primitive, and powerful. The world of human beings and nature is ruled by invisible entities, good and evil spirits, over which the worshiper may gain power. By invoking the good power or powers, he may achieve happiness, peace of mind, a sense of belonging to the universe. By exorcising or repulsing the evil spirits, he may rid himself and his loved ones of disease, calamity, discomfort, and even death.

HEALING

Objectively speaking, I find the healing claims of the pentecostals of little merit. There is, to be sure, much relief of psychosomatic symptoms. Now and then the spontaneous remission of an illness is achieved, but this must be counted as a coincidence. For the most part, claims of healings which are "received" by believers simply do not bear scrutiny. And the "miracle cures," healings that cannot be explained by medical science, prove only that there are occasional events that cannot be explained with the knowledge available to us at this time. They do not prove that the charismatic Christian's interpretation is correct.

"Healings" probably occur as often among primitive people who do not worship Jesus, among heretical Christians who deny his divinity, and by psychic healers, who could care less about the Bible, as they do among pentecostals. Moreover, the acceptance of a healing is an incredibly subjective experience. Many people who have been "healed" at pentecostal services, according to their own testimony or that of their relatives, subsequently suffer the return of their symptoms or succumb to the same illnesses. To a pentecostal, it is the immediate experience that counts, not the interpretation or the subsequent reality. To receive a healing is to be touched by God, even if death occurs the following day. The outsider hears tales of amputated limbs regrown, regenerated lungs, eyes growing in empty sockets, and resurrections from the dead. But many of these stories have been told for many decades. They are almost always about "someone who is a friend of a friend of mine."

The believers I have interviewed who were not healed of cerebral palsy, blindness, Parkinson's disease, cancer of the prostate, or heart disease were admonished to have greater faith, as though faith can be quantified like pounds of flour. Medical attention is often condemned as evidence of lack of faith. "Don't you know that those doctors will kill you?" the believer is admonished. "Only God can heal."

I have comforted the friends and relatives of worshipers who have died of treatable illnesses ranging from lung cancer to diabetes or who have been permanently impaired because they had "received a healing from the Lord" and refused to display lack of faith by seeking medical care. Since some people are refusing to allow their children to be vaccinated or receive immunization for infantile paralysis and other diseases, I expect epidemics of such scourges in the years ahead.

Another abhorrent trend is the refusal of medical supervision in childbirth. Children are brought into the world by unattended mothers, mothers attended only by another woman in the group, mothers attended only by their husbands, or mothers attended by a "midwife," depending on the specific revelation or biblical interpretation that guides the particular sect. The hatred of women, excused by reference to the "curse of Eve"—that is, that women shall bring forth their children in pain and sorrow, is obvious. Women and their babies are dying as a result of this shocking fanaticism.

DELIVERANCE

Deliverance is the dark side of healing. Instead of invoking the goodness of God through faith to obtain temporal benefits, the believer attempts to cast out evil spirits, seen as the cause of all unwanted experiences. All physical and mental conditions, according to this mythical notion, are evil spirits, whose names are, for example, the spirit of hernia, the spirit of leukemia, the spirit of backache, and so forth. By calling upon them by name and invoking the "name of Jesus," the evil spirit is supposed to be expelled, cast out, and bound in the pit of hell.

Every anxiety, depression, and inexplicable experience is attributed to an appropriate evil spirit. According to the catalog of devils presented in the widely distributed do-it-yourself deliverance handbook, *Pigs in the Parlor: A Practical Guide to Deliverance* by Frank and Ida Mae Hammond, virtually every unwanted emotional reaction (ranging from "bitterness" to "embarrassment"), every disease (especially mental illnesses), and every possible use of the mind (including "intellectualism" and "rationalization") are demons that must be identified and expelled from the believer in deliverance sessions. The Hammonds also identify as demons the following: Masonic lodges, ESP, frigidity, Ouija boards, and Buddhism.

In deliverance circles, the expression, "God bless you," uttered when a person sneezes, is taken with deadly seriousness, since each sneeze, cough, or act of vomiting is regarded as the expulsion of evil beings from the human body. Many deliverance charismatics bring brown paper bags with them to worship services in order to confine the demons. (I have trouble imprisoning a sandwich in this manner.) Untoward thoughts are caused by evil spirits. Lust evoked by seeing a woman in a lingerie ad in a catalog is the doing of "the spirit of Sears and Roebuck," and must be exorcised. A mental illness, such as schizophrenia, and substance addiction are really the names of demons, and, as such, may be cast out.

The life of the deliverance charismatic if often one of terror and paranoia. Frogs, toads, snakes, and insects are actually evil spirits. Depictions of them are possessed. Jewelry and clothing made by American Indians or based on Indian designs are crawling with devils because the Indians worship demons. Handmade and manufactured goods from non-Christian countries must also be destroyed, for Japan, Taiwan, the Philippines, Mexico, and other "non-Christian" countries are filled with evil spirits. A broken-down tractor or an automobile that refuses to start or a child's smashed toy is demon possessed.

References to witches in drama, song lyrics that refer to magic, Halloween masks, rock music (when played backwards), fortune cookies, horoscopes in newspapers, the game of Dungeons and Dragons, and so on are infested with evil beings. In 1983, according to an Associated Press report, a wealthy Texan, Cullen Davis, destroyed more than a million dollars worth of gold, silver, jade, and ivory art objects because evangelist James Robison told him that they were heathen idols and thus an "abomination to the Lord."

Deliverance services are lengthy, exhausting, and confrontive. Believers may be held against their wills, pinned down by self-appointed exorcists, and brutally exhorted. One of my clients reports she was delivered from the "spirit of lust" in the following manner: The congregation screamed, "Come out of her, O spirit of Jezebel, I command thee through the blood of Jesus" in every-increasing stridency until they were hoarse. She was physically abused by being thrown about and caressed by unwanted contact with human hands, which were "suddenly seized by Satan." The session, which lasted for hours, panicked her into a nervous collapse.

SPECIAL REVELATIONS

According to Dennis and Rita Bennett, spirit-filled Christians are gifted with both "the word of knowledge," which they define as "supernatural revelation of facts, past, present, or future which were not learned through the efforts of the natural mind," and "the word of wisdom," which they explain as "the supernatural application of knowledge" to specific situations.[4] On the basis of alleged private revelations, all manner of Christians go about declaring authoritatively (and authoritarianly) that God says such and such to virtually everyone.

One of my subjects recently left her husband, who shares her charismatic faith, and has gone to live with a healing evangelist. She is expecting her husband's child as I write, and plans to give the infant away, divorce her husband, and marry the evangelist. Why? Because God told her to do so through a special revelation. Through such revelations marriages are arranged, divorces required, children abandoned, adulterous relationships condoned, and any of the biblical commandments may be selectively disregarded—because someone has received a message from heaven.

Receiving "a word of the Lord" is a game that any number can play. Millions of Christians act as though they have been lobotomized, trusting in the strongest urge of the moment (which they interpret as the voice of God), and acting without any thought of the consequences. An acquaintance of mine once drove on dangerous mountain roads with his wife and children on four bald tires because he had an inner sense of assurance that God would send His angels to protect them.

Pastors tell individual parishioners that God has revealed whom the parishioners should marry, where they should live, what they should do for a living. These people interfere with one another's lives in the most petty and the most serious ways because God has "put it into my heart."

Private revelations have become big business. Several volumes of semipoetic musings have been published by various charismatics purporting to be direct revelations from Jesus. Jesus writes very badly these days. He has lost a lot of his bite and verve since the parables and the Sermon on the Mount. He has become a sickly sentimentalist, who combines pop-psych, advice to the lovelorn, and tritest of moral homilies.

While I was in a hair-styling shop in Nashville recently, captive of a hairdresser with a razor in her hand, I agreed to allow her to read me her messages from Jesus, which she carried in a suitcase full of spiral-bound composition books. The first and most current message, which she recited from memory, was that "we are all cups—some of us full of blessings, some of us half full and some of us empty. Why some of us are cracked cups!" She also had received a remarkable revelation of the spiritual meaning of Walt Disney's *Bambi.*

In addition, I now and then receive telephone calls from women who have received a message for me "from the Lord." I ask them to have God send a copy of His communication to my office. It becomes so easy to move from saying, "I think" or "I feel" or "I want" such and such, to "thus saith the Lord." Among charismatics, every man or woman can function as his or her own cult, with appropriate revelation, ethics, lifestyle, and prophecy.

Exorcism and private revelations received only by the elder, apostle, or prophet of the group are effective means of achieving control and destroying resistance to authority. It is difficult to resist the injunctions of someone who is casting demons out of you. It is much easier to refuse to take your physician's or CPA's advice. At inception, pentecostal healing and deliverance groups are democratic. They quickly become autocratic as prophets receive "words of wisdom," which confirm their special authority.

To criticize or reject the teachings of the prophet is to commit "blasphemy against the Holy Ghost," a sin which "shall never be forgiven . . . neither in this world or in the world to come" (Matthew 12:31-32). The prophet inveighs: "You think you are opposing me. But you are really rebelling against God. And as God smote Miriam with leprosy for opposing Moses (Numbers 12:10), so shall he smite you with death and damnation if you refuse to obey his word through his chosen instrument. Remember what it says in the Bible, 'Touch not mine [the Lord's] annointed' (Psalms 5:15). If you turn your back on God by refusing this word of wisdom or by leaving this ministry, you or your children will die a terrible death or you will become a cripple or a homosexual."

Such manipulation of the flock by charismatic/deliverance preachers has been reported to me in precisely these words and similar ones by diverse groups all over the United States. And through "words of wisdom" sent from above, charismatic preachers avail themselves of multiple wives, concubines, and the financial rewards to which their position entitles them. ("Didn't the Old Testament patriarchs and monarchs have many wives?" they defensively demand. "And didn't God forgive David of adultery and murder. And despite his sins, didn't David remain a man 'after God's own heart'? And besides who is entitled to judge the Lord's annointed—except the Lord Himself?" I have heard these absurdities for more than twenty years.)

Charismatic deliverance is a franchise religion like dispensationalism, to which it is usually connected. The basic ideas and techniques are packaged in books, pamphlets, and tapes that are distributed throughout the country via mail order and sold in Christian literature shops. They are also spread by radio and television broadcasts, healing/deliverance assemblages, and person-to-person recruitment. Deliverance circles are active within many more moderate pentecostal churches such as local congregations of the Assemblies of God and they crop up frequently in mainline denominational groups.

I have in my study a stack of deliverance/dispensational literature given to me by subjects who left tiny (four- to twenty-member) do-it-yourself charismatic groups. If anything is demonic, it is this material. The deliverance groupees became so obsessed with evil that, for all practical purposes, they became worshipers of Satan! A well-known evangelical author, Franky Schaeffer, has said of the new charismatics: "These people have basically made all of life one long unrelated song and dance, in which one must move from one spiritual experience and high to another to validate one's Christian faith. What all this has to do with real life and getting on with being the salt of the earth . . . remains to be seen."[5]

NOTES

1. Kenneth E. Hagin, *Why Tongues?* (Tulsa, Okla.: Kenneth Hagin Ministries, Inc., 1975).

2. Dennis and Rita Bennett, *The Holy Spirit and You* (Plainfield, N.J.: Logos International, 1971).

3. Robert Brandt, *The Pentecostal Promise* (Springfield, Mo.: Gospel Publishing House, 1972), pp. 35-36.

4. Bennett and Bennett, *The Holy Spirit and You,* p. 155.

5. Franky Schaeffer, *Addicted to Mediocrity* (Westchester, Ill.: Crossway Books, 1981), p. 121.

Part Three

THE PLENTIFUL HARVEST

Introduction: Believing in Believing

Cults and sects do not spring forth from the forehead of Zeus full grown and armed. They are the products of America's inability to live without faith. As a nation, we believe in God. We believe in Jesus. We believe in the Bible. We believe in religion. Even more fundamentally, we believe in believing. Believing—that is, being confident and courageous, being positive, having a dream and pursuing it—is central to the American way of life.

A clear example of faith fixation is the vast retail establishment whose very name is derived from "the American Way," the Amway Corporation. It is surely not the income of average Amway distributors that fuels their ardor. For while a few distributors earn enormous sums, the rank and file typically operate at a net loss. Yet they have a dream of wealth which keeps them going.

Above all, Americans respect courage that disregards the odds, the "experts," and common sense. Terminal illness, it is believed, can be cured by vitamins, diet, attitude, or laughter. Anyone can become a millionaire by starting a business from scratch or buying a winning lottery ticket. And if faith breaks down and we fail, there is an alternate set of beliefs that gets us off the hook. The fault lies not in ourselves but in our stars, our biorhythms, our allergies, the system, politics, our diminished capacity, stress, or negative self-image. In no way is the individual accountable or responsible. For if we believe that we have been favored by God with the gifts of luck, chance, and good fortune, we must also believe that tragedy, failure, and misfortune are visited upon us by some equally mysterious, transcendental force.

I would estimate that two-thirds of all Americans believe in astrology—that the individual's destiny is strongly influenced if not wholly determined by the date and time of his birth. No belief is more open to empirical confirmation or rejection. Take any date within the last fifty years. Collect biographical data on any fifty persons born on

123

that date. Select a second date which falls under another sign of the Zodiac. Compare and contrast the two groups. There either are definite similarities between those born on the same date or there are not. There definitely are major general differences between the first and the second group or there are not. Why are such tests not routinely undertaken? Because no one wants the facts. The will to believe is too overwhelming. The need to preserve a transcendental justification, a cop-out that excuses our lack of control over that which we cannot or will not control is too powerful.

Likewise I would estimate that the majority of Americans believe in psychic powers—that certain "gifted" persons can predict the future or locate a missing person or discover the burial site of a murder victim. According to my observations, such magic works in one instance per thousand. Sheer coincidence is a surer guide than any psychic. But who wants to face this reality? The few dramatic successes of psychics receive abundant media coverage but the thousands upon thousands of failures are ignored. Every January the tabloids are filled with predictions for the new year made by America's most celebrated prognosticators. Their batting average is virtually nil. They not only predict events that do not occur but they fail to predict the most significant events that do. At the beginning of 1981, for instance, not one tabloid-accredited psychic foretold the assassination attempts on Pope John Paul II or Ronald Reagan. Considering the abysmal failure of these sages, why do such stories appear year after year?

We want to believe. In something. In someone. In anything. Millions of Americans are conversions waiting to happen.

Religion does not arise ex nihilo. It responds to very real deprivations, fears, frustrations, and desires. The forms in which religion expresses itself owe their substance to the forms available in the existing society as a whole. As revolutionary as new religious movements may appear, it is amazing how culturally influenced they are—even when their attitude toward culture is hostile.

The following chapters examine such mundane realities as sales techniques and interpersonal persuasion in order to disclose the attitudinal backdrop against which today's sect phenomena are projected. Ultrafundamentalism flourishes not only because it is "here," that is, a descendant of America's revivalistic religious heritage; it is also "now," that is, substantially dependent on forms that are *pervasive* and frequently *irresistible* in America at this time.

9

Amway:
Soap Company or Cult?

Several years ago, I was responsible for the administration of graduate-level comprehensive examinations for the Temple University Department of Religion. This job entailed two onerous burdens. First, it was necessary for me to urge reluctant, insecure students to declare their willingness to undergo the terrifying ordeal which would either move them out of academia or one step from the completion of their studies, to the status of A.B.D. ("all but dissertation"). Students had a way of prolonging the inevitable for years.

With our students, who averaged thirty-five to thirty-nine years old, I was the Knute Rockne of graduate examinations, bombarding them with salutes to their readiness, maturity, ability, and need to get out of the academic womb and become self-actualizing human beings.

Second, and much worse than the anxiety of the students, was the unresponsiveness of the faculty, which was obligated to arrange pretesting counseling sessions with each student about to be examined, delineating areas of expertise, required readings, and so forth, on which the student was to be examined. In addition, the contents of the examinations had to be submitted by a specific deadline so that they could be typed, proofread, photocopied and distributed on the occasion of the scheduled examinations. The faculty had a way of being too busy with other matters or too disorganized or simply too neglectful to keep their pretesting appointments, write their questions, or submit them to the examination administrator. Knute Rockne became a nagging mother—begging, cajoling, admonishing, guilt-tripping, lapel-tugging, seducing, and blackmailing colleagues into keeping their commitments.

I phoned each scheduled examinee every three or four days to see to it that none of them slipped off track. When I learned that their mentors were being uncooperative I went directly to their offices and "leaned on them."

Finally, one loose end remained. I will call her Joyce. She was a personable, bright, reasonably attractive twenty-nine-year-old who supported herself as a dorm resident while attending school. And somehow she had avoided comps on six different occasions over a three-year period. There were influenzas, tropical diseases (uncommon in Philadelphia), family problems (despite the fact that she was an orphan with no siblings), emotional traumas, misunderstandings with her professors, automobile accidents. When she found yet another way to avoid the exams that were scheduled in January, I arranged a special March sitting for her alone—no mean task. Three days before the exams, she phoned me in a tone of dark urgency, insisting that it was essential that we meet at the dormitory where she worked. She wore a beatific smile as she informed me that she would not be able to take the examinations because she was leaving graduate school to pursue a business opportunity of her own which, she confidently proclaimed, would not only enrich her but would provide jobs and substantial incomes for her friends in graduate school, and perhaps even, if he played his cards right, her underpaid graduate-school adviser.

My mood at that moment may be described as a ragout combining rage, frustration, disappointment, bemusement, curiosity, and interest. After I expressed the negative emotions at length, I inquired as to the nature and potential bottom line of her new enterprise. She uttered some vague generalities about saving the environment and the free-enterprise system and invited me to a meeting she was conducting in a few days during which this wonderful, idealistic, economic opportunity would be presented. She asked, in a manner that suggested that my life and the future of Western civilization depended on the answer, if I would be there, and if I would bring my wife and friends. Her evangelical zeal for an unknown cause somehow brought out the police interrogator in me, and my persistent questioning forced her to admit that she had become a distributor for a large national company whose products included laundry and dishwashing detergents, personal grooming items, and vitamins.

"You means that you have become a door-to-door salesperson? That's what your new business is, buying soap wholesale, marking it up, and selling it at a profit? And let's see. What is your company called? Amway?" I asked.

Her less-than-honest reply was: "Well, sort of—not exactly. You'd really understand it better if you and your wife would come to our meeting next week. A lot of your friends will be there. (She mentioned several names—graduate students, office staff, and junior faculty.) And there will be some new people who would love to meet you." By now dismay and disgust had become my dominant emotions, and I declined her invitation.

I never saw Joyce again. But other graduate students kept me posted as they effusively rhapsodized about gloriously effective, ecologically responsible, and grotesquely overpriced cleaning, washing, and toiletry products which they were selling at Joyce's inspiration so that they could supplement their meager incomes and lay the foundations for their own independent business enterprises as Amway distributors. Soon secretaries, janitors, students, and faculty wives were all enthusiastic entrepreneurs, merrily selling the products of Amway, Mary Kay, Shaklee, Avon, Jafra, and Tupperware.

It was at this time that I learned the skill which has enhanced my existence—the ability to say no. My personal acquaintances in those days reminded me of the legendary village in Ireland where none of the men worked and the women supported their families by taking in one another's laundry.

THE DREAM

Amway and its imitators are like a bad joke—never taken seriously but often repeated. Again and again, I have seen hard-nosed, rational, cautious, unemotional individuals of every station and background swept up by "the dream," the components of which are the expectation of vast wealth, positive thinking, constant reinforcement through programmed small-group activities and mass rallies, and a product that somehow benefits mankind in ways far beyond the powers of normal, lower-priced commercial items. "The dream" is whatever it is that generates hope, fervor, purpose, identity, and friendship while providing users with health, happiness, love, and peace of mind for less than $15.95.

"The dream" begins with greed, with the mind being thrown into shock by the presence of an individual whose wealth, represented in the crassest manner, defies belief. Our hero wears an expensively tailored suit, a heavy gold wristwatch, diamond-encrusted gold rings, several gold chains around his neck. His pockets are stuffed with wads of hundred-dollar bills. He stands before a huge country manorhouse with servants, a swimming pool, tennis courts, a fleet of expensive cars, a private jet plane. His beautiful wife awaits him, awash in jewels and furs, surrounded by famous and powerful friends. "How have I attained all this? What secret can I share with you? How can you enter the world of 'the dream'?" The answer is simple: "Do exactly as I tell you;

question nothing; never doubt; and allow nothing to come between you and 'the dream.'"

The product is irrelevant. It is keeping "the dream" alive and resisting everything that could possibly rob one of "the dream" that counts. For "the dream" is God's blessing, the divine will, the American Way, family, morality, and the free-enterprise system. Losing "the dream" is falling into Satan's hands, spurning Americanism, advocating communism and free love, and being "a loser." "The dream" is also the supporter of the status quo which, in turn, favors and rewards those who keep the faith. The President and his inner circle praise and promote "the dream," while discouraging and diverting criticism. Hence, "the dream" becomes a cardinal article of faith, a foundation stone of America's civil religion.

I have recently talked to a former Amway distributor. "Amway is a cult," he stated. He should know what a cult is, since he had been a member of the People's Temple and his mother and sister had died in Jonestown. "Amway is a unique cult," he added. "It is a distributors' association that is perceived by the public as being a good clean soap company—a God-fearing company that owns the Mutual Broadcasting Network, uses Bob Hope to do commercials, boasts Gerald Ford and Pat Boone as supporters and President Reagan and former Secretary of State Kissinger as speakers, But there's nothing there. It's just an illusion."[1]

Just an illusion? In 1981 the one million Amway distributors were responsible for retail sales in excess of 1.4 billion dollars! Amway is the second largest distributor of household products in the United States. Only Avon outsells the Amway's network of one million distributors. Surely someone is making money. For without the filthy-rich exemplars of the Amway gospel of greed, the entire structure would collapse.

AMWAY'S LEGAL PROBLEMS

On May 23, 1979, the Federal Trade Commission ordered Amway Corporation to stop fixing retail and wholesale prices and to cease misrepresenting the profitability of Amway distributorships. In the words of an official press release, the Commission found that Amway's claims as to the amount of money distributors are likely to earn had *the capacity to deceive* potential distributors. FTC pointed out that Amway's career manual implies that $200 is a typical monthly sales figure, when in fact the average Amway distributor sells much less.

The claims regarding a distributor's actual income are even further removed from reality, the FTC said.

On July 28, 1982, the Justice Department of the State of Wisconsin filed a lawsuit against the Amway Corporation, Inc., of Michigan and four of its Wisconsin direct distributors for violation of the state deceptive-practices act. The complaint charged the defendants with "misrepresenting individual or personal incomes, utilizing unrealistic hypothetical or projected incomes and failing to adequately disclose to prospective recruits the identity of the Amway Corporation and the nature of the opportunity being offered." At the time the suit was filed, Amway was distributing its extensive line of soaps, detergents, vitamins, and toiletries through approximately 20,000 Wisconsin distributors. An estimated 15,000 new distributors were being recruited annually. They were needed to replenish the ranks, since the turnover rate among Amway distributors is extremely high.

The four Wisconsin distributors were individually charged with misrepresenting their personal Amway incomes and those of other Amway distributors; misrepresenting that a new Amway distributorship has a reasonable chance of netting in excess of a thousand dollars a month on the basis of twenty-five to fifty hours of work; misrepresenting that annual incomes of up to $55,000 may be expected after three to five years. In order to test the defendants' assertions, the Wisconsin Justice Department Office of Consumer Protection conducted a study of the 1979-80 income-tax records of Wisconsin direct distributors. It was found that only 139 direct distributors, *less than one per cent* of all Wisconsin distributors, had an average annual adjusted gross income in excess of $12,000.

The annual adjusted gross income of each of Wisconsin's direct distributorships (each of which consists typically of a husband and a wife) was just over $14,000. However, when business expenses were deducted, the average for all Wisconsin direct distributorships was a *net loss* of $918! Even more damning to "the dream" was the finding that the average adjusted gross income for each of Wisconsin's 20,000 distributorships was $267 a year. The promise of an income of $12,000 a year was achieved by less than seven out of every one thousand Amway distributorships. The Office of Consumer Protection observed: "In order for even one-fifth (4,000) of the 20,000 Wisconsin Amway distributorships to reach the Amway Corporation's projected $1,230 monthly income, each of the 1,652, 261 households in the state would be required to make an annual purchase of $400 worth of Amway products."

Finally, the state attorney general charged that the Wisconsin defendants allegedly urged other Amway distributors to invite potential recruits to presentations and to disguise or not to disclose the nature of the presentation to be given, the nature of the opportunity to be offered, or, when requested, the identity of the Amway Corporation. One of the defendants was quoted as indicating during a 1980 presentation: "When you invite people, don't tell them too much. The idea of products can turn some people off. Don't be a SAP, and mention *S*ales, *A*mway and *P*roducts."

On November 10, 1983, Amway pleaded guilty to criminal charges of defrauding Canada of $23,000,000. It was alleged by Revenue Canada, the nation's tax agency, that Amway cheated on its invoices and distorted the true value of its products by 70 percent. As part of a proposed settlement, the company will pay a fine of $20 million.

PHIL KERNS' EXPERIENCE

Phil Kerns, the former People's Temple member, who is now an evangelical Christian, was recruited for Amway by an evangelist. Phil was tantalized with visions of riches. He was flown from Portland, Oregon, to Chicago, introduced by his evangelist friend to an Amway distributor said to be worth $80 million. From his pockets, the distributor took $50,000 in one-hundred-dollar bills. As Phil recalls, the evangelist declared: "Look, Phil, over $50,000 in cash! Do you want to touch it? Go ahead. It's real—really real! Do you get to carry spending money like that around back home. I'll bet your property-management business doesn't allow you that luxury, does it?" Finally, the rich man said, "Phil, what Mark is trying to tell you is that we would like to make you a millionaire!"

Phil was told to invite his friends and relatives to an opportunity meeting to be held the following Monday night at his home. With visions of golden sugar plums dancing in their heads, he and his wife made the arrangements. The imported speaker promised his audience that whatever they wanted in life, whatever their dreams might be, it would be well within their reach with this "opportunity." As Phil reports, the speaker "brought no products. He brought no literature. As a matter of fact, he brought nothing except his smartly dressed self, wearing boots with 18-carat gold tips and a pinstripe suit. All he did was talk and draw circles—lots and lots of circles."

The first circle represented the distributor himself. Several lines ran from the first circle like spokes on a wheel. To each line another circle was attached, representing additional distributors to be sponsored by the first distributor. Each of these circles became the center of its own constellation of satellites: more circles. And so forth. "With this business," the speaker insisted, "you can quit your job in 90 days. You can be financially independent in two years."

Phil received no sales manual, no stock of soap products. He was told to "sponsor, sponsor, sponsor." Meetings were held in his home five nights a week. If anyone showed interest, Phil arranged to have "opportunity" meetings in his or her home the following night. He continued for eight weeks before receiving his first kits, which included a variety of Amway products and some motivational materials. He was instructed to throw the manual in the trash and to give similar instructions to the distributors whom he had sponsored. He desperately ran from distributor to distributor, pumping up their enthusiasm. But they readily became discouraged and fell by the wayside. His daytime business suffered as Amway demands on his time increased. After three months in the new business, his monthly net was a princely $7.78!

He was encouraged to attend seminars and rallies, where rich and enthusiastic speakers worked their audiences into a fever pitch of zeal, and where the faithful could buy motivational books and tapes. He was to see to it that all his "downlines" distributors attended also. The message had nothing to do with the product and the product had nothing to do with the message. "Keep the dream alive," the speakers proclaimed. "Believe in yourself. Think success. Avoid negativity. The less you know, the better off you are. Do as you are told. Don't let anyone or anything kill your dream."

The more Kerns investigated, the more he realized that the real money was being made through the sale of rally and seminar tickets, books, tapes, and other merchandise sold at the public meetings. Kerns told me of a meeting with his born-again Christian friend, Tom Neill, the afternoon before Neill was scheduled to sing at an Amway rally for 12,000 distributors in Portland. Kerns told Neill that virtually no one in the corps of distributors was making money, that the promise of wealth was a sales gimmick to sell tickets, books, and tapes. He warned that public reaction to eventual revelations of the scam would tarnish Neill's reputation and Christian testimony. According to Kerns, Neill listened for two hours and admitted that while his income as an Amway distributor was only about eight hundred dollars a month, his take from the sale of non-Amway product items ran to six digits a year.[2]

The group hysteria of the mass rallies conducted by various sales distribution networks is well captured by Kerns in his account of an Amway rally:

> Do you people out there want to be free? (the leader asked.) The crowd now sprang to its feet and screamed back to him, "Yes! Yes!" Their arms were stretched outward and upward, hands open, in a pentecostal fashion. Many were swaying and waving their arms back and forth as they responded to the speaker . . . The applause . . . became rhythmic. They all stood and clapped in unison. Some stamped their feet while others beat on the tables! It just kept going on and on . . . It was an orgy of enthusiasm.
>
> Even after the crowd sat back down, their voiced responses continued. Each statement the speaker made generated more excitement in the crowd. The beating of the tables became more intense. Then those sitting at the table closest to me stood again. Hundreds of enthusiastic followers all across the room followed suit. Each was fully engrossed in the leader's words. As I looked out into the sea of faces, every eye appeared to be fixed upon the speaker with a glassy stare . . .
>
> Hundreds were now screaming at the top of their lungs . . . . Dozens of individuals stood on their chairs . . . . They were now whistling, stamping and beating on the tables faster than ever. The noise was deafening. Bodies were twisting, jumping, and dancing to the beat . . . .
>
> "What do you need if you're going to succeed? he (the speaker) roared into the microphone.
>
> The crowd responded instantly. They knew the answer, and without missing a beat they chanted loudly, "Books, tapes, rallies! Books, tapes, rallies! Books, tapes, rallies!"

According to Phil, Amway is a cult. Its converts are brainwashed robots with little interest in anything other than Amway. When questioned about their cult, they become defensive, retreating to mind-numbing cliches. Distributorship leaders govern the voting behavior of the people under them, ordering them to the polls to elect Amway-approved candidates. Hence, through its direct distributors, Amway has become "a big power-brokerage house." Politically, Kerns states, the distributors' voting block is "as conservative as the John Birch Society." Democrats are not welcome in the ranks. Support for President Reagan is a minimal requirement for acceptance among the elite.[3]

At least twice a year, I am contacted by network media personnel who are investigating the "Amway cult." They seriously contend that Amway is as deceptive, disruptive, totalistic, totalitarian, and manipulative as any cult. I am also contacted by resentful family members of distributors, convinced that Amway is a pseudoreligious con game, which is costly in terms of time and money, exploiting the many for the sake of the few. (According to the FTC report, in 1974 less than one-half of 1 percent of the distributors earned $10,000 or more. At the high end, I estimate that one distributor out of every 4,000 makes over $100,000 and one out of every 100,000 exceeds $200,000.)

Although the distributors' rallies encourage a mindless fanaticism and dependence, neither the parent corporation nor the Distributors Association qualifies as a cult. The vast majority of Amway's one million distributors have surrendered to their new business "opportunity" only a corner of their lives. The retention rate is low—about half drop out each year. There are many cheerleaders but few if any all-controlling charismatic leaders.

I think that it is possible and desirable to criticize the abuses within the Amway organization, particularly the exploitation of distributors through the sale of non-Amway product items such as rally tickets, books, and tapes. Manipulation is manipulation whether the term *cult* is applied or not. But in the case of Amway, crying "cult" only confuses the issue. The Amway Corporation would do itself and the public an enormous favor if it would remove snake oil from its product list. But it is difficult for the parent corporation to discipline its distributors when Amway has itself been guilty of misrepresentation.

The lesson that may be drawn from our report of activities in the world of Amway is as follows: Deceptive recruitment, coercive group pressure, authoritarianism, appeals to idealism, promises of earthly rewards, requirements of delayed gratification, exploitation of the gullible, maintaining focus upon "the dream" while ignoring reality, and shunning of nonconformists were not invented by cults, are not a cult monopoly, and flourish within religious sects only because there is so much room for them in the society at large.

NOTES

1. Telephone conversation with Phil Kerns, Sept. 14, 1983. Unless otherwise noted, all Kerns quotations are from his book, *Fake It Till You Make It* (Carlton, Ore.: Victory Press, 1982).

2. Telephone conversation, Sept. 14, 1983.

3. Ibid.

10

Recruitment and Transformation

In the Amway world, recruitment is necessary if "the dream" of fabulous wealth is to be realized. In the world of self-transformation seminars, recruitment is proof that the individual has attained the higher state of consciousness for which he underwent the "experience" in the first place. The purpose of several different workshops/seminars is the unlocking of the "positive," "self-actualizing," "creative," "ambiguity-resolving," "successful" aspects of the subject's personality. If the subject feels that through "the experience" he or she has made gains as an individual, it is not uncommon to sign up for collateral activities, such as intermediate and advanced courses, special topic seminars, social events, and so forth. If these activities benefit the individual further, it is likely that he or she will be enlisted as an active supporter of the ongoing work of the "educational" organization that sponsors the workshops. The subject may become a volunteer assistant, an aide, a facilitator, an unpaid staff member, or even a professional trainer.

As the recruit becomes more active, the educational workshop/ seminar organization mixes and confuses roles. On the one hand, the organization is *therapeutic;* it is a source of solace, insight, self-realization, actualization, the overcoming of inhibitions. On the other hand, the organization is *commercial;* it is a rapidly expanding sales pyramid, which depends upon the earnest recruitment of new customers by previous, satisfied customers. The subject experiences a new freedom to be himself. The sales or registrar staff of the organization interprets this freedom as an obligation to share what the subject has found (or is finding) with the significant others in his life. The registrar's logic is idealistic and self-serving at the same time: Now that you have found peace, joy, meaning, freedom, and enlightenment, you have no choice but to share it with those whom you love and respect. If you resist this suggestion, then you have missed the whole purpose of "the ex-

135

perience."

Soon the organizational recruit is spending all his spare time phoning his friends, relatives, business associates, former college classmates, old girl friends, his ex-wife, his insurance agent, his bunkmates from the summer camp which he attended when he was ten. (Several educational-seminar organizations run "boiler-room operations," rows of cubicles equipped with telephones and supervised by professional telephone solicitors.) Before long, the recruit's discretionary income is devoted to additional courses and workshops, books and tapes, and gifts of seminar/workshop tuition to his loved ones.

How can the subject be sure that he has been perfected, has accepted himself, has realized his potential, has become a winner, or has gotten the message? According to the sales/recruitment staff, the criterion is the refusal of the transformed individual to take no for an answer. Persistence and self-confidence are seen by the recruit and praised by the organization staff as manifestations of enlightenment. They reveal character and integrity where none existed before. The enthusiastic convert wants to talk (and talk and talk) about what has happened to him, but that does not mean that he has become a willing recruiter. Without constant pressure from the sales staff and his peers within the organization, the convert would soon tire of the awkwardness, embarrassment, and rejection, which are the lot of any salesman, and would cease his evangelistic efforts. Hence, the enlightenment business as a business requires the apparatus of motivational sales—pep talks, rallies, banquets, prizes, bonuses, and promises of possible employment by the corporation. After a while, the use of recruits to recruit new recruits becomes an end unto itself. Many a career in sales has been spawned by the volunteer phone bank at seminar-organization headquarters.

However, by manipulating and exploiting its recruits, the educational organization prostitutes its purposes for the sake of the income upon which it depends. The vast majority of the complaints that reach my office concerning est, Life Spring, Summit, isa, Scientology, and others may be traced to overly enthusiastic recruitment techniques—techniques which are often at variance with the stated policies of the organization. Unconverted loved ones resent the time devoted to seminar selling. Fellow recruits and sales staff often drive wedges between enlightened and unenlightened spouses. Marriages crumble and new love matches are made at the organizational center. College students drop out of school because they have "gotten more out of a weekend workshop than from three years at the university." Recent converts hastily recruited as recruiters suffer pangs of guilt when their statistics fall below organizational quotas. Since failure means that they are no better than they were before they invested hundreds or thousands of dollars of their money and countless hours of their time in the organization, many sink into apathy and depression. All too often, the professional recruitment staffs of seminar organizations exploit the disillusioned recruits, whose condition is adduced as evidence of what happens when negativity and lack of commitment spoil the fruits of enlightenment.

THE GREYHOUND BUS STATION

Recruitment depends on motivating individuals to disregard their inhibitions and to place the needs of the group above their own. The use of manipulative techniques by sales organizations and self-transformation groups to foster recruitment is relatively tame compared to the manner in which cults, sects, and pimps employ similar methods to replenish their ranks. The Greyhound Bus Station in San Francisco is a depressing, rundown, dirty, smelly facility located in the skid-row district. Since it is a major port of entry for young people of limited means who have come to California to "look for themselves," it is a gathering place for pimps, con artists, panhandlers, perverts, hustlers, drug dealers, and cult recruiters. For a number of years, I picked up and dropped off my two stepsons at the station every other weekend. On Fridays, I witnessed the Moonies as they approached confused strangers in their early twenties, offering them instant friendship, a meal, and a place to spend the night.

The Moonies look for guitars, cameras, backpacks, and T-shirts with geographic names. I have heard their pitch a hundred times or more: "Oh, hi there. You must be new in town. Do you have a place to stay? That's a nice T-shirt. Are you from Cincinnati? Two of the people who live with me are from Cincinnati. They would love to meet you. I live in this commune. We have lots of room and visitors are always welcome. That's a nice camera. What kind is it? Say, are you a photographer? One of our commune members is a famous commercial photographer. Maybe he can help you get some work. Do you play the guitar? We have these 'singalongs' every night—right after supper. Why don't you come and sing for us?"

The pimps are after younger talent—runaways of both sexes in their early to mid-teens. A short while ago, a fifteen-year-old girl was approached by a suavely dressed stranger. "Hi, there. Gee, you're pretty. Are you alone? What a shame. I'll bet you need a place to stay and a job. I hope you don't think I'm hitting on you but I really like you and I don't want you to get in trouble with the creeps who hang around here. My girlfriend lives near here with her sister. You can stay with them. They'll tell you that I'm cool. I just hate seeing a good-looking kid like you wandering around without a place to stay or any money. Look, let me lend you a few dollars so that you can fix yourself up—have your hair done and get some nice clothes so that you can get a really good job." Within days, the young woman was on the street, selling her body while her flashily dressed friend collected her earnings and supplied her with drugs.

I was returning from a case in Nebraska on the day before Thanksgiving 1980. As I deplaned, I was met by Ed Richards, an elderly vice cop from Detroit. A few days earlier, his son had joined the Creative Community Project, the Moonies recruitment "commune," and Ed had been referred to me for help. His son had been expelled by the group when they discovered he was gay. Before hearing of his son's excommunication from the group, Ed had learned of my anticipated arrival and had planned to intercept me before I got to my luggage so that he could seek my advice. Even though his son was no longer with the cult, he still wanted to talk to me. He had expertly debriefed his son and had learned a great deal about the Moonies' recruitment techniques. He informed me gravely, "I have been in vice for thirty years. And let me tell you, pimps and these Moonies are just the same. The only difference is that pimps sell sex and the Moonies sell bullshit but the bottom line is just the same: How many dollars can we get per ass?"

COERCIVE TECHNIQUES

Ed was the first to point out the similarities between the recruitment of prostitutes and cult members. (My friend, Bernard Walter, an assistant district attorney in San Francisco whose business is the prosecution of pimps, agrees with Ed's analysis.) Ed noted that pimps and cult recruiters look for easily approachable, lonely, naive young people who are wandering aimlessly. Their approach is to inundate the newcomer with attention, affection, and offers of help (money, a meal, a place to stay, clothes, a job).

This positive attention creates emotional dependence and gratitude. It makes it hard for the mark to say no when the pimp or recruiter later reveals his true intentions. The mark appreciates the kindness of his or her new friend and feels special, chosen, and loved. The mark suppresses the warning signals, reservations, and uneasiness which constantly reinvade his or her consciousness. As the price which the pimp/recruiter expects of the mark is gradually disclosed, the mark finds that he or she depends upon the new friend not only for food, lodging, apparel, but for emotional sustenance and self-image as well. The dependent mark has unwittingly allowed the boundaries of his or her ego to be penetrated by an ingratiating and controlling person.

Usually the manipulation by the pimp/recruiter of the mark's emotional dependence is sufficient to insure control of the mark. A person who feels loved for the first time in his or her life will do almost anything to please and placate the source of this love. The pimp uses sex and drugs as symbols of affection and as a means to deepen the dependence. The cult recruiter prefers the application of liberal doses of peer approval, praise, and tokens of status ("Now that you are really one of us, I think you can be trusted with a special responsibility." This may entail looking after new recruits, joining the fund-raising or recruitment teams, giving public testimony at indoctrination sessions, working as the leader's household servant, or some other task.)

At some point, positive reinforcement no longer suffices. The subject becomes indolent, careless, resentful, or critical. Sometimes praise and affection produce only the neurotic need for more praise and affection. The mark becomes confident of his standing with his new master and refuses to follow directions. He malingers, temporizes, and delays. Now the pimp/recruiter must resort to punishment—verbal abuse, humiliations, rejection, threats, beatings, or worse. The clever manipulator uses the mark's own internalized modes of adaptation, that is, the pimp/recruiter mobilizes the mark's fears, insecurities, guilt, and shame. The anxiety level of the mark can be raised by reminders of the mark's past failures, the pimp/recruiter's goodness, and the graphic depictions of the probable disasters that await the mark if he leaves his new-found friends. The message is simple: "Without me, you were a loser; you are a loser; and you will be a loser."

The lesson that the mark cannot survive or prosper on his own is readily accepted by the mark. If the self-fulfilling prophecies of personal disaster are not enough, group pressure is the next step. The other prostitutes or the cult members unite behind the leader and demand conformity. Since the group is the mark's source of comfort and security, as well as the effectual definer of the mark's reality, their unified voice is powerful. All organized groups are coercive. The price of membership in any group is the surrender of individual freedom, the suppression of selfish desire, the suspension of private judgment, and the willingness to "go with the flow."

When psychological pressure is ineffective, there are harsher remedies, uglier enforcers. Acts that no single individual in the group would countenance are routinely meted out by the group. It is a basic rule of crowds that in them individual conscience dies and base impulses spring to life. Pimps and fellow prostitutes do not hesitate to terrorize, torture, disfigure, or destroy their nonconformists. The fact that they are outlaws to begin with further removes their respect for societal standards of behavior. Cults attempt to give the appearance of being law-abiding, while their ethical standards are essential antinomian, that is, the group is a law onto itself; its leadership is accountable only to God. They convince themselves that there is no sin in deceiving, humiliating, threatening, beating, imprisoning, and otherwise overriding the individual's nonconformist tendencies—if such actions are undertaken for the salvation of the individual's soul or for the sake of the group. We should remember that cults are by definition totalistic and totalitarian communities, and that in such communities the ends justify the means even if the means are, in the eyes of the unbelieving majority, morally questionable, repulsive, and sinister.

Leaving a domineering and restrictive group is probably more difficult than separating oneself from a decaying love affair. For the patterns of dependence and interdependence are more complex. Leaving a totalistic group is akin to spurning one's own family. Disillusionment, disappointment, and boredom often rest in one side of the balance scales while in the other side are fear of the unknown, appreciation of the personal gains achieved while in the group, and guilt at the prospect of harming the erstwhile beloved community. The decision to leave or stay may teeter in the balance for months or years.

The fact that members sublimate their uniqueness and entertain attitudes or commit acts which are "out of character" from their pre-group identities is not evidence of any special technology of mind control or brainwashing. Individuals conform to group dictates and suppress their individuality as long as the group continues to serve their needs. When the pain inflicted by the group on a member to maintain conformity becomes greater than the discomfort of his pre-group existence, all but the most self-hating, dependent, and terrorized members will choose to defect.

11

Mr. Blandings Buys
a Swamp Lot

When I was a college teacher, I spent my summers reading and writing in a rented cottage or cabin while my family entertained themselves at the beach or in the woods. A favorite place was Mount Pocono, Pennsylvania, in the Pocono Mountains. Mount Pocono is an area frequented by skiers, hunters, honeymooners, and nature hikers, not too far from New York and Philadelphia. An ugly, modern resort that caters to newlyweds and features big-name entertainers is the chief bothersome evidence of commercialization, but somehow the vastness of the heavily forested and generally unpopulated region is able to hide most of the commercial development. At least, that's the way it was until developers arrived with A-frame houses, power-boat docks, swimming pools, and tennis courts.

I loved the area and seriously contemplated buying a home in a planned new development where I could spend vacations, sabbaticals, or to which I could someday retire. One Sunday, attracted by the builder's advertising blitz, I attended a sales presentation. The development at that time consisted of a parking lot, a single general-purpose building, and some trails scratched out by bulldozers. About twenty of us were the audience that afternoon. First, there were the ice-breaker activities led by an attractive young woman with the artificial warmth of an airline-stewardess trainee. She called upon each of us to introduce ourselves. Then we sang old songs, enjoyed a snack of finger sandwiches served with Hawaiian Punch, exchanged silly remarks and generally acted like a bunch of kids at summer camp.

At the center of the building was an enormous, three-dimensional model of the projected development, complete with tiny but detailed houses, roads, swimming pools, tennis courts, riding trails, a golf course with a club house, and all manner of amenities.

The sales staff unfurled a banner-sized development map which they draped over a bulletin board. They quickly affixed pins to show that many of the lots—particularly the choice locations had been sold. As they explained the sales literature, the prices for various house/lot combinations, and the builder's special which would enable us to save 20 percent if we made our selections today, an auction-like hysteria ensued. "I want lot 6," a man named Ted shouted, "and I'll write you a check right now." The model was impressive, the sales team seemed like nice, friendly people, the area was beautiful, and lots could be reserved for a deposit of only a hundred dollars (to be followed by monthly payments of $250 for ten years). So why not? And besides, I told myself, I had better hurry. Business was brisk. The location that interested me might be gone if I delayed an hour to think about it. (I knew that they made these presentations several times a day). And so my hour in an unfinished quonset hut, some old jokes and camp songs, and a bit of instant familiarity cost me one hundred dollars.

When my best friend, who lives and works in Mount Pocono, told me what he knew about the developer's reputation, I sent a certified letter asking for a return of my deposit. Nearly a year later, a check arrived. When I visited the location fifteen years later, the development still consisted of a few trails scratched out by bulldozers. A few houses had been built on scattered lots, but the promised amenities never materialized.

Look at the elements of the experience. In the course of an hour, a systematic effort was made to make me feel befriended, trusting, entertained, excited, fortunate—and desperate. I was being sold the sizzle and not the steak. I was deliberately induced to feel a succession of emotions (comfort, security, acceptance, wonder, fear of loss, and, finally, assurance) so that I would make the commitment which the sales team wanted me to make. I had allowed the *representation* of something quite tangible and desirable to pass for the real thing. And I had permitted myself to get caught up in the noise, the hoopla, and enthusiasm so that emotions rather than reasons became the basis for my commitment.

Who knows? I could have been lucky. My hundred-dollar commitment could have returned me a net gain of a hundred thousand dollars—if the development had materialized and had been successful. However, if that had been the outcome, my commitment largely would have still been an accident, a "good" decision made for the flimsiest of reasons. Win or lose, *I would have been the victim of my own capacity for self-delusion and my openness to persuasive manipulators.* There is a name for this condition. It is called life. Human beings make mistakes. Or they do nothing. And even doing nothing is a mistake. The most worthwhile ventures in human experience and the worst blunders have been equally inspired by faulty logic, impulsiveness, wishful thinking, and stubbornness. If the results are positive, we praise the risk-taker for his courage, foresight, and wisdom. If the results are disastrous, we shake our heads and wonder why such fools, loonies, and dupes are allowed out on the streets.

Cult and sect recruiters are basically salespersons. They operate according to the same rules of human persuasion. And once they have made their sale—that is, have won a convert—they indoctrinate them in much the same manner as a sales manager prepares a new staff member for a field assignment. The doctrine and ethics of the group, the relationship of the group to the outside world, techniques for fund raising and recruiting, and responses to criticisms of the group are reduced to thirty-second to five-minute capsules which are repeated until they are learned by rote. The bits and pieces add up to highly complex and sophisticated systems. Some recruits' presentations are amazingly comprehensive, internally consistent, and emotionally satisfying. Other converts might as well be speaking random sentences in a foreign language. They make no sense to the convert, and he cannot comfortably present them to anyone else.

A surprisingly large percentage of my subjects admit to me that their new world view is inconsistent and confusing and, further, that their fellow cult members are no more honest, caring, or principled than their precult associates. However, they remain with the group because they have convinced themselves they have no place else to go.

Recently, I talked to a young man who had been sitting in a phone booth at San Francisco International Airport, waiting for a flight to Las Vegas so that he could join a Unification Church MFT (mobile fund-raising team). His family did not want him around; he had neither a job nor a place to live. He had spent about a month with the San Francisco UC, and they had apparently expelled him because of his mental problems. A Japanese-led MFT had offered him a place. He had no conviction about the theological claims of the group and he found their diet nauseating. But no one else wanted him. He had spent four hours phoning everyone he could think of, asking them to dissuade him. He had asked each of them, "If you have something better for me to do, come and get me and give me a place to live, something to do with my life, and a decent wardrobe." There were no takers.

Buying what the sect recruiter is selling, repeating his easy answers as one's own—whether or not the buyer is persuaded—has its advantages. The rote repetition of "an answer for everything" provides a haven from critical thought, a refuge constructed of superficiality, ignorance, compulsiveness, and repression. Allowing oneself to be programmed is a way to escape anxiety, uncertainty, and the pain of endless self-examination.

The late Erving Goffman, America's most acute observer of "total institutions" (prisons, army training camps, mental hospitals, boarding schools, and monasteries) wrote:

> The practice of reserving something of oneself from the clutch of an institution is very visible in mental hospitals and prisons but can be found in more benign and less totalistic institutions, too. I want to argue that this recalcitrance is not an incidental mechanism of defense but rather an essential constituent of the self.

> The simplest sociological view of the individual and his self is that he is to himself what his place in an organization defines him to be. When pressed, a sociologist modifies this model by granting certain complications: the self may be not yet formed or may exhibit conflicting dedications. Perhaps we should further complicate the construct by elevating these qualifications to a central place, initially defining the individual, for sociological purposes, as a stance-taking entity, a something that takes up a position somewhere between identification with an organization and opposition to it, and is ready at the slightest pressure to regain its balance by shifting its involvement in either direction. It is thus *against something* that the self can emerge.[1]

Czeslaw Milosz has noted in *The Captive Mind,* a study of totalitarianism: "Internal revolt is sometimes essential to spiritual health, and can create a particular form of happiness. What can be said openly is often much less interesting than the emotional magic of defending one's private sanctuary."[2]

The problem I have with cult and sect members is not that they have been programmed. Programming is neither a unique phenomenon nor a detrimental one. We are all—cultist, anticultist, or noncultist—programmed to some extent. A great deal of one's success in life depends upon just how well one has been programmed and how marketable one's particular program is in the current labor market. What bothers me is how self-destructive, antisocial, and antirational cult/sect programming is. I take some hope from the observation that the more totalistic and totalitarian the programming is, the more likely it becomes that rebellion will ensue. I do what I can to nourish such rebels. But, in this task, I am only a facilitator. For within fanaticism itself are the seeds of its own destruction.

NOTES

1. Erving Goffman, *Asylums: Essays on the Social Situation of Mental Patients and Other Inmates* (New York: Doubleday, 1962), pp. 319-20.

2. Czeslaw Milosz, *The Captive Mind* (New York: Vintage Books, 1955), p. 76.

12

The Functions of Rumor

Americans love rumors. Without gossip and hearsay, there would be nothing to entertain them while they waited in supermarket checkout lines. In business, rumors are a much more stable medium of exchange than greenbacks. ("I will tell you a secret which reduces your anxiety or gives you power over a competitor, if you will do me a favor of equal value.") Rumors are the response to a situation in which the demand for news is greater than the supply[1] They supplement the usual sources of information, especially when unprecedented events (such as the assassinations of President Kennedy and Malcolm X) destroy our habitual assumptions and rob us of our confidence in authority. And finally, rumors are models, by reference to which we may understand the phenomena of sect conversion and deconversion.

Standing between a rumor and its adherents is more dangerous than roller-skating on the Santa Monica Freeway during rush hour. I remember one occasion when I attempted to disprove the myths claiming that "Paul is dead" and "there are demons in rock recordings." It was an impromptu debate with a pair of surfers in Santa Cruz, California, a community where almost anyone will believe almost anything and the burnt-out hippies of the sixties still wander about in tattered and faded psychedelic garb. I considered their evidence and dismissed it as hearsay, faulty logic, and foolishness. My hearers could not refute my refutation, but they felt no obligation to abandon their "sacred lore."

They repeated the ten-year-old litany of "proofs" for the nonexistence of Paul McCartney. For example, on the album cover of "Abbey Road" the Beatles are shown crossing a street. Paul is barefoot (in the manner of some corpses in England) and out of step with the others; John is dressed in white (as a "minister"); Ringo is in black (which suggests an undertaker); George is in denims and a workshirt (like a gravedigger). A Volkswagen *Beetle* in the background bears the license plate "28 IF," the age of *Beatle* Paul—if he had lived.

I could have spared myself frustration if I had remembered that

147

the opposite of a contrafactual hypothesis can never be proved. Consider the contrafactual hypothesis: "Jesus was a woman from Calcutta." How would one go about establishing that Jesus was not a woman from Calcutta? While I may have cast considerable doubt upon the evidence cited for Paul's demise, I could not prove that he was alive—that is, that the person known currently as Paul McCartney is the same person who was a member of the Beatles known by that name twenty years ago.

I approached the claim about satanic messages in rock and roll music empirically. When I went with the surfers to their apartment, one of them selected a Led Zeppelin recording of the song "Stairway to Heaven," placed it on a phonograph, and manually forced the disk to revolve counterclockwise. We heard garbled sounds suggestive of speech, which the surfers interpreted as "O Mary help us" and "Hear us, O Satan." I was told that these were subliminal messages intended to inspire worship of the Virgin Mary and the Devil. How something recorded backwards could influence my psyche was never elucidated.

I provided several other possible explanations for the "voices." For instance, turning a phonograph record in either direction by hand causes wow and flutter due to the inconsistent speed. Virtually any recorded sound distorted in this manner will begin to sound like some combination of words. The exact "message" is substantially in the mind of the listener. I did not hear the same words that the surfers heard. There is a limited number of phonemes, units of specific sound in a given spoken language. If any twenty-minute recording of spoken or sung speech were to be played backwards, it would not be surprising to find "words" or even short "sentences" amidst the general gibberish. Introduce the element of sudden shifts in pitch caused by the hand attempting to force the turntable to move against the direction of the motor's armature, and eerie noises suggestive of motion-picture sound-effect representations of demons assault the ear.[2] The controversy ended when the surfers resorted to a classic debating technique employed to establish the superiority of one's position: They began calling me names.

My least favorite variety of rumormonger is the conspiracy theorist. I interviewed a few when I co-produced and moderated the television series, "Counterpoint," for CBS several years ago. I remember catching JFK assassination theorist Jim Garrison, the former district attorney of New Orleans, in a number of contradictions. His *Playboy* magazine explanation of the shooting was at variance with his book, *A Heritage of Stone*. He admitted the contradictions but claimed that he had not said what *Playboy* had attributed to him. Now I have been misquoted and quoted out of context often enough to know that mis-representations do occur. But the accusation that *Playboy* had faked an entire interview with Garrison—that the conversation which they reported had never happened—was a bit much for me to swallow. Kennedy-assassination theorizing remains a thriving cottage industry twenty years after his death. Considering the general decline of trust in the government and other forms of authority, it is not surprising. After all, articles, books, and motion pictures about Lincoln's assassination still appear from time to time.

TYPES OF RUMORS

Rumors entertain, explain, justify, express basic emotions, and provide alternative sources of information. A rumor is a factually unverified story based upon conjecture, speculation, wishful thinking, or malice.[3] Rumors may be categorized as follows:

1. Pipe dreams—expressions of the wishes or hopes of the teller. For example, General Motors has a new automobile engine which gets a hundred miles to a gallon of gasoline; the Russians will soon withdraw from Afghanistan.

2. Bogies—reflections of fears and anxieties. For example, we will completely run out of sources of energy including petroleum, natural gas, coal, and uranium by the end of the century; John F. Kennedy and Marilyn Monroe were murdered by the CIA; the KGB is putting LSD in our drinking water.

3. Wedge-drivers—manifestations of hatred toward specific groups—ethnic, racial, professional, and others. Examples include the following: the Jews are responsible for the recession of the early eighties; a white child was castrated by blacks (or a black child was castrated by whites) in a public restroom in Detroit; the AMA and the federal government have suppressed cures for cancer and heart disease in order to keep physicians profitably employed treating these conditions.[4]

4. Iksyds (an acronym I coined, meaning "I know something you don't")—entertain or impress the hearer and thereby confer status upon the teller. Iksyds are also tokens which may be exchanged for other iksyds or other favors. One of the best-known iksyds is the "Paul McCartney is dead" tale, which flourished from about 1969 to 1975 and which is still heard today. Another is the "alligators in the sewers" myth: People have been bringing baby alligators home from Florida and flushing them down their toilets when they tire of the little crea-

tures; the animals have survived and grown to giant proportions in the sewers of several northern urban cities where they are a danger to sanitation workers.

The necessary conditions for the successful spread of rumors are ambiguity, interest, and arousal. First, there must be lack of consensus, a distrust of the usual sources of information (the media, the government, big business). Second, the rumor must, in some way or to some degree, personally make a difference to the hearer. Third, there must be present in the hearer an emotional arousal, a state of anxiety due to specific circumstances or habitual personality factors. The individual must be excited about an impending change or disappointed by recent events or confused by occurrences which refuse to conform to the usual categories by which experience is interpreted and absorbed. Or the hearer must be the sort of perpetually overwrought individual who is always searching for a scapegoat to blame for his sense of pervasive distress.

When the necessary preconditions are present, the rate of "information flow" is startling. The disoriented, personally concerned, anxious, and excited listener immediately becomes the teller who instinctively selects a new hearer who also possesses the preconditions. To cite a parallel concerning the transmission of factual news: When John F. Kennedy was assassinated, nearly 90 percent of the American population received the news within forty-five minutes of the first announcement, and more than half of this total received the news by word of mouth and not through the media.

Stanley Milgram demonstrated in an experiment dealing with the "small-world problem" that messages were easily transmitted from subjects in Wichita, Kansas, or Omaha, Nebraska, to target individuals in Massachusetts even though subjects and targets were unknown to one another. The subjects phoned individuals believed likely to be in contact with the target and this individual repeated the process. The targets were reached through a chain of contacts requiring an average of only five intermediaries. In some cases, only two intermediary links were required.

The response to the Kennedy killing demonstrates the incredible speed of word-of-mouth communication when it is vital and significant to teller and hearer. And Milgram's experiments reveal the invisible linkages along which messages travel more surely and swiftly than by first-class mail. Earth-shaking news, messages of potential personal import, and rumors avail themselves equally of these preestablished pathways. I suspect that the more intelligent a person is, the more he lends himself to rumor-transmission. Why? Because rumor-spreading is a process of seeking a perspective from which to understand an ambiguous situation. Educated persons are more likely to look for explanations than are the uneducated.[5] Likewise, more college-educated individuals find their way into the ultrafundamentalist sects with which I deal than do uneducated persons.

The social scientists, Ralph L. Rosnow and Gary Alan Fine, report that "most rumors are born, have a period of prominence, and then disappear." Rumors are eventually disproved, grow boring and irrelevant, or exhaust themselves through overexposure. Some rumors are self-fulfilling prophecies, bringing about the very state of affairs which they report. Rumors about shortages of consumer goods, the weakness of financial institutions, the rise or fall of the stock market, impending changes in fashion, the waning popularity of a movie star belong to this category. In these cases, rumors trigger actions that result in the rumor proving true. But not every rumor elicits responses. Rumors are often met with apathy or active resistance. George Katona, an economic psychologist, has observed:

> Mass behavior consisting of cumulative and self-justifying expectations may be viewed as a form of catastrophic behavior. The masses resist speculative fever or despondency unless their sanity is crushed by a series of repeated shocks. The basis of mass sanity may be found in the desire to understand the reasons for developments that take place. News and rumors which are not clearly understood may be accepted for a short while, but they will not sustain action by very many people over long periods.[6]

But what if sanity has already been crushed by inexplicable, unprecedented, and shocking events? What if the individual no longer feels at home in his accustomed world? What if he can no longer accept the justifications, cliches, and explanations offered by traditional sources of authority? When the foundations of his existence are shaken in this manner, his very notions of right and wrong, true and false, acceptable and unacceptable are placed on hold. And at such times, rumors and systems of rumors provide the only perch on which individual and group psyches can rest. For many Americans, now is such a time.

NOTES

1. Ralph H. Turner, "Collective Behavior," *Encyclopaedia Britannica*, Macropedia, vol. 4, p. 842.

2. In 1982, California Assemblyman Phil Wyman introduced legislation to require any records that contain messages discernible when played backwards to be labeled accordingly. He was particularly alarmed by reports that the Led Zeppelin's "Stairway to Heaven" pays homage to Satan. Wyman stated that the song contained the lyrics, "Here's to my sweet Satan." A similar bill passed the Arkansas House of Representatives 86 to 0 but was defeated in the state Senate.

In a UPI story dated May 3, 1982, Sandra Michioku attacked the song "Snowbound," which she claimed contains the message, "Oh, Satan, move in our voices." Allegedly the message can be heard if the record is played backwards.

The Chicago *Tribune* retained a recording studio to test a number of records by playing them backwards. Most of the transcription proved unintelligible. The engineers found no messages—until they were told exactly what to look for *(Tribune,* June 6, 1982).

3. This discussion of rumors is based upon *Rumor and Gossip: The Social Psychology of Hearsay* by psychologist Ralph L. Rosnow and sociologist Gary Alan Fine (New York: Elsevier Scientific Publishing Company, Inc., 1976).

4. The names of the three classes of rumors just discussed are derived from Robert H. Knapp's analysis of rumors gathered by the Massachusetts Committee on Public Safety during World War II, "A Psychology of Rumor," *Public Opinion Quarterly* 8 (1944), pp. 22-37.

5. Turner, "Collective Behavior," p. 842.

6. George Katona, "The Relationship Between Psychology and Economics," in *Psychology: A Study of a Science,* ed. S. Koch, vol. 3 (New York: McGraw Hill, 1959), p. 660.

Part Four

DEFUSING THE GOSPEL
TIME BOMB

13

Why Fanaticism Fades

Religious experience begins with intensity. It proceeds to symbolism—the need to articulate, explain, and express by attaching vague feeling states to concrete images, pictures, doctrines, rules, and patterns of living. At this point, the individual's commitment enters into tension with the life experiences previously recorded in the individual psyche, that is, the individual's history and interaction with this surrounding milieu. Out of constant interaction between religious feeling-states on the one hand, and dogmas, doctrines, moral maxims, religious rites, and rituals on the other hand, there arises a personal reinterpretation of reality that is both individual (based on a given person's experience) as well as social (in that it partially accepts, partially rejects, and partially recreates that which the group instills).

Starting with the emotionally powerful conversion experience, the individual frames all other experiences by reference to it, in a process that is both hierarchical and asymptotic. In other words, faith is both the unconditional commitment, and the interpretation or frame of reference for valuing all experiences. It is the total act that unites every element in a centered self. Its central element, that in which we believe, is not chosen. It overwhelms us and we see all other aspects of our lives in a new and valued perspective.[1]

Having been overwhelmed by the central element, it is then the vocation of a religious person to "compose" intellectually and existentially a world view that satisfies his rationality by its completeness (inclusion of all experience), consistency, and simplicity, and which remains, at the same time, intensely satisfying.

Even the most zealously defended world view—at least in principle—counts evidence that goes against it. Even though a world view is accepted unconditionally, it is nonetheless subject to possible revision and even falsification. To accept unconditionally means only the opposite of to accept conditionally, that is, as a hypothesis based upon probability. Experience, whether one wants it to be or not, is an ever-widening movement to which a structure of reality constantly reacts.

Not even a world view initially accepted without reservation is exempt from this process. Thus, faith grows, faith matures, sometimes faith dies—even within the most restrictive, authoritarian setting.

When a person commits himself or herself to a way of life, to a way of seeing the world, that person does so with ultimate seriousness. Of course, it is the case with an act of personal faith that the data which is subsequently gathered does not always fit the scheme comfortably. So one has to reinterpret the scheme as incomplete or abandon it altogether. A believer may constantly modify his beliefs and so gain higher levels of theological sophistication. However, if through constant modification his faith becomes an embarrassing patchwork of unresolved inconsistencies, then the human tendency to demand simplicity will require that the convert tailor a new garment.

To cite an illustration from the physical sciences: It was not long ago in the history of humankind that there were two incompatible views regarding the relationship of the earth and the sun. One view held that the earth was the center of the universe and that the sun and all the planets revolved around the earth. This, of course, was the Ptolemaic concept. And then came the Copernican theory, which held that the sun is the center of a planetary system and that the earth is merely a member of the system; therefore the earth revolves around the sun. There was in that stage of man's experience no way in which the issue could be resolved by observation. No one could stand outside the solar system and confirm if Ptolemy or Copernicus was right.

Now the Ptolemaic astronomers were very shrewd people; through their calculations they were able to explain every known phenomenon—to predict eclipses of the sun and the moon, to predict the positions of the planets, and so forth. But their calculations were complicated, because as astronomy developed, as people could actually peer out into the universe with telescopes, there were more and more phenomena to account for. And in order to fit them into the Ptolemaic system, the Ptolemaic astronomers had to claim as a corollary of their system that the sun and the planets revolved around the earth in a series of epicycles—cycles within cycles. On the basis of their revised theory, the Ptolemaic scientists were able to calculate and predict just as accurately as the Copernican scientists. Why then did the Copernican system triumph over the Ptolemaic? For only one reason: it was simpler. It is much easier to become a Copernican astronomer than a Ptolemaic astronomer. But it is possible to interpret the data from either point of view.

Though there is value in simplicity, there are limits as well. Because reality itself is rich and varied, a system of truth must mirror that variety and richness. In other words, a world view must attain a high degree of sophistication. It must be able to allow ambiguities, paradox, awe, and mystery. However, completeness, consistency, and simplicity are not enough. There must be something about a world view which we can feel in our innards. Even when the convert clings to his faith as inviolate and permanent, he cannot escape automatic processes that adjust personal reality to the way things are. No matter how tenaciously the cult or sect disparages the mind, there are rules at work to which a world view is subject. These rules can be phrased in the form of questions: Does our way of describing reality suppress, violate, invent, or deceive? Is it complete? Consistent? Simple? Does it satisfy?

Even without the deconversion attempts of deprogrammers and exit counselors, the fact remains that every convert is a potential counterconvert. The new believer finds that he is anchored by circumstances and responsibilities to a mundane world that stubbornly refuses to disappear. One day the rapture is gone. The easy answers answer nothing. The new cliches become old, hackneyed platitudes. In Eric Hoffer's words, "take away our holy duties and you leave our lives puny and meaningless."[2] Our existence has again become dreary, difficult, and joyless. The magnificent illusion is gone.

The contradictions, inconsistencies, and doubts present within every act of faith cannot be repressed without paying a high price—the suppression of critical inquiry, the loveless fanaticism that will tolerate any act of evil. When the inadequacy of one's faith comes crashing down upon the believer, he or she has several choices: (1) The believer may moderate his faith, that is, expect less of the object of devotion and more of himself. (2) The believer may counterconvert, that is, compensate for disappointed expecations by loving what he formerly shunned and hating what he previously adored, an attitude similar to "negative formation" (the lifestyle based on the assumption that whatever one's parents prohibited should be engaged in freely, and whatever they encouraged should be avoided). (3) The disappointed believer may find a worthier object of total devotion, compared to which the old cause was "merely an illusion"; such reconversion may become a pattern or "conversion career." (4) The believer may become cynical. (5) The believer may despair. (6) The believer may reconsider and return to his group. (7) The disgruntled believer may outgrow the group and discover a creative freedom to be his or her true self.

Why does an individual lose faith? Why is he or she no longer able to interpret the world through a previously meaningful frame of reference? As we have noted, no world view can be strictly proved or refuted. Nevertheless it is constantly subject to reality-testing. Commitment to a community of faith initially releases enormous energy, and the routinization of religious experience is characterized by a spate of passion and activity. Yet the fact remains that the active phase that follows religious conversion is creatively sterile.

Eric Hoffer has noted that the strength of the "true believer" derives from his "conviction that life and the universe conform to a simple formula—his formula. He is thus without the fruitful intervals of groping, when the mind is as it were in solution—ready for all manners of new reactions, new combinations and new beginnings."[3] Without such intervals of creative groping, the expressions of the life of faith are likely to be no more than repetitions of the forms already used within the community of faith. Only such intervals can enable the individual or the community to attain new levels of fulfillment. But these intervals are dangerous to the faith that prompted them in the first place, and there can be no guarantee that faith will survive them. If the community stifles creativity, it will lose its most valuable members. If it grants opportunities for introspection, it may lose them anyway.

The primary sources of dissatisfaction with a faith are delayed fulfillment, hypocrisy, and too much of a good thing. As we noted earlier, religion consists of both the manifestation and the betrayal of ideals that arise from the individual's encounter with the real. Since such ideals are impossible by definition, their actualization may never be more than approximated. Religion is based on the awareness of a gap between what *is* and what *ought to be*. Moreover, it is a program for overcoming the gap—gradually, progressively, and asymptotically. The impossible version is always the elusive dream. Otherwise it would not be worthy of man's unconditional devotion. But not everyone is cut out for the endless quest. And many sects and cults make the mistake of promising utopia tomorrow or next week or after the next million dollars is raised. When the kingdom reaches into the distant future, many are discouraged and leave.

However, the real tragedy of many religions is not the failure to realize hopeless goals, but the perversion of these goals. The quest for the divine will becomes the quest for power and prestige. The religious group becomes an end in itself instead of a means to the end of human perfection and service to others. This usurpation of the place of God by the particular religious form is the greatest source of unsettling ferment within religious communities. The dissatisfaction with the world and oneself which led the convert to the community of the faithful cannot endure hypocrisy. Its existence can only be denied for so long. Finally inconsistencies between what the group espouses and what it really does will deprive the recruit of his motivation to sacrifice himself for the sake of the group.

Dissatisfaction with the group's progress in attaining its goals and an unwillingness to countenance hypocrisy are not the only ambiguities that undermine the convert's faith. Much more fundamental are the obstacles arising from the "too much of a good thing" syndrome. Every valuable function performed by religion gives birth to a parallel dysfunction. Religion enables individuals to face powerlessness, frustration, and deprivation. Sociologist Thomas F. O'Dea describes six functions by which religion gives security and assurance to human beings to sustain their morale:

> 1. Religion, by its invocation of a beyond which is concerned with human destiny and welfare and to which men may respond and relate themselves, provides *support, consolation,* and *reconciliation.*
> 2. Religion offers a *transcendental relationship* through cult and ceremonies of worship, and thereby provides the emotional ground for a new *security* and firmer *identity* amid the uncertainties and impossibilities of the human condition and the flux and change of history.
> 3. Religion *sacralizes the norms and values* of established society, maintaining the dominance of group goals over individual impulses. It thereby reinforces the legitimation of the division of functions, facilities, and rewards characteristic of a given society . . . thereby aiding order and stability; and . . . the reconciliation of the disaffected.
> 4. Religion . . . may also provide standards of value in terms of which institutionalized norms may be critically examined and found seriously wanting.
> 5. Religion performs important *identity* functions. . . . individuals, by their acceptance of the values involved in religion and the beliefs about human nature and destiny associated with them, develop important aspects of their own self-understanding and self-definition.
> 6. Religion is related to the growth and maturation of the individual and his passage through the various stages distinguished by his society.[4]

But, as O'Dea notes, these functions give rise to corresponding dysfunctions. By providing emotional support and consolation, religion may provide an island of security in an essentially insecure world. Such consolation may encourage a neglect of worldly obligations and an insensitivity to the responsibilities of everyday existence. It may provide a sense of identity based upon authoritarian principles, which produces a rigid and intolerant personality. Religion may sanction the status quo, thereby discouraging needed social changes, or it may so overstate its criticism of a present society that it produces nothing but despair. Religion may institutionalize and routinize immaturity by providing the individual with *answers* when he needs to grapple with fundamental *issues* for himself. The strong sense of identity it produces may be totally inappropriate to the individual's life situation.

The functions and the dysfunctions of religion stand in constant dialectical tension. Only the most insensitive fanatic is immune to this stress. For the most part, religious sects either adjust to the world in which they find themselves or they disappear. Likewise, the individual consciousness constantly modifies its stances, commitments, values, attitudes and feelings, or it wastes away. Atrophy is not unknown but it is rare. During the period of their inception sects see themselves as the sole source of truth and goodness. They set themselves apart from the world, which they regard as beyond redemption. But if the group survives its first generation, it comes to terms with the world and takes its place among the established sects and denominations. It has a stake in being accepted and respected.

Likewise, only the most alienated, spiteful, and masochistic individuals can maintain a stance of unreasoning zeal. Sect members grow and mature through and despite the best efforts of their family members and friends to deconvert them; through and despite the best efforts of their fellow cultists to protect them from reality; and despite the cultist's own resolve to sacrifice the qualities that make him human. The processes we have described are automatic. They work whether we will them to work or will them not to.

NOTES

1. Paul Tillich, *The Dynamics of Faith* (New York: Harper Torchbooks, 1958), p. 8.

2. Eric Hoffer, *The True Believer* (New York: Perennial Library, 1951), p. 23.

3. Ibid., p. 140.

4. Condensed from Thomas F. O'Dea, *The Sociology of Religion* (Englewood Cliffs, N.J.: Prentice-Hall, 1966), pp. 14-15.

14

Systems of Rumor

In many ways, ultrafundamentalist sects are unified systems of rumor. They advance alternative explanations of the way things are and ought to be, but these explanations have not been confirmed and probably cannot be. Whether they are true or false assertions subject to empirical proof (or disproof) or poetry that cannot be verified or falsified, they give the appearance of being explanations which, at least potentially, satisfy the individual's need for rationality. In addition, they are programs for action that invite commitment and promise release of pent-up emotional energy. Once such belief systems are planted in the soil of a disoriented, concerned, anxious, and excited psyche, they are governed by the same dynamics as the successfully disseminated rumor. Further, the activities through which the new belief system is routinized are like fads. The rituals through which the belief is acted out are intense and frequent. Since the behavior of the faddist appears ridiculous, irrational, or evil to those not caught up in it, social disapprobation follows. Such disapproval often has the effect of pushing the faddist deeper into his obsession.

Like rumors, the hold of sects on the lives of their adherents is notoriously difficult to uproot. Just as the power of rumors arises from the need of the rumormonger to resolve ambiguity and attain status, so the power of sects arises from the needs of their members and what they project upon the group and its leadership as satisfaction of these needs. Belonging to a sect confers status, identity, belonging, control over "evil" forces, direction, security, and meaning. Sects appeal to basic human needs: the individual's desire to be loved, accepted, and respected by others as well as the need to feel that his or her life has significance and importance in the greater scheme of things. Once the individual joins any group that offers acceptance and self-respect, that person is powerfully influenced by his or her own tendencies to submit to authority and conform to the expectations of peers.

Sects provide the anxious individual with unambiguous father figures, who give love in return for obedience. In addition, they give the convert the support and approval of an instant family of brothers and sisters. In groups based on a shared subjective experience, the recruit feels a suspension of normal inhibitions. He is like a spectator caught up in a surging crowd. The new situation creates its own rules, fills the participant with a sense of power and immunity, and moves him forward as though preordained. While a mob may vent its frustrations on the system by looting or burning buildings, the sect turns inward, gloating at the intense shared experience as though ecstasy were an accomplishment.

Group leaders maintain their power by appealing to the primal terror of their followers, the fear of losing the love of a parent. All too often they resemble abusive parents, the kind who manipulate their children for their own ends, damage their offsprings' self-esteem, program them for failure, and then blame the victims for the shame and guilt this emotional treatment induces. The follower projects power, significance, insight, and spirituality on the leader because he wants the leader to have these traits. Reliance on a godlike figure relieves the disciple of responsibility, anxiety, and confusion. Also, enhancing the image of the leader by protecting his own desires and fantasies, the follower enhances his own frail image. How much better is it to be chosen by "Jesus Christ returned" or by "God's only end-time apostle" than by a Christlike teacher or a spiritual brother who is, after all, only a mere mortal like the follower.

The true mind-bending power of ultrafundamentalist sects derives not so much from the disciple's submission to authority as from the dynamics of conformity. Philip Zimbardo, a major investigator of social control, has noted:

> . . . under specified conditions, less social pressure can produce more attitude change. The most profound and enduring changes in attitudes occur under two conditions: when people perceive they have free choice in deciding to behave in ways that are against their values, beliefs, or motives, and when the force applied is just strong enough to accomplish the task. The pressure may be as innocuous as having the experimenter in an authoritative white coat say, "this is an important experiment . . ." or touch the person's shoulder and say confidingly, "Do me a favor." People want to be good sports and team players.[1]

Moreover, Zimbardo reports, "when people can be subtly induced or seduced into publicly behaving in ways that are contrary to their needs or usual standards, it produces an uncomfortable state of cognitive dissonance." This inner discomfort must somehow be resolved.

It is well known that when attitudes and behavior are inconsistent, there is a tendency to change attitudes to conform with acts rather than acts to conform with attitudes. The individual resolves the inner tension by rationalizing his behavior as his own free will. In two classic psychological experiments, individuals invented dozens of personal reasons for apparently irrational acts: (1) giving in to group pressure and claiming that lines of nonidentical length were identical; (2) administering potentially dangerous electric shocks to other subjects because the laboratory instructor told them to and their peers went along. Once induced to act contrary to former inhibitions, the individual justifies his subsequent behavior as though his motivations were in no way influenced by the group.

Moreover, as psychologist Lee Ross and others have demonstrated in their "perseverance" experiments, individuals tend to maintain their convictions about ambiguous situations despite disconfirmation of the empirical basis of their beliefs, rational argumentation against their convictions, or the presentation of new evidence.[2]

If, for example, a "psychic" is introduced to a college class and performs various feats of "mind reading" through his alleged powers, a certain percentage of students will believe that he is what he claims to be. If he returns to the class the following day and reveals that he is a fake and that his "mental magic" was achieved through standard stage-magician's tricks, a substantial percentage of the students will refuse to believe his disavowals of psychic ability. Apparently, when we are duped, we prefer to remain duped by redefining our sense of reality so that we do not have to abandon the "truths" we feel are now part of our own being. Thus we are able to maintain our self-respect—even if the cost is the denial of the truth. In sum, once they are formed, beliefs tend to persevere.

Am I arguing that fanatic convictions are indestructible? Not at all. Like rumors, they definitely may be counteracted. For example, Percy H. Tannenbaum has noted how attitudes are changed as the result of cognitive incongruity.[3] Consider a hypothetical example in which one respected authority makes a negative statement about another accepted authority. Imagine that the U.S. Public Health Service were to issue a statement that regular brushing of the teeth destroys beneficial enzymes and is harmful to the health of the whole body. The conflict between these two accepted authorities, the U.S. government and the dental profession, could cause a shift in the American public's attitude, which in turn could produce a change in behavior (a rejection of dental hygiene).

Such being the case, Tannenbaum asks, how can this negative shift in attitude be eliminated or reduced? In extensive experimentation he found that there are four effective procedures, which appear to have a cumulative ameliorative effect when used in combination: (1) denial of the assertion; (2) derogation of the source; (3) logical refutation of the assertion; and (4) strengthening the original concept through counter-argumentation.

These same four steps are the basis of conversion, deprogramming, and much antisect propaganda. The standard technique for recruiting consists of (1) attracting the individual's attention by focusing upon his disorientation, concern, anxiety, or excitement; (2) gaining his confidence through shows of affection and approval; (3) setting up his accustomed beliefs in straw-man fashion by belaboring the negative aspects of his present life and the shortcomings of the society in which he lives; pinpointing parents, college, friends, the media, or whatever as the source of this distress; (4) presenting a new system as an escape from the psychic pain of the old; (5) representing the founder/prophet of the group as a trustworthy and enviable guide in contrast to a prior authority; (6) enjoining attitudinal and behavioral compliance with the new system; and (7) rewarding the desired response with peer approval and affection.

There is no special magic, hypnosis, or "technology of mind control" at work here. Rumors are spread and discredited in the same way.

ROLE OF THE DEPROGRAMMER

The deprogrammer creates a situation to which the subject cannot but respond with attention, anxiety and confusion. Life in an ultrafundamentalist sect is an endless process of intellectual accommodation, interpersonal relating, personal striving, assimiliation of novel experiences, reevaluation and reintepretation of ideology, and spiritual transformation. The deprogrammer reduces the complex socio-theological-psychological life of the sect to a list of assertions and then proceeds to deny these assertions and to ridicule their source. He refutes them through arguments, evidence, and the testimony of previous defectors, and he strengthens the original world view (values, attitudes, associations, affective ties, family relationships, friendships, career orientation) which the convert spurned when he joined the sect.

Since deprogrammers are usually more successful at tearing down new commitments than at shoring up previous attitudes and patterns of behavior, their deconverted subjects are frequently left in a state of ambivalence, depression, and undirected anger. Such "floating" is blamed upon the "damage to the central nervous system," allegedly wrought by cult brainwashing. If we discredit a rumor being spread by a highly anxious individual—one who considers the rumor a valuable possession, an expression of his being and worth—similar affective states will be manifested.

What the agent of deconversion is witnessing in the former sect recruit are *mourning* phenomena. Whenever an individual is suddenly separated from someone or something that defines his personhood, he suffers "floating" symptoms. According to Elisabeth Kübler-Ross, an individual who learns that he has a terminal illness passes through a succession of emotional states: denial, isolation, anger, bargaining, depression, and, finally, acceptance. All profound shocks to our sense of identity and security elicit similar responses.

When a marriage ends, the psychological aftermath incorporates a huge range of feelings: rage, sadness, depression, a deep sense of guilt and personal failure, shame, regret, fear and distrust of the former beloved, nostalgia, self-justification, and, ultimately, acceptance. With acceptance, the individual is able to cope once again. Why should separation from the friends, accustomed routines, beliefs, mores, pains, and pleasures of an all-consuming lifestyle be less any traumatic?

The sect recruiter and deprogrammer both reduce reality to the level of rumor and gossip so that they may destroy the subject's presuppositions and implant their own. When examined dispassionately, we discover that the assertions, denials, arguments, and evidence of both are cognitively unimpressive—almost trivial. For instance, the high divorce rate does not prove that most people are unhappy and that they should become members of shepherding groups and allow their leaders to select ideal mates for them. A high divorce rate may equally be cited as evidence that many people were once unhappy, did something about it, and are now much happier. Further, even if divorce is caused by unhappiness, there is no empirical evidence that sect-arranged matches are any more fulfilling or that they are longer lasting.

The logic of the sect recruiter and the deprogrammer is based upon the "fallacy of the missing middle." In terms of conventional philosophical logic, to jump from the assertion "Socrates is a man" to the conclusion "Socrates is mortal," requires the connecting premise "All men are mortal." The logic employed by recruiters and deconverters is based on certain assumptions: the potential convert is not loved by his parents; the potential deprogramee cannot find happiness unless he returns to his career goals; the sect leader is superior to ordinary human beings; the sect has failed to achieve its goal.

By presenting such premises the recruiter/deprogrammer acts as though he has destroyed the entire system of thought, belief, attitudes, and behavior from which the premises have been plucked. However, from a logical point of view, it should be recognized that the acceptance of any premise does not require the abandonment of an entire lifestyle nor does it necessitate the acceptance of an alternative. And, logic aside, the discarding of personal commitment, attitudes, and patterns of behavior is a painful process psychologically, irrespective of whether it leads to new commitments or to freedom from repressive authoritarianism.

Gossip and rumor are highly susceptible to countergossip or counterrumor. Gossip and rumor lose much of their power when they are denied, when the motives of the gossipy individual are uncovered, when arguments or sophistries are presented against the gossip, and when the trustworthiness of the target of the unsupported gossip is reasserted. However, it is imperative that the counterattack on lies or speculations should never repeat the rumors the counterattack seeks to lay to rest. Strange as it may seem, arguing against a rumor is one of the most effective ways of spreading it.

Much sect recruiting and much deprogramming repeat the mistake of spreading a rumor by its denial. The sect indoctrinator urges that the convert break off all contact with the "evil" world outside the sect—family, friends, associates, and media. So, of course, many sect members sneak into public libraries, bootleg letters to friends, and contact "negative" persons or "persecutors" of the group like me. Likewise, the deprogrammers' insistence that the defector end all ties with friends in the group and zealously avoid thinking about sect life, ritual, prayer, and chanting contributes to a great deal of nostalgia for the group and to an obsessive ongoing identification with the group. The human mind is perverse in dealing with negative commands. When suggestions are constantly underscored with emphatic prohibitions, the mind sometimes does exactly what it is told not to do.

Many former sect members adopt roles as anticultists with a zeal just as fanatic as their former role within the group. In a sense, all the attention that has been focused on their former group by the agents of deconversion has left the ex-cultist obsessed with that group. They need a new rumor—a new story about themselves meaningfully related to the world in which they find themselves. In sum, they need a sense of direction, identity, and hope for the future. They do not need substitute dependencies. They need freedom.

ALTERNATIVES TO DEPROGRAMMING

Are there better ways than fighting fanatic belief with anticult propaganda, rhetoric, hysteria, and coercion? Freedom Counseling Center was founded to provide sane and effective alternatives. Our approach may be summarized in three words: *patience, process,* and *farewell.* When we are contacted by concerned relatives, we counsel patience. We urge them to be supportive of the individual who has joined the sect and scrupulouly neutral toward the group. Hostility, anger, guilt-tripping—the conditioned reflexes of parents engaged in familial strife—simply do not work and they are counterproductive. It is better to seek to understand the family and the personal problems—the human needs—that made the subject susceptible to the lure of the sect in the first place. It is wiser to restore communication by evidencing interest and eschewing doctrinal debate. And it is efficacious to wait.

In the lives of most sect converts, fanaticism is a short-lived phenomenon. We earlier compared rumors and sects with fads. As we observed, the faddist's behavior is excessive and obsessive. Before long, it elicits resistance and opposition from outsiders. The critics of the fad question the sanity of the faddist, the motives of those who promote the fad, and the social significance of the activity. Conservatives issue warnings that the fad is distracting people from more productive effort. Liberals declare that it is distracting the faddist from a need to change society in basic ways.

And all the while the debate is raging, the fad is fading into obscurity by itself. Heedless of the invective of the fad critics and the ridicule of the media, the faddist discovers for himself that the creative possibilities for self- and group-expression are finally exhausted. The fad has come to an end. Often the frenzy peaks suddenly, drops off markedly, and is followed by a counterobsession. Promiscuity gives way to stern moralism. Miniskirts are replaced by maxiskirts. And a sect can lose its hold on its followers just as unexpectedly. Unless the ultrafundamentalist group changes its style from ecstatic-charismatic to democratic-bureaucratic or the leader is particularly adept at introducing innovations or finding new audiences for his idiosyncratic message, the sect loses all but its hardcore zealots in short order.

Where do the disciples go? A few turn their backs on all religious zealotry. Others seek new apostles, stricter discipline, or more ecstatic states. Some wander the no man's land between mainstream mores and fringe religiosity for years. For them, conversion becomes a career. But most simply lose the sense of urgency and ardor that characterized their sect involvement. They accept responsibility for their own lives and move on. They have grown up.

The real nemesis of fanaticism is personal development. People change. They find that the faith that suited them when they were anxious postadolescents who could not handle their freedom no longer serves them when they become adults with adult opportunities and demands to face. And they rebel against authority and conformity. Most converts come face to face with a major crisis in the first six months of their involvement. Suddenly they realize that they resent being treated like children (although at the same time, they love the comfort, security, and approval of being treated like children). In that moment, about half of all sect converts lose their sense of belonging. They begin asking questions, shirking duties, criticizing hypocrisy and compromised ideals. Their "brothers and sisters" in the sect overreact to displays of the convert's reindividuation by declaring them rebellious, negative, selfish, undedicated, demon-influenced. They may be threatened with divine wrath or corporal punishment. The wayward member becomes resentful. The gulf widens. The rebel is told that God will punish him, that he will lose his salvation or special standing in God's elite, that he will go crazy or die a terrible death. Fear works. The rebel submits and tries to repress his doubts and to redouble his efforts. But it is never the same again. Punishment and threats simply cannot produce what approval and acceptance once obtained. For most converts, the end is at hand.

In the past five years, I have spoken to numerous sect members in every stage of involvement. I have discovered to my surprise that most of them left their fanatic groups after our conversations. When I asked myself what I was doing that was contributing to these defections, I noted that it would be easy to take me for a sort of "delicate deprogrammer." For I often resort to files full of media-reported atrocity stories, tape recordings of the testimonies of former members, rational and biblical arguments against sect doctrines, and consultants who had belonged to the same groups.

But unlike deprogrammers, I never tell converts that they are helpless victims of powerful techniques of mind control. Instead I help them to understand why they gave the group power over their lives, why they wanted the group to have this power, and how the processes of submission to authority and conformity work. I help my clients accept responsibility for their own lives—for the past that led them to the sect, for the months of fanatic excess, and for the future that lies ahead. I enlist my clients in no anticult crusade and offer them no new dependency. On this basis, I share with them whatever information I have concerning their groups—weighing the data as carefully and as critically as if it were evidence in a jury trial. Once I have helped them through the reevaluation of their experiences and the creation of their own image of a hopeful future, I say goodbye.

Many of my clients agree to see me, secretly hoping that I will give them "permission" to do what they really want to do—leave the group behind them. Others want a forum where they can try to outsmart and outargue a professional critic and whom they view as an agent of their parents' attempt to regain authority over them. Some are starved for attention, as much as they were before they were recruited. Others are confused, scattered, and uneasy. They are exactly where they were before they joined the group. They are looking for a new rumor, for a better explanation of the facts, for a way of finding themselves related to the world in a significant manner.

At Freedom Counseling Center, I always ask parents to consider seriously whether they should intervene at all on behalf of their adult offspring who have become involved in a cult or sect. I warn them that if a single demon is exorcised (metaphorically speaking) from their son or daughter, perhaps seven others, each more destructive, are lying in wait. For as long as people are lonely, as long as the difference between good and evil is a blur in our minds, as long as we feel unloved and incapable of loving, as long as our quest for personal significance is frustrated, the inner ear will strain to hear rumors, new gospels, whispers of hope. In times like these, rumors abound.

NOTES

1. Philip Zimbardo, "Mind Control in 1984," *Psychology Today,* Jan. 1984, p. 69. See also Leon Festinger, *A Theory of Cognitive Dissonance* (Stanford, Calif.: Stanford University Press, 1957); Stanley Milgram, *Obedience to Authority: An Experimental View* (New York: Harper, 1974); and Streiker, *Mind-bending: Brainwashing, Cults, and Deprogramming in the 80s* (New York: Doubleday, 1984).

2. See Lee Ross and Mark R. Lepper, "The Perseverance of Beliefs: Empirical and Normative Considerations," in *New Directions for Methodology of Behavioral Science: Fallible Judgment in Behavioral Research,* ed. R. A. Shweder and D. Fiske. (San Francisco: Jossey-Bass, 1980).

3. Percy H. Tannenbaum, "The Congruity Principle Revisited: Studies in the Reduction, Induction, and Generalization of Persuasion," in *Advances in Experimental Social Psychology,* ed. L. Berkowitz, vol. 3 (New York: Academic Press, 1967).

15

Decade of Shocks

We have been warned that those who ignore the lessons of history are doomed to repeat them. But what if the lessons are obscure or unfathomable? What if history teaches no lessons but only leaves us bewildered as it destroys our most cherished assumptions?

In a recent book, *Decade of Shocks: Dallas to Watergate, 1963-1974,* a popular historian and television writer, Tom Shachtman, re-immerses us in the ten years that cost us our national innocence, the period that began with the assassination of John F. Kennedy and ended with the resignation of Richard M. Nixon. Before the "decade of shocks," our lives were governed by basic assumptions pertaining to ourselves, our economy, our national leadership, and our place in the world. These assumptions, as Shachtman lists them, were:

1. a belief in the safety, sanctity, and legitimacy of our leaders;
2. a belief that minorities would stay in their "place";
3. a belief in the basic health and superiority of the American economy;
4. a belief that we are, and would continue to be, militarily superior to the rest of the world;
5. a belief that small nations could not by themselves affect their own future or alter the world's strategic balance;
6. a belief that our environment and natural resources are virtually limitless;
7. a belief that the problems of the day would be solved through the application of technology;
8. a belief that youth would take its place, as previous generations had, and without undue upset, on the accepted ladders to success;
9. a belief that the supremacy of the nuclear family in our society would not appreciably alter;
10. a belief that our society is the best possible configuration to help us realize our potential, and that we are a model for the rest of the world.[1]

Shock after shock has loosened the hold of these assumptions

171

upon our lives, our attitudes, and our patterns of behavior. The kill-ings of President Kennedy, Robert Kennedy, Martin Luther King, Mal-colm X, and the attempted killing of George Wallace during the dec-ade of shocks, as well as attempts on the lives of Gerald Ford, Ronald Reagan, and Pope John Paul II, have destroyed the assumption that any leader is safe. And with the loss of confidence in their safety has gone the loss of confidence in our own. Urban riots, the loss of black patience and white resourcefulness, the repudiation by middle America of the Great Society and War on Poverty programs have left in their wake increased racial tension and ever greater black-white polariza-tion. Judicial gains have been made, but the will to deal with America's shameful heritage of racism seems to have faded.

Our industrial-technological hegemony has been severely endangered by foreign competition and the American worker's declining dedication to quality workmanship and productivity. We helped rebuild the in-dustries of our former enemies as part of a grand design to build impregnable defenses against the threat of communist expansion, but we failed to develop our own industrial base during the same period. The growth of ecological consciousness has led us to question whether we have the boundless resources we counted on and whether free enter-prise and big business realized just how fragile the ecosphere is.

Suddenly everything is carcinogenic—cigarettes, diet soft drinks, food additives, asbestos, and a whole string of products. As though the specters of polluted air, poisoned food, diseased bodies were not enough, we were rudely awakened to our loss of energy independence when OPEC raised the ante. Our fate, it seemed, was neither in our stars nor in ourselves but in the hands of small third-world nations who raised our energy costs significantly, sparked worldwide recession and runaway inflation, and filled our hearts with panic and hopeless-ness. The oil embargo and the growth of terrorism destroyed our notion that small nations did not matter.

The debacle of our involvement in Vietnam contributed as much to the deterioration of our assumptions as any single factor during the decade of shocks. Before Vietnam we believed that it was our destiny as a nation to stem the tide of communist imperialism. Vietnam not only revealed the inability of our gigantic military might to defeat movements of national liberation of which our government did not approve, but it also provoked a youth revolt against political leader-ship. This burgeoned into the rebellion of the young against every form of authority. Sexual promiscuity, open drug experimentation, rock-and-roll music, the repudiation of the work ethic, campus riots, attacks upon the traditional family, the flight from the cities and the suburbs to agrarian and crafts communes were but some of the fruits of the youth-led dissent of the decade. Everywhere the once powerless demanded a bigger piece of the action from the powerful. Ghetto residents, college students, women, farm laborers became more assertive and uncompromising.

The answer was not a new vision of a society that worked for everyone but an incensed political backlash. The majority wanted the Vietnam war to end as honorably as possible and wanted the clock turned back to the Eisenhower interregnum. We elected Richard Nixon. He finally brought home the troops, impounded funds which Congress appropriated for social programs, and used the power of his office to punish those who opposed the status quo. But he confused the enemies of our old assumptions (enemies a majority wanted crushed) with the foes of Richard Nixon. In a stunning succession of events, he won a resounding victory at the polls—carrying every state but Massachusetts—but lost control of his underlings, the media, and Congress. In order to evade punishment, he resigned in disgrace, bequeathing the majority of Americans a distrust of authority that almost matched the disillusionment of the young at the height of antiwar dissent. There was also a numbing sense of despair and indecision.

The republic survived and continued. Charisma gave way to routine. Leaders whom we could love or hate, whose rhetoric inspired and terrified, whose example lured us to action—such leaders had been swept away. The solid, faceless institutions of our democracy were all that remained. There was comfort in that but not much. We ignored the vapidity and failures of the two one-term presidents, licked our wounds, hoped that hard times would give way to old times, let the avuncular presence of Walter Cronkite reassure us that even if life could not be beautiful it would nevertheless go on—and elected Ronald Reagan. Perhaps we would be strong, good, capable, secure, safe, and sane once more.

But shock after shock had assaulted our assumptions, leaving us staggering like inebriates and dividing us into incessantly warring camps. First, there are the "seekers," who accept the demise of the old values and who murkily pursue a better way. Second, there are the "preservers," who desperately cling to the old assumptions and who claim that "if we reassert our will and nerve we can once again attain military, economic, and moral superiority";[2] and third, there are those who are too immersed in the demands of daily life to respond to anything but the latest "crisis."

America, as a nation, a civilization, a world power, an industrial colossus, a keeper and champion of democratic dreams, and a moral influence, has been directionless for the past decade. What guides us? It is not possible to return to the simplistic solutions of the past. Our arrogant posture of moral superiority, while displaying the traits of a neighborhood bully instead of a great civilization, must be set aside so that we as a nation may attain a new maturity. Neither "seekers" nor "preservers" have provided us with a vision of a hopeful future. The seekers have the passion but few workable programs. They are romantics who think they can undo reality by their temper tantrums or by appealing to "new age" irrationality. The preservers have the right words but have lost the melody. Wanting to go home is admirable. But where has home gone?

Religious cults and ultrafundamentalist sects arose as part of our stumbling in the midst of political assassinations, racial violence, inflation, the Vietnam war, the counterculture, women's liberation, and the failings of technology. Cults and sects articulate the national confusion, build upon the confusion, and, each in their own way, attempt to transcend the confusion. Their fanaticism is their own but their madness is ours. The communities of new believers are seekers as well as preservers. They find new ways of living, governing, parenting, and surviving based on their idiosyncratic religious visions. They would have no need to look if old or new assumptions derived from the wider population worked for them—or if they worked for the wider population. They keep that which appeals to them as the best of the old by rebaptizing it and imbuing it with holiness.

NOTES

1. Tom Shachtman, *Decade of Shocks: Dallas to Watergate, 1963-1974* (New York: Poseidon Press, 1983), p. 289.
2. Ibid., p. 290.

16

Can the Gospel Time Bomb Be Defused?

housands of small sects like Truth Station and the Bible Truth Fellowship exist. Some are charismatic/deliverance, others charismatic/shepherding, yet others noncharismatic/dispensational, still others charismatic/heretical fundamentalist, etc. Although their theologies are more alike than different—being derived from the familiar matrices of fundamentalism, revivalism, dispensationalism, and the charismatic movement—they come in an astonishing variety of sizes, shapes, stripes, and degrees of intensity.

There are black-ghetto sects, white suburban sects, small-town sects, rural sects, in-the-middle-of-nowhere sects, farming sects, sects that sell Mexican pottery at gas stations, sects with only a few housewives who study the Bible over coffee, and sects with thousands of members that rent auditoriums in principal cities and place full page ads in daily newspapers. What they generally share is a common appeal to the Bible as the inerrant Word of God, the final arbiter in all matters of faith and practice. But that is only the surface. What these groups are basically concerned with is power—how to get it, how to enjoy it, how to use it, and how to retain it.

Consider their leaders. Their credentials are not college or seminary training, professional certification, or ecclesiastical approbation. Rather they possess the three "B"s—britches, breath, and Bible. Ultra-fundamentalism is a bastion of male dominance. Male shepherds lord it over their flocks. Wives are submissive to their husbands and children obey their fathers. (Yes, there are some women sect leaders. They sneak in by designating themselves prophetesses. But in the New Testament that probably meant someone who went into an ecstatic state now and then and babbled; it scarcely meant the authoritarian leader of an authoritarian sect.)

Sect leadership is an equal-opportunity path to stardom. Few people can be wealthy. Few can be elected to high public office. Few can be a movie star or television celebrity. Few can survive the rigors of professional education and become a doctor or a lawyer. But anyone can buy a Bible, preach his or her version of the Gospel, start telling others how they ought to live, and reap financial benefits and other rewards. Putting a Bible into the hands of some people is like giving them a loaded revolver. Ted Patrick is right about one thing. He once told me, "The Bible is the most dangerous book ever written." That is true, since appeals to it confer instant power, prestige, influence, and control.

The second *B* is breath. Sect leaders like to talk. They are in love with the sound of their own voices. The more they talk the more they believe what they are saying. It comforts them. People who have nothing to say like to listen. People who are under stress, estranged, lonely, depressed, and dislocated like to listen. It comforts them also. This is the best and simplest explanation I can give for brainwashing, coercive persuasion, mind control, and revivalistic religious phenomena.

Mao was wrong. Power does not come out of the barrel of a gun; it comes out of a seemingly confident person talking to a person lacking in confidence. One person says to another: "I love you." The words express the speaker's inner state. At the same time, they create a new inner state in the speaker *and* they evoke an inner state in the hearer.

The spoken word is powerful. It can create or destroy. A man may be feeling self-confident and secure, but if a friend tells him he looks tired and anxious, he may disagree with his friend but his inner state changes. When a second friend tells him that he looks tired and anxious, he takes a tranquilizer and goes to bed.

Religious words express the brute facts of human experience. We are creatures of circumstances, profoundly conditioned and limited by what life has given us. Our power to control our emotions, our situations, other people, and the world in which we live is severely limited. We want more than we have—more things, more money, more prestige, more pleasure, more peace of mind—and we are often frustrated in our attempts to acquire and to control what we want. And, finally, we are desperate for meaning—for some glimpse of the big picture, in reference to which all our strivings, accomplishments, relationships, frustrations, and desires have some significance.

Whether each individual life has meaning or not, we need to live *as if* it does if we are not to give way to despair and self-destruction. And when we are feeling the threat of meaninglessness intensely, when we are bored with life, sick of ourselves, disoriented in a rapidly changing world, bereft of comfort, it is at these points that promises of a bright future and an easy answer are as welcome as the first robin of spring after a winter of blizzards. The invitation from a self-confident stranger to accept comfort, security, assurance, and self-transformation is magic. For hundreds of thousands of Americans, living according to a myth that may ultimately prove inadequate and unfulfilling is better than living with no myth at all. For what else is left? Confidence in government leaders has steadily waned in the aftermath of Eisenhower's lying about the U-2 plane, Kennedy's initial denial of our involvement in the Bay of Pigs, the sordid deals and resignation of Spiro Agnew, the disgrace of Nixon's tapes and Watergate. Appeals to patriotism are somewhat hollow in the light of Vietnam. Love is scarcely a safe refuge in a society where half of all marriages end in divorce.

This nation lost its perennial optimism. Successive generations have always believed that things were better for them than for their fathers and that life would be even better for their children. Not anymore. For there is not any "more." Our conversations today are filled with images of scarcity, lowered expectations, disappointed hopes, uncertainties, and fears. We are the stuff of which apocalypticism and escapism are made. Why, then, is it so surprising that apocalypticism and escapsim are so prevalent on the religious scene?

Consider the third *B*—the Bible. The Bible is many centuries old. Virtually nobody reads all of it. Most people don't even read some of it. Almost everybody believes that it is sacred or holy or divine or special or the ultimate truth. But nobody really understands what it says because of its archaic concepts and language (in the case of the still popular King James version). Its concepts—with the exception of a few generalities of universal significance like the Ten Commandments and the Golden Rule—are properly suited to cultures that ceased to exist long ago.

When I was a child in Chicago, my parents brought home a Gideon Bible from a hotel room in Detroit. It lay around our apartment for years. My father tried reading it aloud to his three children. Somewhere in Leviticus we got bored. My Christian friends talked about the book—it was supposed to be the be-all and the end-all.

Then at the age of fifteen, when I was involved in a frantic search for personal meaning, I carried the book to a Youth for Christ rally. I wanted to dedicate my life to something. I was feeling trapped and lacking direction. But the magic book was no help. It was unintelligible. The evangelist cracked the code. He gave me a way of appropriating the archaic book for myself. I knew no other way either of making the book my own or getting my life under control. I had no sense of sin at fifteen—though the youth evangelists made a big thing of it that night. (One of them would later be accused of sexually molesting young boys, the other of stealing church funds.) But I did know that I had no sense of identity or direction or purpose. All I needed was an invitation to dedicate my life. It was that simple. By accepting the authority of the evangelists' understanding of the Bible that night, I embarked on a road which would lead eventually to the academic study of religious experience and the counseling of families disturbed by cults and sects.

There are hundreds of millions of copies of the Bible. And there are people who feel good about themselves when they tell others how to live and others heed their instructions. And since anyone can pick up this book and become an expert on how someone else ought to live, a lot of people, ranging from unimpressive nobodies to gifted visionaries to organizational geniuses, pick up the book and immediately start telling everybody else how to live. And millions of bored, depressed, lonesome people heed the word.

How to determine the truth is controversial in every field, whether it is astronomy, psychiatry, dermatology, or mutual funds. The experts never agree and the rest of us tolerate their wrangling. But usually there are standards, authorities, rules of the game, tests of reality. When it comes to religion and the Bible, every man is his own court of last appeal. The Reformation and the Bill of Rights guarantee it. There are no standards of right and wrong biblical interpretation (except in seminaries). There is virtually no standard as to what constitutes a religion or who is and who is not an ordained clergyman. No one claims more authority than the founder-prophets of biblical sects, and never are claims based upon flimsier foundations. But to those desperate for direction and confident leadership, it makes no difference.

I know of one sect whose supposedly unique "divinely revealed" system of biblical interpretation is an obvious amalgam of Adventism, Mormonism, and the Jehovah's Witnesses. Many of the faithful are as aware of it as I am. They calculate the cost of entertaining such notions versus continuing to have a sense of identity, purpose, and direction. To such persons, suppression of rational inquiry is a small price to pay for comfort and meaning.

It costs hundreds of thousands of dollars to buy a McDonald's franchise, and then the only thing you have to offer the public is fast food. Bibles are available for the taking, meeting places can be found without cost, customers are eagerly awaiting the new merchant, and the product is peace, security, assurance, and renewal.

Why are the sectarians so successful in winning converts, demanding obedience, and creating havoc? There are many reasons. By demanding more, they grant more. But above all there is their special secret. They are more biblical—from a literalistic, simplistic point of view—than are traditional groups. The Gospels overflow with apocalypticism. Many, many verses in the New Testament deal with the Second Coming. But that millenial fervor died with the first generation of Christians. The church "in the world" rather than the church "about to be wrested from the world" became the norm for Christian theology for nearly two thousand years. Apocalypticism was left to the crackpots. It was usually ignored by establishment priests and ministers. If it had not been so, Christianity would have remained a tiny eschatological cult that probably would have disappeared long ago. The fact is that the major Christian churches have too much of a stake in the real world to concern themselves with the possibility of the demise of the social order. Death is enough of an eschatological worry for the average Christian.

When it comes to charismatic gifts such as speaking in tongues, performing miracles, healing the sick, and casting out devils, the pentecostal churches are definitely closer to the milieu of the New Testament than are traditional churches or noncharismatic fundamentalists. The Gospels and the Book of Acts are essentially records of ecstatic and magical acts. The Jesus of the Synoptic Gospels is an apocalyptic preacher of the impending destruction of the social order and of the coming of God's Kingdom. The imminence of the rule of God is revealed in disruptions in the limits between seen and unseen worlds. Demonic and divine manifestations are inseparable from Jesus' apocalyptic message. He heals the sick, casts out demons, raises the dead, multiples food, controls the elements, and so forth.

In the Acts of the Apostles, the ascended Christ is replaced by the Holy Spirit, a kind of invisible Jesus who goes about with the faithful performing magical deeds similar to those of the Jesus of Matthew, Mark, and Luke. And the Church of the Book of Acts has the gift of tongues. However, Luke's account is confused. It moves from the intepretation of tongues as the ability to be heard by another person in the hearer's own language (a gift of simultaneous translation) to the notion of a trancelike state akin to drunkenness. Ecstatic trance or altered states of consciousness that produce inarticulate babbling is meant in the only other major New Testament reference to tongues, Paul's first letter to the Corinthians, chapter 14. If the church in New Testament times had been as obsessed with charismatic gifts as today's charismatics are, Christianity would be studied today with the other dead cults of antiquity.

The New Testament was written in a world accustomed to possession, trance, visions, oracles, resurrections, and miracles. The church grew and developed in those parts of the Hellenistic, Mediterranean world that regarded charismatic manifestations as evidence of divine power. The greater or more ecstatic the manifestation, the more authentic the message. Cecil B. deMille would have understood this. For a while the apostolic church was in danger of becoming just another mystery cult or mystical-magical brotherhood. Only when a succession of ordained, orthodox bishops was accepted did Christianity spread as a major faith. Within two centuries the ecstatic states and the charismatic gifts were virtually forgotten by all but a few sectarians. And so the situation remained until the charismatic renewal of the early twentieth century.

Like all sectarians, the pentecostals claim a portion of the Bible as though it were the whole Bible. They reduce the Christian life to the recreation of trance states and the performance of miracles. Together with the dispensationalists, they have alienated traditional Christians, including the Anglican, Reformed, Evangelical, and Roman Catholic communions. Since early pentecostalism drew heavily from the have-nots of society—displaced agrarian elements, immigrants, blacks, the uneducated, and the working poor—it is not surprising that the charismatics were essentially antiestablishment. It is also not surprising that these populations, which were never far from folkways and animistic outlooks, felt at home in sects that romantically recreated the ecstatic elements of the early church.

Today's charismatic/deliverance and shepherding groups include the dispossessed of former times but they also embrace vast new markets among the psychologically deprived—the products of divorce, disruptions in the labor market, alienating mobility—all the wholesale confusions and aimless drifting found in our society. My clients and acquaintances in biblical sects are not farmers newly settled in the rooming-house districts of big cities or recently arrived immigrants. They are aerospace scientists, engineers, lawyers, photographers, teachers, nurses, small-business owners, musicians, actors, secretaries, school administrators, counselors, housewives, and TV newsmen.

How can such seemingly intelligent people allow themselves to get involved in this nonsense? I am asked that question or a variant about once a day. I think I have explained the needs that impel individuals to surrender self-control for group domination. To put what I have been saying another way—we want the unconditional love many of us received from our grandparents and the strict limits many of us never got from our mothers and fathers, busy as they were in supporting our new standard of material comfort. We want to be loved. We want to be accepted.

And, finally, we want to get high. This is the new element that scarcely existed twenty years ago. When I was converted to evangelical Christianity, I sought the company of Christians with whom I could feel comfortable. This was not a conscious motive but it is obvious in retrospect. I wanted to be able to be myself "in Christ." but it was a struggle. The antiworldly, antiaesthetic, and irrational tendencies of such fundamentalist religiosity made me uncomfortable. I felt compelled by my evangelical peers to give up my acting, my writing, my attendance at plays and movies (which I deeply loved), my self-assertion, my convivial relations with non-born-again Christians, my sense of humor, and my intelligence. In the groups with which I was involved—Youth for Christ, HiCrusader Bible Clubs, the Plymouth Brethren, the Conservative Baptists, and Moody Bible Institute—there were few peers or elders who advised anything other than crucifying myself with Christ. I put up with it for about three years and then became a different kind of Christian. I was proud of my gifts and eager to use them to help others.

How did I feel about charismatics? It is not as though they did not exist in the late fifties and early sixties. I attended a few ecstatic celebrations of worship with my friends. I sat in at store-front explosions of shouting, stamping, screeching blacks seized by the spirit, getting tranced out, writhing on the ground for the love of Jesus. I attended hundreds of revival meetings with Bible-thumping, screaming enthusiasts working the faithful into hysteria with cries of "Hallelujah, brother and sister," "Praise the Lord!" and spontaneous outpourings of testimony and prayer. I watched black Baptists, caught up in colorful patterns of rhythm, string together meaningless snatches of Bible imagery and scriptural quotations while the choir sang and the congregation went wild.

But I knew in my heart that even though I shared their faith, I did not want to be like these people. After all, I was a self-disciplined middle-class Jewish kid, who wanted to plumb the depths of my faith not through displays of raw emotion but through the use of what I am. And, for all my fanatic devotion and involvement in a goodly share of ill-conceived evangelistic enterprises, I did not want to be a misfit. (Once I distributed 15,000 pieces of gospel literature in Chicago's Austin High School in one day, and I spent a great deal of time during my first year of college preparing "gospel rafts." These were sealed tin cans with religious tracts and my personal testimony, which I released in the Chicago River.) Finally, I did not want to be taken for an out-of-control wacko. I did not want to spend the rest of my life with dropouts, has-beens, and never-wases, justifying my alienation and inability to cope on the grounds that I was special in the sight of God because I was obnoxious.

And besides who got high on Jesus—or on anything—in those days? The message among evangelicals was cool it—or else join some fringe group. We were a crew-cut, coat-and-tie, long-skirt-with-stockings, antibooze, anti-sex-before-marriage, socially-acceptable, you-would-want-your-daughter-or-son-to-marry-us elite cadre, not only of future suburban denominational churchdom but of conformity to the Eisenhower status quo as well. We were as likely to freak out on Jesus as we were to use marijuana or shoot up with heroin.

So where did the charismatic/apocalyptic gospel bomb come from? The key is in my subject statistics. The age of the average convert to a cult such as the Moonies, the Hare Krishnas, Divine Light Mission, or Scientology is twenty-two. But the average age of a convert to the biblical sects I would classify as ultrafundamentalist is thirty-three. That means that the charismatics were born around 1950, were eighteen around 1968, and married around 1973. They were conditioned by a very different set of circumstances, mores, norms, and cultural forms than was a Moonie, who was born in 1961, or a born-againer such as myself, who was born in 1939.

The converts to ultrafundamentalism come from the counterculture and the antiwar riots, the street people and the human-potential movement, the third-wave and users of recreational drugs, people who regard astrology as just as helpful as psychiatry, ones who let it all hang out and believe that irrationality, old wives' tales, organic food, and free love would lead us into the "age of Aquarius." The journalistic perception of the Jesus movement of the early seventies was that it was discontinuous with the counterculture, that is, that it reformed drug burnouts, street people, and disillusioned student activists. That may be true in part, but the larger reality is that the warm fires of Jesus-freak revivalism and charismatic ecstasy were fueled by the experiences that were part and parcel of everyone growing up in the sixties and seventies.

It is no longer disgraceful to get high. Ecstasy is fashionable. It is the parents of today's cultists and biblical sect members who are out of step. Most deprogrammings are acts aimed at cutting the enthusiast off from the source of his high more than at anything else. Intensity is a cardinal sin only if you programmed your children to graduate from college and become professionals. Is it really true that the boring, normal kid is the happy, self-fulfilled kid?

But unbridled enthusiasm is no more a guarantee of health,

wealth, and goodness than is the unrestricted consumption of hot-fudge sundaes. When I can no longer tell the difference between ecstasy and the behavior of the inmates of a ward for the chronically mentally ill, I am profoundly troubled.

What, if anything, can be done? Religion is a "let the buyer beware" market. The best antidote to bad religion is good religion. Would irrational, destructive, and antisocial religion be flourishing today if there were serious competition from established religion? Would the headlong pursuit of rumor, fanaticism, and superstitition persist if the forces of liberal humanism entered the fray in significant numbers and with zealous dedication? Why should the Bible, religious experience, and enthusiasm continue to be the monopoly of the vandals?

It is a shame that the counterfanatics have been the clearest voice opposing sectarian abuses. For we as a nation cannot afford to accept the solutions of the vigilantes. No one has the right to impose standards of religious orthodoxy on others. But that is not to say that I am opposed to the regulation of antisocial behavior. I do not think that our society is obligated to tolerate theft, fraud, negligence, and death in the name of religion.

In many states, parents may refuse to allow their children to be vaccinated and may permit their children to die of treatable illnesses; pregnant women and their infants may be denied medical attention; men may beat their wives and children beyond the boundaries of acceptable discipline. If a nonreligious person were to perform any of these antisocial acts, he would be liable to prosecution. But if the perpetrator contends that his actions were matters of religious scruple, there is no penalty. I remember one situation in Vermont, where a member of the ultrafundamentalist Northeast Kingdom Church was tried for burying his child's body in the ground without the proper death certificate or embalming. His defense, members of the commune related to me, was that he was exercising his freedom of religion because as head of his family he had full authority over his children and besides God had told him what to do. Although he was convicted, he received a lenient sentence.

There is precedent in case law for the government to interfere when religious fanaticism crosses the boundary into the illegal. We do not have to stand by when book-burnings or polio epidemics become a way of life. Further, the failure of government at all levels to enforce the laws impartially for believer and nonbeliever alike is shocking. Zoning ordinances, immigration laws, wage-and-hour statutes, tax regulations, banking rules, child-snatching laws, automobile-registration requirements, and more are routinely disregarded by local, state, and national law-enforcement officials when it comes to cults and sects. The government is afraid to be seen as persecuting dissidents or minorities. It finds it impossible to deal with the distinctions between legitimate religion and religions that feel they are beyond the laws of man. When it comes to religion, government suffers from what one preacher terms "the paralysis of analysis." It thinks and thinks and thinks until the problem, hopefully, will go away.

It is ironic that the same law-enforcement officials who tell me they do not want to become involved in church-state quarrels are the first to turn the other way when the kidnapping of a sect member occurs. Allowing a child to die of a removable tumor and turning a twenty-three-year-old son over to the vigilante mind-benders are both regarded as "family matters," with which officials choose not to concern themselves. Does our society really care so little when the issues are life and death, civil rights, or a latter-day inquisition?

Fanatic religion invites fanatic repression. Fanatic repression threatens the very fabric of democratic society. The silence of the unconcerned allows the gospel time bomb to tick on.

17

Ultrafundamentalism and the Future

The context for understanding ultrafundamentalism is conservative Protestantism. The conservatives are one of the three major camps into which American churches are divided. These three groups are:

1. liberals—Methodists, Episcopalians, Unitarians, and members of the United Church of Christ.
2. moderates—Disciples of Christ, Presbyterians, American Lutherans, and American Baptists.
3. conservatives—Missouri-Synod Lutherans, Southern Baptists, Southern Presbyterians, Roman Catholics, and members of sects.[1]

If the adult membership of Protestant denominations were counted according to these three divisions, I would estimate that there are about 22 million liberals, 28 million moderates, and 23 million conservatives. If America's 50 million Catholics were added, the conservative camp would swell to 73 million—more than liberals and moderates combined. This would mean that 18 percent of the Christian population is liberal; 23 percent is moderate; and 59 percent is conservative.

What generalizations taken from sociological studies can be made about the liberals, moderates, and conservatives?

LIBERALS

Liberal Protestants rate low in orthodox belief. Their confidence in the existence of God lags behind other Christians. Only about a half of them believe in the divinity of Jesus. Few liberals believe that Jesus will definitely return to earth or that the devil exists. Less than half think that belief in Jesus as one's personal savior is necessary for salvation. Very few are committed to belief in life after death, the virgin birth, or the miracles of Jesus.

Liberals place much greater emphasis on interpersonal and social realities than do moderates and conservatives. Liberals are more interested in educational, social and political institutions as instruments of human betterment than are the moderates and conservatives. Glock and Stark comment, "There is a slight tendency for Protestants to be either orthodox and nonethical, or ethical and unorthodox."[2]

The ritual commitments of liberals mirror their theological stance. Liberals attend church, say grace, and read the Bible less frequently than other Christians. They are also less likely to believe in the efficacy of prayer, to have "experienced" God, or to claim that they have been saved. They are also less likely to have felt that they were being punished by God for their sins. In fact, nearly one-fourth of them report that they have had neither salvation experiences nor experiences of God during their entire adult lives. In addition, their knowledge of the Bible and general religious knowledge lags behind that of other Christians.

In the area of financial support for their churches, the term *liberal* seems ill-suited. Their per-capita income is the highest of the three groups, but their giving is the stingiest. The members of liberal churches constitute religious audiences rather than primary groups that provide a focus for their members' day-by-day activities. For the most part, their fellow parishioners are strangers to them. Few of their friends are members of their churches and few of their social/fraternal activities are church-based. Liberals provide the warm bodies and the cold cash for numerous social and political causes. But their dedication to institutional religion, ritual commitment, church financial support, and religious knowledge is so scanty that they cannot be counted upon to maintain the personal and corporate expressions of traditional religion in America or to exert a distinctly Christian influence upon American society in general.

MODERATES

Moderates are average in all respects. They are more committed theologically, ritualistically, and financially to their faith than the liberals, but they are less committed than the conservatives. Although they consider religion very important to their lives, some do not attend church or say grace before meals on a regular basis. They believe in life after death but do not allow their conviction to interfere with their pursuit of the good life. They assert that concern with an afterlife should be of paramount importance but admit that they are more concerned to live comfortably. They are slightly more affluent and better givers than the liberals, and their level of involvement with church activities is somewhat higher.

Assuming that moderates are much like the statistical average of a 1979 *Christianity Today*-Gallup Poll, we would add that moderates are inclined to regard the Bible as inerrant but are unlikely to regard it as a test of their religious or ethical convictions. Most moderates read the Bible less than once a month. Few of them, less than 30 percent, can identify the source of the quotation: "Ye must be born again" (the words of Jesus to Nicodemus found in the Gospel of John, chapter 3); and only 42 percent can name five of the Ten Commandments. About one in ten use what their church teaches as a basis for testing the truth of their own beliefs.

CONSERVATIVES

Conservatives are firmly convinced that God exists, that Jesus is divine, that he will return to earth, that the Bible is the inerrant Word of God, that the devil exists, that acceptance of Jesus as savior is necessary for redemption, and that being ignorant of Jesus will prevent salvation. They are twice as likely as Protestants in general to believe that being Jewish is an obstacle to salvation.

They tend to consider their relation to God as being more important than relations with their fellow human beings. Although Catholics are weak in some areas, the ritual commitment, involvement in church activities, Bible reading, prayer, and giving of conservatives considerably outrank the liberals and moderates. More of them report conversion experiences, feeling the presence of God, having felt that God was punishing them or that the devil was tempting them.

The numerical strength of conservatives is apparent in the Gallup Poll conducted in 1979 on behalf of *Christianity Today*. It produced the following data: Out of 155 million adult Americans, one-fifth or 31 million are "evangelicals." According to *Christianity Today*, an evangelical is one who believes that Jesus is the divine Son of God, or is both fully man and fully God; that the only hope for heaven is personal faith in Jesus Christ; that the Bible is the Word of God and is not mistaken in its statements or teachings. Further, an evangelical is one who reads the Bible and attends church services at least once a month.[3] Although "evangelicals" are more likely to be found in the conservative denominations listed above, they are by no means restricted to these groups.

Further, the poll reveals that almost one-fifth (29.4 million) of the adult population of the United States consider themselves pentecostal or charismatic, even though most (23.5 million) report that they have never spoken in tongues. Approximately one-quarter of the population (39.5 million) have undergone a conversion experience that included "asking Christ to be their personal savior." The divinity of Jesus is accepted by four-fifths of the adult population (124 million); and the inerrancy of the Bible by 65 million.

The poll revealed the following information about evangelicals: (1) 62 percent are female; (2) only one-fourth have completed college; (3) almost half live in the South; about one-fourth in the Midwest; (4) half live outside of metropolitan areas; (5) three-fourths are married; one in twenty is divorced or separated.

The poll also noted that 85 percent of the evangelicals read the Bible at least once a week; and 80 percent attend church weekly. Sixty-two percent could identify the source of "Ye must be born again"; but only half could name five of the Ten Commandments. Among the unexpected findings of the poll were the following: about one "evangelical" in eight is a Roman Catholic; more than one-third of all evangelicals consider themselves pentecostals or charismatics, but 62 percent have never spoken in tongues.

Conservative Protestants are twice as knowledgeable in religious matters as other Protestants. Very high percentages report that a majority of their closest friends are members of the same church. For conservatives, the church is a primary group in which they find friendship, intimacy, involvement, and permanence. It is a bastion against the loneliness, alienation, and boredom of modern urban life.

Pollster Gallup feels that the 1980s "could be described as the decade of the evangelicals, because that is where the action is." He elaborates:

The fact that 20 percent of all adults today are evangelicals—and their influence certainly extends beyond that number—and that we find in our surveys of teen-agers that they are more evangelical than their elders, all indicate that the movement will gain in strength. Given the fact that evangelicals give more of their time than do nonevangelicals, that they are more likely to want their pastors to speak out on social and political issues, and that they are more ready to speak to others about their faith, it is hard to escape the conclusion that evangelicals will have much to do with how religion shapes up in the U.S. in the 1980s. If evangelical ministers are able to mobilize the large number of evangelicals, their effect on the shape of the 1980s could be profound.[4]

What are the short-term and long-term implications of a nation in which one-fifth of the population identifies itself as evangelical or conservative Protestant? What are we to make of the vast numbers who feel comfortable identifying themselves as pentecostals or charismatic-Christians? The editors of *Christianity Today* speak of the present situation as "an opportunity that might not come for another hundred years, if ever." An opportunity for what? To convert the other four-fifths of the population to evangelical/charismatic convictions? To impose a shallow, regressive vision of theocracy on the disorganized majority? Or to achieve a vision of equality, caring, and service to others based on the moral authority of Jesus and the prophets?

CONSERVATIVE CHRISTIAN TRIUMPHALISM: POSSIBLE CONSEQUENCES

Church membership in America has grown from just over half the population in 1950 to more than two-thirds today. And the evangelical population has swollen to 44 million (31 adults and their 13 million children). Does this conservative religious upsurge bode ill or well for our divided and sleepwalking society? What is the worst that could happen to our society as the result of growing evangelical influence? According to a "worst case" analysis, the growth of evangelicalism both in numbers and influence would mean the following:

1. more "Christian right-wing" political-action committees that work to destroy the reputations of honest public servants because the office-holders fail to dot their *i*'s and cross their *t*'s in the prescribed Christian manner, that is, by militantly opposing gay rights, women's rights, the Supreme Court ban on Bible reading and prayer in the schools, and so forth;

2. more concern about preparing for eternity and less attention to social realities; hence, less criticism of the status quo; and less compassion for the poor, the elderly, the handicapped;

3. a return to strident "good guy versus bad guy" rhetoric in American foreign policy, as policymakers try to present themselves as thermo-nuclear-armed soldiers of the cross in the moral crusade against "godless communism";

4. a growth of irrationalism and anti-intellectualism in all spheres of life, with a commensurate decline in American achievements in science, industry, and literature;

5. a "manifest destiny" mentality which considers born-againers as citizens with rights and all others as inferiors deserving neither the

protection nor the benefits of American institutions, and a coincident fresh wave of anti-Semitism;

6. a devaluation of the arts to the level of propaganda for evangelism;

7. the imposition of evangelical standards of morality on nonevangelicals by making crimes of such "sins" as adultery, premarital sex, and so forth;

8. censorship of television, books, and movies to avoid offending evangelical sensibilities, and increased boycotts of sponsors of offending programming;

9. pressure on public schools to teach creationism and not to offer sex education, and pressure on schools and libraries to remove "offensive" books with explicit sexual material, obscenities, or references to witches, demons, or blasphemers;

10. the outlawing of homosexuality and the repression of gays through the criminal-justice system;

11. the abolition of liberalized abortion policies;

12. the requiring of Bible reading and prayer in public schools;

13. the granting of federal aid to evangelical elementary and high schools, thereby reinstituting segregation;

14. the growth of such excesses as religiously sanctioned child abuse, wife abuse, neglect of health care, avoidance of innoculations, and so forth;

15. the appeal to a higher authority as justification for the avoidance of laws, regulations, codes, taxes, and ordinances which the evangelical finds undesirable or inconvenient;

16. the encouragement of vandalism and violence against non-Christians, especially "militant gays, ultra-liberals, atheists, porno pushers"[5] and others, by the self-appointed guardians of Christian virtue;

17. the rewriting of history to support the myths that Christianity was the faith of our founding fathers, that we have always been a Christian nation, and that faith in God is the basis of our Constitution and way of life.

Admittedly, the preceding list constitutes a "worst case" scenario. The left and the center may be dormant, but they are not dead in either the political or the religious realms. I am not predicting that any of these fears will come to pass, but I am concerned that we face a period in which political and social movements increasingly react to the demands of the more boisterous evangelicals. It is not so much that public policy will be determined by the Christian Right as that the institutions of our republic, including legislatures, courts, police, the media, professional groups, and the presidency, will spend ever greater amounts of time and effort in outguessing and placating the Moral Majority.

The damage of McCarthyism, to cite an example from the past, was not limited to those unfortunate victims of the witch hunt who lost their livelihoods, reputations, and future opportunities. The fear of anticommunist zealots made moral cowards of millions who simply chose to wait for the storm to pass. When it did, these survivors were among the first to deride the red-baiters. But the fact remains that because of McCarthyism critics of the status quo were more restrained in their efforts, artists were less radical, the churches were less prophetic, the media were more temperate. In general, the passionate were prone to keep their passions to themselves. When opposition to injustice was liable to get one branded a "red" or a "pinko" or a "fellow traveler," discreet quiet seemed the better part of valor. And when opposition to anticommunism was inevitably misinterpreted as procommunism, only the bravest or most foolhardy would challenge the McCarthyites.

I know that the Moral Majority no more represents the rank and file of America's conservative Protestants than Donald Duck does the poultry industry. The observer of the Moral Majority should note that it is a coalition which has attracted elements from several movements, including special-interest lobbyists (opponents of abortion, gay rights, sex education, pornography, centralized government; proponents of prayer and Bible reading in the schools, amending the Constitution to acknowledge America's theistic and/or Christian foundation, and so forth), the political Right, fundamentalists, conservative Protestants, and the Christian Right. The Moral Majority is a point at which several disparate movements intersect. It draws some from each of the groups but includes many who belong to none of the others.

For example, a small percentage of Southern Baptists support the Moral Majority but a larger percentage does not. A few Jews belong to the political Right as well as the Moral Majority, but they are not fundamentalists. Many fundamentalists are right-wing Republicans but most are not. Most fundamentalists, conservative Christians, and right-wing Republicans have little or nothing to do with the Moral Majority.

Further, the Moral Majority controls no important component of evangelicalism. *It has yet to win the support of any conservative denomination, seminary, established fundamentalist publication, or any association of evangelicals.* Although its membership is not overly impressive, it is clear that the organization articulates the rage and confusion of a much larger audience. It is not only the size and scope of the Moral Majority's potential constituency that bothers me but the manner in which the reactions of those who hate, fear, and oppose the Moral Majority give significance to the movement by their very reaction.

Returning to my list of feared consequences of conservative Christian triumphalism, it should be borne in mind that most Moral Majority members, together with some fundamentalists, some conservative Protestants, radical Rightists, and even some Majority-endorsed political figures live in a world dominated by fear and hate. They believe and act as though the following were true and universally applicable:

1. Man's legitimate primary concern is salvation; all other concerns are secondary.

2. Major social problems can only be solved by God; preaching the gospel is the most significant way of improving human beings and society.

3. The Bible is the only book anyone needs to know, and any secular learning or science not based on the Scriptures is worthless.

4. The state exists to punish sinners, and sinners are those who violate the laws of God found in the Bible.

5. Those who produce or distribute books, magazines, or movies that encourage immorality should be treated as a threat to society and be censored and/or prosecuted.

6. Secular humanism (any teachings which encourage human beings to depend on their own abilities and resources to solve their own or society's problems) is satanic and certainly should not be allowed to dominate the school curriculum.

7. The Bible, creationism, and Christian morality should be the only proper foundation for education.

8. Homosexuality and abortion are crimes against God and society.

9. The state must never be allowed to interfere with the rights of Christians to regulate their families, businesses, and private property according to the Word of God as it is interpreted by the conscience of each believer.

10. Ultimately the individual is answerable only to God and not to any secular authority.

11. Anyone who disagrees with these convictions is not fit to hold public office.

There are millions of Americans who believe the preceding and act as though these beliefs were the law of the land. It is important that we understand not only that these Americans make these convictions binding on themselves and their families but that they are governed by a moral imperative that requires they extend them to the rest of us. I believe that numbers, reason, history, and the ideological foundations of our society as embodied in our Constitution and manifest in our social institutions and laws are against them. But I do not look forward to having to listen to the acrimony of the continuing rhetoric of those to whom evangelicals look for leadership. It is possible that this small and unrepresentative faction will hold public attention and silence the outcries of conscience as did an equally small and unrepresentative faction in the 1950s. My instinct tells me that the boisterous evangelicals are putting few nickels into the jukebox but are selecting most of the songs.

Still, the prospects of an evangelical takeover of the country are slim. For evangelicalism is politically and socially reactive rather than revolutionary or creative. Further, as rapidly as conservatives grow, so they also decline.

THE CONSERVATIVES: GROWTH AND DECLINE

Conservative Protestant groups are more conversionist than Roman Catholics, moderates, and liberals. They not only believe; they are committed to the exclusivity and uniqueness of that which they believe. They put their faith into action by offering others the opportunity to share their gospel of salvation through faith. Conservative religious groups recruit incessantly. Their evangelistic efforts win recruits who find homes in an ever-increasing number of sects and movements. Sects divide into newer sects, the options steadily mounting. Evangelical numbers grow steadily. And decline rapidly!

Evangelicals' ability to gain converts is not matched by a capacity for holding onto them. They successfully evangelize the unchurched and the dispossessed. But as their recruits become more middle-class in attitude and mores and, hence, more socially acceptable and mobile, they and their children feel less at home with the conservatives. With the passage of time, the young revivalistic recruit marries, has a family, acquires property and goods, becomes less interested in the fervor and excitement of the sectarian group, and desires to be accepted by his neighbors. He becomes a moderate. Even those who remain within evangelical churches cool off and lose the ardor of the sawdust trail.

The vast majority of evangelicals, according to the 1979 Gallup Poll, report that "their life-changing religious experience" was "gradual," not "sudden." And for all their church attendance and belief in biblical inerrancy, they are not significantly ahead of the general population in their ability to name five of the Ten Commandments. Moreover, a startling 40 percent did not know that "Ye must be born again" were the words of Jesus to Nicodemus. Why not? The average evangelical hears a sermon on the third chapter of the Gospel of John several times a year.

However, with the passage of time, the relative impersonality and boring respectability of liberal forms of Christianity—the lack of demands and the theater-audience level of participation—allow the financially more secure Episcopalian, Methodist, or Congregationalist to wander farther and farther away from any sense of religious identity. The church becomes a place where people are married and from which representatives are sent to offer opening prayers at public events or to participate in funerals. But as some of the liberals or their children drift away, they become potential converts to high-demand forms of Christianity. In this way, the conservative camp, on the one hand, and the combined liberal-moderate camps, on the other, exchange members in about equal numbers. But since the intense, assertive conversionist is more vocal, recognizable, and active, the appearance is given that the whole society is being moved irresistibly toward the religious right. To draw such a conclusion would be erroneous.

The truth is that the religion of the conservative encourages him to act on the basis of his convictions, while the religion of the liberals and moderates fosters a complacency that borders on apathy. The irony is that conservatives have the ardor to accomplish a great deal but few concrete programs worth doing. Conservative activism is largely religiocentric and socially irrelevant. Conservatives spend their time with fellow conservatives, give their money to conservative causes (their church, its programs, and conversionist activities), and react to non-conservatives as threats or as potential converts.

At the same time, the politically and socially active liberal or moderate draws little energy from his faith, acts as though his faith were largely irrelevant, and reacts to the conservative as an impediment to human progress.

The conservative is fervent, reactionary, and irrelevant. He is against hedonism and self-indulgence, against divorce and welfare, and largely indifferent to needs for social change. The liberal-moderate is socially responsive but spiritually shallow. He is for a plethora of good causes. His attention is unfocused and scattered. He has no vision or plan for the future of the society—just the hope that people will learn to get along with one another and that the economy will improve.

I once hoped that fundamentalists could be urged to become more socially responsible and that liberals could be persuaded to stop their social posturing and to pay attention to the need to inculcate moral and spiritual values. Instead evangelicals learned from the liberals how to organize mass protests, develop narrow, single-issue constituencies, and manipulate the media. And liberals became ever more reactive and powerless. In many ways, the religious center and the left are in danger of becoming a mentality of resistance to the Christian right and evangelicalism, just as fundamentalism once degenerated into mere opposition to modernism.

I suspect that something is happening to middle America which gives the appearance of a resurgence of revivalism, but which has other explanations. The leaderless, powerless, and frightened majority—the real majority—is desperately trying to preserve the values of the past. They were reared to respect progress and success. Progress and success, in turn, were represented to them as the fruits of hard work, optimism, and the peculiar tilt of reality that favored Americans above all people. The pursuit of success depended largely on the ability to postpone immediate gratification for the sake of long-term gains, as well as the belief that the dice were loaded in our favor. Thrift was encouraged as a counterbalance to the tendency to spend today's paycheck for today's trivial pleasures—alcohol, entertainment, poorly produced or instantly obsolescent merchandise, gambling, and so forth.

Sexual experimentation was discouraged, and marriage was encouraged. Monogamy offers stability, predictability, security, and comfort. It is to sexual gratification and interpersonal intimacy what a savings account is to earnings. And for some reason—probably because we as a nation have never outgrown our sexual adolescence—sexual inhibition became the standard against which all other delayed gratifications were measured. For if the control of sexuality were lost, all resistance to the impulse of the moment would crumble with it.

Evangelicalism has long been the religion of middle America. But this cannot be explained because its tenets are widely known and accepted or because the revivalistic conversion is ubiquitous. If a person is trying to hold onto the virtues and values of the past, revivalism is simply more comfortable. If one is attempting to rear children who will postpone sexual gratification, save money, get a college education, and avoid drugs, born-again religion seems more supportive and less threatening than any of the alternatives—even if the individual has never experienced crisis conversion or has never given any thought to whether the Bible is inspired, inspiring, or simply a masterpiece of world literature. Because the evangelical posture seems to protect and defend a way of life whose foundations have been eroded by events of the past two decades, middle America says that it believes what the evangelicals believe. But, for the most part, middle America identifies with what the born-again symbolize, and not with what they experience or believe.

How has the rise of evangelical influence and the political activism of the Moral Majority influenced the ultrafundamentalists? The truth is that even if every American were an evangelical, ultrafundamentalism would still condemn and reject the nation in general and the evangelicals in particular. Ultrafundamentalists are true sectaries. They reject, despise, and scorn the present world as the domain of Satan. And they have turned their backs on the evil world system, including the government and the churches. They await a coming of Christ which, according to their eschatology, will be preceded by accelerated apostasy, false religiosity, and the persecution of the faithful remnant by the combined forces of state and church under the control of the Antichrist. The ultrafundamentalist scorns the alleged evangelicalism of more than 40 million Americans as the diabolical counterfeit foretold in the Bible from which the true Christian has no choice but to flee.

And yet the evangelical and the ultrafundamentalist are bound together like quarrelsome Siamese twins who cannot be separated. The more evangelicalism spreads, the farther ultrafundamentalism advances. Ultrafundamentalism is evangelicalism taken to extremes— some of them logical, some ridiculous but harmless, others ridiculous but scarcely harmless. The cardinal emphases of ultrafundamentalism are derived from revivalism. Crisis conversion, the centrality of the Bible, dependence on religious authorities, pessimism about the human condition, and self-distrust are pushed to limits well beyond those acceptable to evangelicals. Evangelicalism is uneasy with the authoritarianism, the totalitarianism, the paranoia, the self-righteousness, the insanity, the abuses of power of their ultrafundamentalist brethren. But what is to inhibit the ultrafundamentalist? Surely not his inner state, which manipulative groups can turn on and off like a faucet; nor the Bible, which is pliant and coercive in his hands; nor his fellowship with other born-again Christians, whom he spurns.

As much as fundamentalists oppose and condemn the ultrafundamentalists, they are unable to disown them. For in ultrafundamentalism are combined all the excesses and weaknesses of evangelicalism: subjectivism, anti-intellectualism, biblicism, repression, elitism, fear of the outside world, and social irrelevance. Ultrafundamentalism represents the triumph of *thanatos,* the death urge, over *eros,* the impulse toward life. Its repressive and regressive tendencies are derived from revivalism. For revivalism in all its forms expresses the terror of mankind when faced by the creative possibilities of existence. Despite its stage-managed celebrations of fervor, revivalism fears the chaotic, the intense, and the sensual. It backs away from the stirrings that mark the boundary between the solitude of singular existence and the power of external reality, that is, other selves, new possibilities, and unprecedented opportunities. Revivalism is obsessed with self-control at the cost of self-expression and intimacy. It is a religion of self-hatred and distrust of others. It seeks a state of bliss in which we are at rest on the bosom of an accepting parent, who demands of us only that we sacrifice our essential humanness. Revivalism is a perversion of the message of the cross. Jesus set an example of loving service. He was willing to lay down his life for others. He did not set an example of self-crucifixion or self-mutilation.

Revivalism is routinized repression. Consider the functions of negation in the revivalistic way of life. Revivalistic ethics are entirely negative. The good man is the man who avoids vice and worldliness. For the evangelical "immoral" means just one thing: violating middle-class sexual taboos. Evil is thus reduced to banality. What honor is there in resisting it? The believer's sense of identity also depends on negation. He is much more secure in *what he is not* than in what he is. Status by negation leads to separatism, revivalism's incurable divisiveness. His friends are not those who offer opportunities for mutual growth. Rather they are those with whom he shares common enemies. Revivalism's mores, norms, values, and attitudes are further examples of negation; the evangelical is most comfortable in being against than in being for. After all, accomplishments are unnecessary. "Only one life; 'twill soon be past, only what's done for Christ will last." And it is infinitely easier to condemn as worldliness artistic effort, literary expression, scientific discovery, or attainment in any field than it is to create for oneself.

But impulse does not disappear because it is repressed. It finds new forms of expression. The Moral Majoritarian decries pornography but he is fascinated with the sexual lapses of his brothers and sisters. It is immoral to enjoy sexual pleasure outside the sanctity of marriage, but it is edifying to hear the testimonies of sinners who have found the path of righteousness, especially to hear how deeply and deliciously they were sinking in sin before love lifted them. And it is amazing how much more sinful some pasts become with each retelling. Further, while the Christian should shun the ways of the wicked, it is acceptable for him to discuss them for hours so that he will be able to guard himself against temptation should he meet it in the future. When I was a teenager, there was more sex and violence in the pulpit of the evangelical youth organizations which I frequented than there was in movies or television at the time. At Youth for Christ rallies and HiCrusaders I was subjected to a never-ending parade of converted dopers, hookers, wiretappers, hoodlums, faded beauty queens, and night-club entertainers, who thrilled us with their testimonies of miraculous conversion from lives of degradation. Is it not just such exploitation which turns sin into pornography?

The preoccupation of revivalism with sin—particularly sexual trespass—charges the air of the evangelical's world like electricity. Evangelicals can work off their frustrations in crusades against vice, in private devotion centered on Jesus as the lover of one's soul, or in ecstatic public services of song and praise. But for an increasing number of evangelicals, repression is the pressure cooker and pentecostalism is the safety valve. Cut off from the natural expressions of humanity in intimacy, interpersonal relationships, creative expression, and sensual delight, the evangelical finds solace in outpourings of charismatic gifts.

Ultrafundamentalism is evangelicalism gone cultic. Evangelicalism is middle-American repression institutionalized. And middle-American repression is awash in self-contradictions and uncertainty. For it is not only the decade of shocks that has undermined the value structure of the middle, it is middle-America's desire to have it both ways: to spend tomorrow's substance for today's trinkets and yet to have whatever is required to pay off destiny's note. It was not secular/liberal humanism or women's lib or the counterculture or the sexual revolution or rock-and-roll music which weakened the hold of traditional values. It was middle-American hypocrisy—professing the work ethic, living on credit, and hoping that a winning lottery ticket would free us from grim realities.

Evangelicalism provides millions with just the right rumor to allay their anxieties. Repent and believe—and nothing else matters. But additional millions are too angry and distressed to look to heaven for solace in the midst of all that has gone wrong. They need a scapegoat, someone to blame for things having gone awry. (In truth, no explanation is needed. We did it to ourselves.) To these millions, these merchants of blame—the Moral Majority and vast segments of revivalism and the right—appeal. Blame the gays, the pornographers, the advocates of liberalized abortion, the secular humanists, the pointy-headed intellectuals, the women's libbers, communism, socialism, and so forth. But do more than blame them, the Moral Majority and their allies urge. Stop them. Set the clock back to 1953 and all will be well.

There is yet another constituency of blame-seekers—one which knows that there is no going back. These are the ultrafundamentalists.

This constituency takes the dilemmas of the present with even greater seriousness than do either the evangelical center or the Christian right. Ultrafundamentalism accepts the scapegoating of the Moral Majority. It adds to the list: Roman Catholics, ecumenical Protestants, most other born-againers, blacks, the "Jewish-Zionist-Bolshevik conspiracy" to dominate the world's financial institutions, the Trilateral Commission, the Club of Rome, the Freemasons, all government above the county level.

Ultrafundamentalism is a parasitic growth on evangelicalism, just as evangelicalism is on middle-America's hopes and fears. Ultrafundamentalism is the athlete's foot of the body politic. Should the health of the society suddenly change for the better, all religion based on anxiety and scapegoating will decline. Ultrafundamentalism, Jerry Falwell's blend of revivalism and politics, even the moderate evangelicalism of Billy Graham will wither away, finding their place along with Millerites, "Know Nothings," the Anti-Saloon League, and Father Coughlin's National Union for Social Justice in the history of forgotten causes.

But what if the climate does not change? What if no great moral equivalent of war, no stirring cause, no hopeful vision of the future, no sense of new frontiers and challenging opportunities bursts upon us? Will our society stumble along until some tragic disaster forces it to unite? Or until some hero on horseback appears? Or until its average citizens eschew cheap grace and miracles in all spheres of life and settle down to the hard tasks of reevaluation and renewal?

NOTES

1. For a more detailed presentation of the three groups, see Charles Y. Glock and Rodney Stark, *American Piety: The Nature of Religious Commitment* (Berkeley and Los Angeles: University of California Press, 1968); Glock and Stark, *Christian Belief and Anti-Semitism* (New York: Harper, 1966); Lowell D. Streiker and Gerald S. Strober, *Religion and the New Majority: Billy Graham, Middle America and the Politics of the 70s* (New York: Association Press, 1972); Martin E. Marty, Stuart E. Rosenberg, and Andrew Greeley, *What Do We Believe? The Stance of Religion in America* (New York: Meredith Press, 1968); George Gallup, Jr. and David Poling, *The Search for America's Faith* (Nashville, Tenn.: Abingdon, 1980).

2. Glock and Stark, *American Piety*, p. 75.

3. "The Christianity Today-Gallup Poll: An Overview," *Christianity Today*, Dec. 21, 1979, p. 13.

4. "We Poll the Pollster," *Christianity Today*, Dec. 21, 1979), p. 11.

5. These words are used in a fund-raising letter distributed by the Christian Voice Moral Government Fund. A "declaration of war" distributed by Jerry Falwell's Old-Time Gospel Hour vows to fight against the following evils: legalized abortion, pornography, homosexuality, socialism, and the deterioration of the home and family. Both documents can be found in Perry Deane Young's gripping book about the resurgence of fundamentalism in American politics, *God's Bullies: Political Politics and Religious Tyranny* (New York: Holt, Rinehart and Winston, 1982).